Transmedia Storytelling East Asia

C000313720

This book offers a thorough investigation of the recent surge of webtoons and manga/animation as the sources of transmedia storytelling for popular culture, not only in East Asia but in the wider global context.

An international team of experts employ a unique theoretical framework of media convergence supported by transmedia storytelling, alongside historical and textual analyses, to examine the ways in which webtoons and anime become some of the major sources for transmedia storytelling. The book historicizes the evolution of regional popular culture according to the surrounding digital media ecology, driving the change and continuity of the manhwa industry over the past 15 years, and discusses whether cultural products utilizing transmedia storytelling take a major role as the primary local cultural product in the cultural market.

Offering new perspectives on current debates surrounding transmedia storytelling in the cultural industries, this book will be of great interest to scholars and students of media studies, East Asian studies and cultural studies.

Dal Yong Jin is Distinguished SFU Professor. Jin's major research interests are on digital platforms and digital games, globalization and media, transnational cultural studies, and the political economy of media and culture. Jin's books include *Korea's Online Gaming Empire* (MIT Press, 2010), *New Korean Wave: transnational cultural power in the age of social media* (University of Illinois Press, 2016), *Smartland Korea: mobile communication, culture and society* (University of Michigan Press, 2017), and *Globalization and Media in the Digital Platform Age* (Routledge, 2019).

Routledge Research in Digital Media and Culture in Asia
Edited by Dal Yong Jin, Simon Fraser University

Transmedia Storytelling in East Asia
The Age of Digital Media

Edited by
Dal Yong Jin

Routledge
Taylor & Francis Group

LONDON AND NEW YORK

First published 2020
by Routledge
2 Park Square, Milton Park, Abingdon, Oxon OX14 4RN
605 Third Avenue, New York, NY 10017

First issued in paperback 2022

Routledge is an imprint of the Taylor & Francis Group, an informa business

Publisher's Note
The publisher has gone to great lengths to ensure the quality of this reprint but points out that some imperfections in the original copies may be apparent.

Library of Congress Cataloging-in-Publication Data
A catalog record has been requested for this book

ISBN 13: 978-1-03-240022-8 (pbk)
ISBN 13: 978-0-367-24653-2 (hbk)
ISBN 13: 978-0-367-24654-9 (ebk)

DOI: 10.4324/9780367246549

Typeset in Sabon
by codeMantra

Contents

Figures

Tables

Contributors

Andrew Hillan is a PhD candidate in the School of Communication at Simon Fraser University in Vancouver, British Columbia. He also holds a B.A. and an M.A. in Political Science from the University of Western Ontario. His current areas of research converge on video games – particularly the history of micro-transactions in gaming media. He enjoys examining and playing with vintage coin-operated games, slot machines, arcade games, and trading card games, in attempts to better understand how concepts of in-game spending have evolved in conjunction with playing experiences and gamer identities across different media over time. He also enjoys teaching and helping students to embrace critical approaches and grapple with complex concepts at the big-picture and micro-levels of media and communication.

Barbara Wall is an Assistant Professor in the Department of Cross-Cultural and Regional Studies at the University of Copenhagen. Her primary fields of research include narrative studies (canonization, intertextuality, parody, transmedial narratology), digital humanities, circulation, translation and adaptation of literary works of fiction in East Asia, and reframing of tradition in North and South Korea. She has published various articles in the *Journal of Japanese and Korean Cinema, International Journal of Communication,* and *Acta Koreana.*

Brett Hack is an Assistant Professor in the Program for Applied Global Education and Coordinator of the Multilingual Learning Center at Aichi Prefectural University in Japan. His writing on Japanese popular media and culture has been published in *Mechademia* and *Contemporary Japan.* His current research focuses on the cultural rhetoric of anime, manga, and related fictions in the context of neoliberalism and nationalism in contemporary Japan, and combines textual and comparative media approaches with insights from anthropology and social theory. His teaching activities fuse media literacy and production with intercultural communication and global citizenship initiatives.

Bruce Fulton is an Associate Professor at the University of British Columbia. As the inaugural holder of the Young-Bin Min Chair in Korean Literature and Literary Translation, he offers instruction in Korean-to-English literary translation and both traditional and modern Korean literature. His research interests lie in modern Korean fiction and its translation; intertextuality and intermediality in Korean literature past and present; and non-mainstream Korean literature, such as women's literature, military camptown fiction, and the literature of the Korean diaspora.

Dal Yong Jin is a Distinguished SFU Professor. He completed his PhD at the Institute of Communications Research at the University of Illinois in 2005. Jin's major research and teaching interests are on digital platforms and digital games, globalization and media, transnational cultural studies, and the political economy of media and culture. Jin has published numerous books and journal articles, book chapters, and book reviews. Jin's books include Korea's Online *Gaming Empire* (MIT Press, 2010), *New Korean Wave: Transnational Cultural Power in the Age of Social Media* (University of Illinois Press, 2016), *Smartland Korea: Mobile Communication, Culture and Society* (University of Michigan Press, 2017), and *Globalization and Media in the Digital Platform Age* (Routledge, 2019). He is the founding book series editor of Routledge Research in Digital Media and Culture in Asia, while directing Center for Policy Research on Science and Technology (CPROST) at SFU.

Jane Yeahin Pyo is a PhD student in the Institute of Communications Research at the University of Illinois at Urbana-Champaign.

Jeehyun Lee recently received her MA in Media and Communication at Korea University and starts her PhD degree in the Department of Communication at the University of Washington in fall 2020. Her research interests include feminist media studies, digital culture and identity, and transnational popular culture. Her collaborative research projects have been presented at various academic conferences and published in the *International Journal of Communication and Asian Women*.

Ji Hoon Park (PhD, University of Pennsylvania) is a Professor of Media and Communication at Korea University. His research focuses on the cultural implications of visual representation with a specific emphasis on race, gender, and sexuality in the media. His academic research has been published in journals such as *Journal of Communication, Media, Culture & Society, Tourism Geographies*, and *Continuum: Journal of Media and Cultural Studies*. He also directed documentary films such as *When the West Brings Civilization Back to Africa* (88 min, 2008), *Latina, Rome, and Their Family* (25 min, 2004), and *I Am Who I Am: My Life as a Transsexual* (53 min, 2003) that aired on U.S. public television and screened at international film festivals.

Jinying Li is an Assistant Professor of Modern Culture and Media at Brown University. She focuses her teaching and research on media theory, animation, and digital culture in East Asia. Her essays on Asian cinema, animation, and digital media have been published in *Film International, Mechademia, the International Journal of Communication, Journal of Chinese Cinemas, Asiascape, Asian Cinema,* and *Camera Obscura.* She co-edited two special issues on Chinese animation for the *Journal of Chinese Cinemas,* and a special issue on regional platforms for *Asiascape: Digital Asia.* She recently completed her first book, *Geek Pleasures: Anime, Otaku, and Cybernetic Affect* (to be published with Indiana University Press), and began her second book project, *Walled Media and Mediating Walls.* She is also a filmmaker and has worked on animations, feature films, and documentaries. Two documentary TV series that she produced were broadcasted nationwide in China through Shanghai Media Group (SMG).

Ju Oak (Jade) Kim is an Assistant Professor in the Department of Psychology and Communication at Texas A&M International University. Her research and teaching interests include global media industries, transnational media, digital convergence and production culture, media representations of race, gender, and ethnicity, East Asian media connections, and Korean media and cultural studies. Her work has appeared in the *International Journal of Communication, Culture, Theory, and Critique, International Journal of Korean Studies, The Journal of Popular Culture, Journal of Fandom Studies,* and *China Media Research.* She holds a PhD in Mass Media and Communication from Temple University and an M.F.A. in Television Production from Brooklyn College.

Marc Steinberg is an Associate Professor of film studies at Concordia University, Montreal, Canada. He is the author of the award-winning book *Anime's Media Mix: Franchising Toys and Characters in Japan* (University of Minnesota Press, 2012), which historically situates the practices of merchandising or the media mix in relation to the anime industry. His second monograph, *The Platform Economy: How Japan Transformed the Commercial Internet* (University of Minnesota Press, 2019), tracks the platform-led transformation of film, media, and Internet cultures. Offering a comparative study of platformization with a focus on Japan as the key site for global platformization, the book systematically examines the managerial, medial, and social functions of platform theories and platform practices.

Minji Jang is a Researcher at the Korea Creative Content Agency.

Shige (CJ) Suzuki (PhD, University of California Santa Cruz) is an Associate Professor who specializes in comparative literature, film, and popular culture, teaching courses on Japanese literature, film, and culture, as well as the Japanese language. In addition to teaching at Baruch, he has taught at the University of Colorado at Boulder, Lehigh University, and Elon University. Dr. Suzuki has published several articles and book chapters both in Japanese and English. Recently published articles on comics include "Tatsumi Yoshihiro's Gekiga and the Global Sixties: Aspiring for an Alternative" (2013) in *Manga's Cultural Crossroads* edited by Jaqueline Berndt and Bettina Kümmerling-Meibauer; "Learning from Monsters: Mizuki Shigeru's Yōkai and War Manga" (2011) in *Image [&] Narrative*; and "Envisioning Alternative Communities through a Popular Medium: Speculative Imagination in Hagio Moto's Girls' Comics" in *International Journal of Comic Art* (IJOCA).

Tae-Jin Yoon is a Professor at the Graduate School of Communication and Arts, Yonsei University, Korea. His major research and teaching interests are popular culture, digital games, and television studies, among others. He has recently published books on Korean television dramas (2016; as a contributor), digital game studies (2015), and the history of radio dramas (2015). His recent publication includes *The Korean Wave: Evolution, Fandom, and Transnationality* (2017) which he edited with Dal Yong Jin.

Taeyoung Kim is a PhD candidate in the School of Communication, Simon Fraser University. His thesis analyzes the nexus of neoliberal globalization and developmentalism in South Korean cultural industry policies in the era of the Korean Wave. His research interests also include political economy of culture, multiculturalism and the revival of nationalism, and increasingly, impacts of digital technologies on culture. His research has been published in *International Journal of Communication and The Journal of Arts Management, Law, and Society*.

Yongsuk 'Alan' Lee is a PhD student at Korea University and the Chief Creative Officer at Mongjakso, independent TV Drama and film Production in Seoul, Korea. Before moving to Mongjakso, he was one of the executive producers and directors working for the drama production center at SBS in Korea. He has produced and directed dozens of TV shows such as Sitcoms, mini-series dramas, daily soap operas, and Korean historical dramas. He earned his master's degree in Media Studies at the News School in New York.

Preface

Transmedia storytelling has been one of the most significant academic discourses and media practices in the 21st century. While Western countries, including the U.S. and those in Western Europe, are major players, East Asian countries have recently developed their own transmedia storytelling and become new sources for global popular culture. In the age of digital media and platform technologies, Japan, Korea, and China have unexpectedly jumped onto the transmedia storytelling bandwagon. Japan started its own transmedia storytelling practice based on its manga and anime. Later, Korea began to develop its unique transmedia storytelling due to the rapid growth of webtoon. China, based on its novels, also contributed to East Asia's increasing emphasis on transmedia storytelling in the cultural industries.

Due to the explosion of transmedia storytelling based on East Asian popular culture and digital technologies, I developed an international conference in Vancouver, Canada, in June 2018 and a journal, special issue, on East Asian Perspective in Transmedia Storytelling, which was published in the *International Journal of Communication* in March 2019. As many scholars in the fields of media studies and Asian studies continue to study Asia-based transmedia storytelling, we decided to further develop our discourses as a form of edited volume. Since several scholars wanted to join this project, we accepted a few new papers, in addition to those that were already published or presented; therefore, the current edited volume is a timely contribution to the literature and to the readers who are interested in Asia-based transmedia storytelling.

As the primary goal of this book is to offer historical, theoretical, and contextual analyses of transmedia storytelling in the Asian context, we mostly attempt to explore whether cultural products utilizing transmedia storytelling take on a major role as the primary local cultural product in the global cultural market in the 21st century. Some of the chapters naturally historicize the evolution of East Asian popular culture according to the surrounding digital media ecology, driving the change and continuity of the cultural industries over the past two decades. Others provide new perspectives on transmedia storytelling coming from East Asian countries, which means that they also develop new approaches to transmedia storytelling so that the readers will be able to learn several key theoretical frameworks and can apply them to other regions' transmedia storytelling discourses.

As explained, some parts of the book were published in the special issue. The chapter contributors, of course, developed, extended, and revised their original work to enhance their discussions and interpretations. The original works published in the journal special issue and included in this edited volume are as follows.

- Jin, Dal Yong (2019). Transmedia Storytelling in the Age of Digital Media: East Asian Perspectives Introduction, 2085–2093.
- Barbara Wall (2019). Dynamic Texts as Hotbeds for Transmedia Storytelling: A Case Study on the Story Universe of The Journey to the West, 2116–2142.
- Kim, Ju Oak (2019). The Storyteller Who Crosses Boundaries in Korean Reality Television: Transmedia Storytelling in New Journey to the West, 2143–2160.
- Jin, Dal Yong (2019). Snack Culture's Dream of Big-Screen Culture: Korean Webtoons' Transmedia Storytelling, 2094–2115.
- Pyo, Jane Yeahin, Jang, Minji, and Yoon, Tae-jin (2019). Dynamics Between Agents in the New Webtoon Ecosystem in Korea: Responses to Waves of Transmedia and Transnationalism, 2161–2178.
- Park, Ji Hoon Lee, Jeehyun, and Lee Yongsuk (2019). Do Webtoon-Based TV Dramas Represent Transmedia Storytelling? Industrial Factors Leading to Webtoon-Based TV Dramas, 2179–2198.
- Suzuki, Shige (CJ) (2019). Yōkai Monsters at Large: Mizuki Shigeru's Manga, Transmedia Practices, and (Lack of) Cultural Politics, 2199–2215.
- Fulton, Bruce (2019). The Multimedia Life of a Korean Graphic Novel: A Case Study of Yoon Taeho's Ikki, 2231–2238.

This current book project is made possible because of two enthusiastic editors at Routledge. Erica C. Wetter has been very supportive since our meeting on the book project at the IAMCR (International Association of Media and Communication Research) conference held in Eugene, Oregon, in 2018. During our meeting, she recommended that I develop the special issue into an edited volume, which was very encouraging. Suzanne Richardson as the editor in charge of the project has also been very supportive and conducted external reviews to get constructive feedback on the project. Without their support and interest, the current book would not be the same. We hope that this book is meaningful to the readers, including scholars, students, and policy makers in various academic fields.

Dal Yong Jin
Simon Fraser University

1 East Asian transmedia storytelling in the age of digital media—introduction

Dal Yong Jin

Transmedia storytelling is not new. At the dawn of the 1940s, the U.S. film industry had already exploited other media in order to maintain firm control of the products that were appealing to audiences (Freeman, 2015). Since then, transmedia storytelling has rapidly grown. In the early 21st century, major elements in the cultural industries have changed; however, transmedia storytelling has continued to play a key role in producing contemporary cultural products for major Hollywood studios and small local cultural producers.

Transmedia storytelling has become one of the hottest media practices in recent years, as the transmedia phenomenon—which is a remediation of one particular cultural form as original to other cultural forms—has become a very significant media trend in the global cultural industries (Freeman, 2015; Jin, 2019). The rise of each new medium—print, film, radio, television, and smartphone—introduced new forms of media and entertainment, which triggered the development of the adaptation of media content based on novels and manhwas. Furthermore, the current multichannel and digital platform era gave rise to a new form of storytelling dubbed transmedia, which unfolds a narrative across multiple media channels (Knowledge@ Wharton, 2012).

In the 21st century, East Asia has become a major hub for transmedia storytelling due to Japanese manga, animation, and light novels, and later Korean webtoons (web comics) as well as Chinese novels. In Japan, many cultural forms like films and digital games have relied on manga and/or anime, and several Asian countries have utilized these cultural forms to develop their own films and television programs. South Korea (hereafter Korea) has especially developed a new type of transmedia storytelling as webtoons have gained popularity. Several movies, such as *Secretly, Greatly* (2013), *Misaeng Prequel* (2013), *Inside Men* (2015), *Along with the Gods: The Two Worlds* (2017), and *Cheese in the Trap* (2018), which were transformed from webtoons, achieved huge success, and many film directors and television producers are energetically developing webtoon-based cultural products. Tencent—a Chinese Internet-based technology and cultural enterprise—is also increasingly involved in the production of webtoons and has funded the production of webtoon-based digital games and animation. Japan has long prided itself on being a manga powerhouse; however, due to Korean webtoon's popularity in Asia, many Japanese people have witnessed that Korean webtoons make "forays into Japan, where they have quickly carved out a fan base among digital native youth who are increasingly shunning the traditional print formats in favor of titles read on apps" (Osaki, 2019).

Analyzing the explosion of transmedia storytelling based on several Asia-based cultural materials, including Korean webtoons and Japanese manga/anime, this book focuses on the emergence of East Asian transmedia storytelling. The chapters included in this volume commonly attempt to investigate the recent surge of East Asian popular culture like webtoons and manga/anime as the sources of transmedia storytelling for the creation of popular culture. The primary purpose of this book is to explore whether cultural products utilizing transmedia storytelling take on a major role as the primary local cultural product in the East Asian cultural market and beyond in the 21st century. Some chapters also historicize the evolution of regional popular culture according to the surrounding digital media ecology, driving the continuity and change of the manhwa industry, now focusing on webtoons, over the past 15 years. Therefore, as the foundational basis for the chapters in the volume, this introductory chapter discusses the major characteristics of transmedia storytelling. The major aim here is to provide several key dimensions of webtoon and anime- or manga-based transmedia storytelling to help readers understand the nature of the emerging transmedia practices as a new trend.

Transmedia storytelling and media convergence

As transmedia storytelling has heavily relied on media convergence, cultural production and consumption have depended on digital technologies. Contemporary transmedia storytelling is especially based on digital storytelling, referring to "a two-to-four-minute multimedia story in which photographs, film and drawings are used to convey a personal story, personally narrated by the storyteller" (Hancox, 2017, p. 53). For example, webtoons, which are major sources of big screen culture, such as television dramas, digital games, and films, are deeply interconnected with the increasing role of digital storytelling, and therefore, it is crucial to understand transmedia storytelling in conjunction with media convergence.

While there are several different characteristics, media convergence is about the mixing of digital technologies and content to achieve endless transformation to maximize the benefits to both users (in a new way of convenience) and developers (in a new way of capital accumulation) in the digital media era (Jenkins, 2006; Jin, 2013). Several scholars have continued to emphasize the nexus of media convergence and transmedia storytelling in the age of digital technologies.

To begin with, transmedia as a combination of "trans" and "media" implies that contents from several media forms, including film, broadcasting, manga, animation, webtoon, and game, converge beyond their independent medium boundaries (Cho, 2018, p. 310). As Evans (2011, p. 1) points out, "transmediality describes the increasingly popular industrial practice of using multiple media technologies to present information concerning a single fictional world through a range of textual forms." In particular,

> transmedia storytelling is the technique of telling a single story across multiple platforms and formats using current digital technologies. From a production standpoint, transmedia storytelling involves creating content that engages an audience using various techniques to permeate their daily lives.
>
> (Ram, 2016)

Freeman (2017, p. 32) also points out that

> at the present moment, therefore, it is digital platforms that most emphatically and most frequently build fictional story worlds across media; online promoters exploit digital tools like social media and film websites to plant in-universe artefacts about a given story world.

As Freeman (2015, p. 215) argues, "transmedia storytelling is perhaps the most aesthetically theorized component of media convergence, and one that has gained significant academic presence over the last decade." As Mikos (2016) and Jenkins (2006, pp. 2–3) address, one of the major characteristics of media convergence is "the flow of content across multiple media platforms," and the flow has been actualized through transmedia storytelling in the 2010s. In this regard, Evans (2011, pp. 1–2) explains, "it may relate to practices such as franchising, merchandising, adaptations, spin-offs, sequels and marketing."

More specifically, transmedia storytelling is a popular technique in cultural production as "doing transmedia means to make the project's contents available on different technological platforms, without causing any overlaps or interferences, while managing the story experienced by different audiences" (Giovagnoli, 2011, p. 8). Transmedia, and therefore, transmedia storytelling "has promise as a democratizing force," offering new opportunities for increased diversity and meaningful participation in media and communication (Baker & Schak, 2019, p. 202) as:

> (1) New tools and technologies enable consumers to archive, annotate, appropriate and recirculate media content. (2) A range of subcultures promote do-it-yourself media production, a discourse that shapes how consumers have deployed those technologies. (3) Economic trends favoring the horizontally integrated media conglomerates encourage the flow of images, ideas and narratives across multiple media channels and demand more active modes of spectatorship.
>
> (Jenkins 2014, p. 269)

However, transmedia storytelling needs to be understood not only as the flow of story from the original text to several different platforms, but also as the expansion and/or compression of the original story to fit into platforms' unique attributes. As Jenkins (2011) himself later argues, the media industry has rapidly changed; thus, "the current configuration of the entertainment industry makes transmedia expansion an economic imperative, yet the most gifted transmedia artists also surf these marketplace pressures to create a more expansive and immersive story than would have been possible otherwise." Transmedia storytelling as stories told across multiple media "is not just an adaptation from one media to another: it is a narrative expansion" (Scolari, n.d.). This does not mean that all transmedia experiences are expansive. As Scolari (2013) clarifies, "many audiovisual contents, rather than expanding the story, reduce it to a minimum expression, like in trailers and recapitulations." In the snack culture era, the collision of old and new media produces a large number of textual splinters (Miller, 2007), and therefore, sometimes, compression occurs throughout transmedia storytelling.

Meanwhile, transmedia storytelling involves not only text but also characters (Shige, 2019; Steinberg, 2012) and visual images; therefore, the current focus on the adaptation of textual story is limited, nor does it reflect the contemporary emphasis on visual images. This means that it is critical to comprehend that transmedia storytelling is not a simple adaptation from an original source, in particular text, to another platform, but necessitates sometimes expansion and at other times compression to fit into each platform's visual attributes.

Korea has recently advanced a new type of transmedia storytelling as webtoons have gained huge popularity. Cultural producers in Korea, such as film directors, television drama producers, and digital game designers, have paid attention and adapted webtoons for their own cultural forms. As webtoons have created one of the most unique youth cultures in the early 21st century, the local cultural industries have relied on webtoons as a new source. This phenomenon is sudden and rampant. In other words, the webtoon has become one of the most recent sources for transmedia storytelling. As Stavroula (2014, pp. 28–29) addresses, "technology advancements have created new forms for stories," and "a digital story is a short form of a digital production narrative. Digital stories combine moving images with voice, music, sound, text, and graphics." Webtoons are the latest and one of the most important forms of Korean transmedia storytelling (Jin, 2015). The discussion of transmedia storytelling in conjunction with media convergence in the cultural industry will shed light on the extension of the current debates on transmedia storytelling.

Major characteristics of transmedia storytelling in the 21st century

From Hollywood majors to the small local cultural industry firms, transmedia storytelling has played a key role in producing contemporary cultural products. As several scholars (Freeman, 2017; Jenkins, 2006; Jin, 2013; Steinberg, 2012) point out, the nexus of media convergence and transmedia storytelling in the age of digital technologies has been conspicuous. Digital technologies and participatory culture have rapidly developed, and transmedia storytelling has gained momentum.

The convergence of popular content and digital technology has been increasing, and in this regard, Jeff Gomez, CEO of Starlight Runner Entertainment, states, "transmedia storytelling is something that the Digital Age is now demanding of us all" (Hughes, 2013). Unlike old forms of transmedia storytelling, again, contemporary transmedia storytelling has been deeply related to digital media, including platform technologies—such as social media, search engines, smartphones, and relevant apps—which will continue to grow, although there are still non-digital parts that play a role in transmedia storytelling practices.

In addition, again, transmedia storytelling can be understood not only as the flow of story from the original text to several different platforms, but also as the expansion and/or compression of the original story to fit into each platform's unique attributes (Jin, 2019). In other words, transmedia storytelling also involves text, characters, and visual images (Jin, 2019; Shige, 2019; Steinberg, 2012). Transmedia is not simply retelling the same story through a different medium, as in adapting a book to film. Nor is it just franchising, involving merely sequel after sequel. Rather, at the heart of transmedia storytelling is the interactive "story world"—the process of expansion of stories beyond one particular medium to diverse platforms (Jenkins, 2006; Park, 2016), which blurs the boundaries between fiction and non-fiction, creator and audience, and narrative and non-narrative (Prior, 2013).

Meanwhile, as Phillips (2012) and Cho (2018) point out, transmedia storytelling is different from cross-media storytelling or OSMU (one source, multi-use) because it not only adapts and/or slightly modifies the original text but also provides new stories. For example, *Twilight* and *The Lord of the Rings* movies can be categorized as cross-media as they simply adapt the original novels. In contrast, *Avengers* can be identified as transmedia storytelling as the movie is much different from the original graphic novel in stories and characters while continuing to expand the story world through diverse media platforms.

East Asia had shown a relatively weak tradition in transmedia storytelling over the past several decades; however, it has become a norm in the local cultural industries in East Asia, including Japan, Korea, and China as both popular culture and digital technologies have greatly grown. Based on manga/anime, Japan developed digital storytelling as many Japanese film directors and television producers adapted media products into big screen production. Japanese manga has long been the center of transmedia practices in the Japanese cultural industries, followed by a few Asian countries;

there are several reasons why the adaptation of manga has become such a popular custom. First, manga sources can save time and money by acting as blueprints for the planning and development of a franchise. Secondly, a manga original can act as a storyboard during the production process, allowing investors and production staff to easily create adaptations and advance towards a clear collective goal.

(Joo et al., n.d., p. 16)

Adaptation from manga into live action films and TV dramas indeed has a long history. Cinema has also increasingly had to compete with television to become the core medium of adaptation from manga originals. Cinema received new attention as an adaptation vehicle for manga originals across the same period, with the aid of increasing numbers of new multiplex cinema screens. Thus, direct adaptation into live action films became a popular trend in the mid-2000s (Joo et al., n.d., pp. 17–19).

In the Korean context, webtoons have become popular, and many cultural industry corporations, such as film, broadcasting, and gaming companies, have developed their cultural products based on webtoons. Thanks to their popularity, many webtoons, including the works of Kang Full and Yoon Taeho, have been made into movies and television dramas. From political dramas to murder thrillers, these movies show diverse genres and styles (Jin, 2015, p. 203). Cultural creators like film directors, drama producers, and game designers have deeply paid attention to webtoons for their own cultural forms. For them, webtoons as the original source content are easy to adapt to another cultural form, like film, television drama, games, and musicals, and therefore, transmedia storytelling based on webtoons has blurred the boundaries between genres, platforms, and even entertainment. In other words, "transmedia storytelling is either a storytelling strategy or the world that crosses the multiple media and genre by expansion of story world to extend, strengthen and spread the enjoyment" (Park, 2016, p. 116).

As a reflection of the growth of Korean webtoons, many cultural creators, including filmmakers in East Asia, have rapidly developed their cultural content based on webtoons. Chinese and Korean film versions of the fantasy love story *The Witch*—based on webtoonist Kang Full's original story—were underway as part of a coproduction deal between Korea's NEW and China's Huace (Lee, 2017). Tencent's QQ, a Chinese online content provider, published *Undead King*, a Korean comic, and Mileland, the company that brought *Undead King* to China was in negotiations with Chinese companies to produce video games with characters from the same webtoon in 2015 (Lee, S.A., 2015). The popularity of Korean webtoons has been rapidly rising, spilling into dramas, movies, and games in Korea, followed by several East Asian countries. As of June 2015, more than 50 webtoons were already recreated into more value-added movies, dramas, and games, and the trend has continued (Kim, 2015).

While Korean TV dramas draw inspiration from varied sources, webtoons are one of the most popular sources of inventive storylines.

This in-demand form of instant entertainment began in Korea in the early 2000s and now attracts international attention, alongside other forms of Korean pop culture, at least partly because of the dramas and films it inspires.

(MacDonald, 2019)

Of course, adaptations do not always please global fans.

It is crucial to investigate whether East Asia will continue to develop local-based transmedia storytelling, and therefore, we have to carefully contemplate the future of storytelling. Manga/anime and webtoons certainly become transmedia platforms that create a virtuous cycle in which manga and/or cartoon characters and stories can move into television, film, and digital games. Manga and webtoon are now treasure troves of unprecedented stories for other tropes of popular culture. These cultural contents come with an established fanbase and the formats themselves are narrative and visual maps that the cultural producers are easily able to use as a foundation (Song, 2016). Many film producers and corporations are keen about well-made manhwas and webtoons because they can leverage meticulous information for movies and digital games as they have detailed pictures.

Organization of the book

The organization of the book is as follows. Chapter 2 uses *The Journey to the West* as a case study to discuss the dynamic nature of transmedia storytelling, which is often promoted as the future of storytelling. By employing Henry Jenkins' notion of transmedia storytelling, this chapter shows how it is a transmedia story that started to unfold hundreds of years ago. Barbara Wall analyzes the ways in which *The Journey to the West*, which is conventionally identified with a Chinese novel, has transformed into other media content so that most people are familiar with *The Journey* universe through films, comics, or computer games. This chapter suggests that by approaching them as what Roland Barthes calls dynamic texts we can develop tools for comprehension and analysis, although Jenkins (2011) argues that transmedia stories are too broad to be grasped. In this chapter, she demonstrates how such a tool might work by applying Barthes' concept to Korean variations of *The Journey*, and in particular by using tree diagrams and an animation to create a visual map of the story's elements.

Chapter 3 uses the Korean reality TV franchise, *New Journey to the West* (NJW), to unpack how the Korean media industries have initiated transmedia and intertextual experiences in the realm of reality television. This chapter spotlights Young-seok Na, a television producer of *NJW* who has developed locally engaged transmedia storytelling, revamping characters and episodes from his previous works, coalescing Korean television channels and online streaming sites, and integrating a Chinese classic and its Japanese manga adaptation into a Korean reality show franchise. By analyzing the six seasons of *NJW*, (tvN), its prequel, *2Days and 1Night* (KBS2), and its spinoff series, *Kang's Kitchen* (tvN) and *Youth over Flowers* (tvN), it proposes that the aura of a reality show director as a storyteller is essential in creating a transmedia entertainment brand and, more importantly, in engendering the regionally bounded transmedia storytelling.

In Chapter 4, Dal Yong Jin historicizes the emergence of snack culture. By employing media convergence supported by transmedia storytelling as a major theoretical framework alongside historical and textual analyses, he divides the evolution of snack culture—in particular webtoon culture—followed by its transformation into big screen culture, into three major periods according to the surrounding new media ecology. Then, he examines the ways in which webtoons have become one of the major resources for transmedia storytelling. Finally, it addresses the reasons why small snack culture becomes big screen culture with the case of *Along with the Gods: The Two Worlds*, which has transformed from a popular webtoon to a successful big screen movie.

Chapter 5 aims to analyze the textual elements that operate across different forms of a given transmedia franchise, and how the transformations in these elements can be linked to corresponding transformations in the industrial and cultural contexts surrounding them. The three textual elements that prove essential to study and understand the specific case of the Japanese series *Sword Art Online* (SAO) are its story, characters, and setting. This franchise's unique use of these elements will be examined for how each one changes based on the specific media they appear on, and how they help shape—and are reciprocally shaped by—the professional and amateur collaborations and subcultures of fans who support its expansion across various media platforms. It will be seen that, unlike story or characters which are typically found to be the most important contributing factors to a franchise's transmedia expansion, it is the setting of *SAO's* fictional videogame world and its premise that appeals most to fans of this series and maintains this franchise's continued success through various adaptations.

Chapter 6 analyzes many different forces and agents that shaped the webtoon ecosystem into what it looks like today. It addresses the ways in which the structure is constantly evolving, as the webtoon is gaining great popularity in and out of Korea and the number of different agents entering the production field is growing. Starting off with an observation of how the webtoon ecosystem was structuralized, it attempts to portray the lives of agents residing in the large structure of the webtoon ecosystem. It identifies webtoon creators, producers, and platform companies as three core agents that constitute the production field. Based on nine in-depth interviews with each type of agent, the authors aim to capture their vivid experiences based on identity and power relations.

Chapter 7 examines why Korean TV producers use webtoons for dramas, focusing on industrial factors leading to dramatization of webtoon. It finds that several key industrial factors lead to webtoon-based TV drama production: the big success of earlier webtoon-based dramas (e.g., *Misaeng*, *Cheese in the Trap*), the limited pool of top drama scriptwriters, the use of the webtoon as a cost-saving option (as opposed to hiring a top script-writer), the strategy of reducing the risk of hiring a mediocre scriptwriter, the use of the webtoon as a deal point when production companies set out to pitch a show, and the effectiveness of promoting TV dramas on the basis of the existing reputation of a webtoon. It emphasizes that the proliferation of the mobile phone and the migration of traditional cartoonists to the mobile platform contribute to the emergence of the webtoon as a reservoir of creative stories.

In Chapter 8, Bruce Fulton discusses "The Multimedia Life of a Korean Graphic Novel" focusing on Yoon Taeho's *Ikki*. The chapter suggests that the multimedia life of the Korean graphic novel *Ikki* exemplifies the prospects for Korean graphic novels both at home and abroad. He discusses Yoon Taeho's utilization and engagement with the highly developed internet infrastructure in Korea, as well as the success of *Ikki* as a work of creative writing that resonates strongly with the trauma and abuse of power that have characterized much of contemporary Korean history. Bruce anticipates that the multimedial opportunities enjoyed by Korean graphic novels today, combined with the translation of representative works into languages such as English, Japanese, and Chinese, will allow these works to take their place alongside better-known components of Hallyu that are increasingly driving popular cultural production worldwide.

Chapter 9 examines the topic of female conscription that has been a controversial issue in Korean society. That being said, this chapter examines the discursive relationship between feminism and militarism in cultural products. As a case study, it analyzes *Beautiful Gunbari*, a Korean *webtoon* about the fictional lives of female soldiers. Throughout the analysis, this study finds that female soldiers are considered as less competent regardless of their talents since cartoonists continually emphasize aspects of femininity that have been characterized as weak or submissive. Despite fitting into military life seamlessly, female characters are objectified by male voyeuristic gazes. Such a representation of female soldiers emphasizes preexisting gender hegemony despite the recent trend of depicting woman as strong or competent in other media genres.

Chapter 10 proposes to critically reflect on *meta-modelling* and *auto-theorization*, asking to what degree these audiovisual experiments of auto-theorization push media mix theory or transmedia theory in new directions, and to what degree they repeat existing paradigms. This chapter suggests that with series such as *Re: Creators* industrial meta-modelling has itself become a genre (or meta-genre) within the incredibly dense universe of Japanese franchising, all the while offering a novel site for the theorization of Japan's and East Asia's transmedia practices. In other words, it follows work such as Lamarre (2018), who examines animation and game works to discover their models of media systems contained therein. And yet this also treats this series symptomatically, paying close attention to the manner in which it singles out the government as having a unique role in the management of media practice (a role that is part fiction and part fantasy, but reflective of the Japanese government's ideal outcome of the Cool Japan initiative for the support of Japanese contents), even as it usefully shines a light on the committee-based management of a media mix franchise.

Chapter 11 engages in a discussion of *yōkai* (preternatural monsters in Japanese folklore) characters in Mizuki Shigeru's manga and their transmedia expansion *not* as an expression of Japanese cultural tradition, but as an outcome of transmedia adaptation practices in the modern period by creators, media companies, and other social agents. It argues that recent Japanese transmedia practices are principally propelled by the specific style of character drawing found in the manga medium *and* the character-centric multimedia production scheme, which makes manga(-originated) characters including *yōkai* characters, versatile for moving across different media platforms. By analyzing the transmedia practices that have used Mizuki's *yōkai* manga as "original" sources, this chapter addresses what has been gained and lost when *yōkai* migrated to different media platforms.

In Chapter 12, Brett Hack considers the short-lived but influential subgenre of anime-based transmedia fiction called *sekai-kei* or "world-type," situating its affective dynamics against the sociocultural shifts within Japan during the late 1990s and early 2000s. *Sekai-kei*'s standard narrative of a traumatized young couple implicated in an a fantastic, vaguely defined "world" conflict is often seen as a mere symptom of the depressive solipsism which plagued Japan's so-called "lost decade" of economic recession and social collapse. Shifting attention to the subgenre's fundamentally *visual* form of cognition, he suggests that the original *sekai-kei* texts are an instructive manifestation of otaku transmedia's distinctive social imagination processing the simultaneous neoliberalization, globalization, and digitization of society. He attempts to show how *sekai-kei* fiction constructs subjective visuality within a macroscopic transmedia environment that is nonetheless grounded in the basic interactional desires and anxieties of the everyday, building phenomenological "worlds" with nonhierarchical assemblages of sensory experiences, mediated images, fictional genres, and scalar social relations.

Finally, in Chapter 13, Jinying Li examines the transmedia series, *One Hundred Thousand Bad Jokes*, as a case study to analyze the emerging new strategy of intellectual property (IP) in the transmedia system, and compare it with the existing model of media mix that has been established in anime culture in both Japan and China. The case study demonstrates a strategy shift from the character-world relation in media mix to affective resonance in the platform-based IP system, which operates through affective modules as enframing devices to establish, sustain, and manage affective parasocial contact with users. This shift marks the ongoing process of platformization that has fundamentally reshaped the ways in which media contents are created, distributed, and consumed.

References

Baker, D., & Schak, E. (2019). The hunger games: Transmedia, gender and possibility. *Continuum, 33*(2), 201–215.

Cho, H. Y. (2018). Study on application patterns of transmedia storytelling with focus on media extension using webtoons. *Journal of the Korea Entertainment Industry Association, 12*(3), 309–322.

Evans, E. (2011). *Transmedia television: Audiences, new media, and daily life.* London, UK and New York, NY: Routledge.

Freeman, M. (2015). Up, up and across: Superman, the Second World War and the historical development of transmedia storytelling. *Historical Journal of Film, Radio and Television, 35*(2), 215–239.

Freeman, M. (2017). *Historicising transmedia storytelling: Early twentieth-century transmedia story worlds.* London, UK: Routledge.

Giovagnoli, M. (2011). *Transmedia storytelling: Imagery, shapes and techniques.* Pittsburgh, PA: ETC Press.

Hancox, D. (2017). From subject to collaborator *Transmedia storytelling and social research. Convergence: The International Journal of Research into New Media Technologies, 23*(1), 49–60.

Hughes, M. (2013, March 15). What made Oz so great and powerful? Starlight runner's Jeff Gomez tells us. *Forbes.* Retrieved from http://www.forbes.com/sites/markhughes/2013/03/15/whatmadeozsogreatandpowerfulstarlightrunnersjeffgomeztellsus/

Jenkins, H. (2006). *Convergence culture: Where old and new media collide.* New York, NY: New York University Press.

Jenkins, H. (2011). Transmedia 202: Further reflections. Retrieved from http://henryjenkins.org/2011/08/defining_transmedia_further_re.html

Jenkins, H. (2014). Rethinking 'rethinking convergence/culture. *Cultural Studies, 28*(2), 267–297.

Jin, D. Y. (2013). *De-convergence of global media industries.* London, UK: Routledge.

Jin, D. Y. (2015). Digital convergence of Korea's webtoons: Transmedia storytelling. *Communication Research and Practice, 1*(3), 193–209.

Jin, D. Y. (2019). Snack culture's dream of big screen culture: Korean webtoons' transmedia storytelling. *International Journal of Communication, 13,* this Special Section.

Joo, W. J., Denison, R., & Furukawa, H. (n.d.). *Manwha movies project report1: Transmedia Japanese franchising.* Norwich, UK: University of East Angelina.

Kim, M. S. (2015, June 30). Webtoons' become S. Korea's latest cultural phenomenon. *Al Jazeera.* Retrieved from https://www.aljazeera.com/blogs/asia/2015/06/korea-latest-cultural-phenomenon-150630055653457.html

Knowledge@Wharton. (2012, July 3). Transmedia storytelling, fan culture and the future of marketing. Retrieved from http://knowledge.wharton.upenn.edu/article/transmedia-storytelling-fan-culture-and-the-future-of-marketing/

Lamarre, T. (2018). *The anime ecology: A genealogy of television, animation, and game media.* Minneapolis: University of Minnesota Press.

Lee, H. W. (2017, November 3). Why South Korean filmmakers are adapting local webtoons into movies and TV shows. *The Hollywood Reporter.* Retrieved from https://www.hollywoodreporter.com/news/why-south-korean-filmmakers-are-adapting-local-webtoons-movies-tv-shows-1054466

Lee, S. A. (2015, June 15). Online comics goes global. *Korea.net*. Retrieved from http://m.korea.net/english/NewsFocus/Culture/view?articleId=128046

MacDonald, J. (2019, February 12). Webtoons provide abundant storylines for Korean film and drama adaptations. *Forbes*. Retrieved from https://www.forbes.com/sites/joanmacdonald/2019/02/12/webtoons-provide-abundant-storylines-for-korean-film-and-drama-adaptations/#5edba0995dc4

Mikos, L. (2016). Television drama series and transmedia storytelling in an era of convergence. *Northern Lights*, 14, 47–64.

Miller, N. (2007, March 1). Minifesto for a New Age. *Wired*. Retrieved from https://www.wired.com/2007/03/snackminifesto/

Osaki (2019, May 5). South Korea's booming 'webtoons' put Japan's print manga on notice. *The Japan Times*. Retrieved from https://www.japantimes.co.jp/news/2019/05/05/business/tech/south-koreas-booming-webtoons-put-japans-print-manga-notice/#.XOYZZ9MzY1g

Park, K. S. (2016). A study on webtoon transmedia storytelling strategy. *The Korean Journal of Animation*, 12(3), 97–117.

Phillips, A. (2012). *A creator's guide to transmedia storytelling: How to captivate and engage audiences across multiple platforms*. New York, NY: McGraw- Hill.

Prior, K. S. (2013, October 18). The new, old way to tell stories: With input from the audience. *The Atlantic*. Retrieved from https://www.theatlantic.com/entertainment/archive/2013/10/the-new-old-way-to-tell-stories-with-input-from-the-audience/280682/

Ram, A. (2016, November 8). Asia to be a major player in transmedia content. *Digital news media*. Retrieved from https://www.digitalnewsasia.com/personal-tech/asia-be-major-player-transmedia-content

Scolari, C. (2013). Transmedia storytelling as a narrative expansion interview with Carlos Scolari. Retrieved from http://www.nordicom.gu.se/sites/default/files/kapitel-pdf/10_scolari.pdf

Shige, S. (2019). *Yōkai* monsters at Large: Mizuki Shigeru's manga, transmedia practices, and (lack of) cultural politics. *International Journal of Communication*, 13, this Special Section.

Song, M. (2016, January 9). South Korea embraces webtoons as the new trend in dramas. *Koogle TV*. Retrieved from http://www.koogle.tv/media/news/south-korea-embraces-webtoons-as-the-new-trend-in-dramas/

Stavroula, K. (2014). *Transmedia storytelling and the new era of media convergence in higher education*. London: Palgrave.

Steinberg, M. (2012). *Anime's media mix: Franchising toys and characters in Japan*. Minneapolis: University of Minnesota Press.

Part I
Asian culture and transmedia

2 Dynamic texts as hotbeds for transmedia storytelling

A case study on the story universe of *The Journey to the West*

Barbara Wall

Transmedia storytelling is often associated with digitalization, "Web 2.0," or simply the "future" (Costa-Zahn et al., 2011). New production and reception practices have definitely opened the doors to new transmedia storytelling experiences, while media convergence makes storytelling across multiple platforms inevitable (Jenkins, 2006, p. 104). In his essay "Transmedia 202: Further Reflections" (2011), however, Henry Jenkins argues that transmedia storytelling was possible even before "the rise of networked computing and interactive entertainment" (para. 18).

Transmedia storytelling has become such a popular term that it runs the risk of meaning everything and nothing. Before we can turn to the question of what belongs to the field of transmedia storytelling, however, we first need to know what transmedia storytelling is. *Transmedia* literally means "across media." It goes without saying that stories were told across different media long before digitalization, but for storytelling to be truly "transmedia," it is not enough to simply cross media forms. In this article, I use Jenkins' more specific definition of transmedia storytelling, which he developed in his seminal monograph *Convergence Culture: Where Old and New Media Collide* (2006) and continued to refine later on. According to him,

> transmedia storytelling represents a process where integral elements of a fiction get dispersed systematically across multiple delivery channels for the purpose of creating a unified and coordinated entertainment experience. Ideally, each medium makes its own unique contribution to the unfolding of the story.
>
> (Jenkins, 2011, para. 4)

Although the term *transmedia storytelling* might seem to be fairly inclusive, according to Jenkins' definition, a repetitive reproduction of a story across different media alone does not belong to the realm of transmedia storytelling. In Jenkins' definition, he clarifies that each medium should make "its own unique contribution to the unfolding of the story" (Jenkins, 2011, para. 4). Although every reproduction or adaptation of a story in a different medium inevitably extends or adds to the existing story to some degree, Jenkins emphasizes that transmedia storytelling requires that the story world is further developed through each medium. Each new text or new variation has to make a "distinctive and valuable contribution to the whole" (Jenkins, 2006, p. 96) and it has to add to our understanding of the story as a whole. Jenkins calls this characteristic "additive comprehension," which is a term coined by game designer Neil Young. Every new variation has to participate in the world-building process. Jumping across different media alone is not enough to make a transmedia story. Based on this definition, I argue that transmedia storytelling is not only "The Future of Storytelling" as, for example, the *Transmedia Manifest* (Costa-Zahn et al., 2011) suggests, but it is also part of the history of storytelling.

Here, I offer *The Journey to the West* as case study of a transmedia story that started to build its world hundreds of years ago. In addition, although this study is based on Jenkins' definition of transmedia stories, I would suggest that Jenkins fails to extrapolate from his definition of transmedia storytelling any useful methods for approaching transmedia stories and working with them. In Jenkins' writing, transmedia stories seem to be ungraspable and are usually referred to as abstract "story worlds" (Jenkins, 2011), "infinite story universes" (Costa-Zahn et al., 2011), or "bottomless texts" whose depth and breadth make it "impossible for any one consumer to 'get it'" (Jenkins, 2006, p. 127). Complementing Jenkins' theory of transmedia storytelling, I propose a way to grasp a transmedia story by making use of Roland Barthes' concept of dynamic texts. In essence, I argue that we can understand dynamic texts as hotbeds for transmedia storytelling.

I first give a short overview of the story universe of *The Journey to the West* and then introduce Barthes' theory of dynamic texts and explain how this concept can inform a receptive and critical approach to transmedia stories. Specifically, I show how the variations that build the universe of a transmedia story can be understood as creative recombinations of integral elements that recur in the variations of the story. In conclusion, I directly apply this concept to a selection of Korean variations of the story and visualize the story universe of *The Journey to the West* by mapping it with the help of radial tree diagrams.

The story universe of *The Journey to the West*

The Journey to the West 西遊記 (China: *Xiyouji*; Japan: *Saiyūki*; Korea: *Sŏyugi*; Vietnam: *Tây du ký*) is a story world that has been part of the literature and art of several Asian cultures for centuries under a title that translates to "Journey to the West." I intentionally use the abbreviated English title *The Journey* in this article to emphasize that this story persisted without regard to the boundaries of periodization and national literatures. In the academic realm, *The Journey to the West* is generally identified with the Shidetang edition of the 100-chapter novel allegedly written by Wu

Cheng'en in China at the end of the 16th century, and so, by using the short-ened title I emphasize that the dynamic story universe at the center of this work is importantly distinct from the static Shidetang variation of the story.

For readers who are unfamiliar with *The Journey* story universe novel, the Shidetang edition provides an adequate orientation to the basic elements. The novel tells the story of the Monkey King Sun Wukong who protects the Buddhist monk Tripitaka during his odyssey from China to the Western Heaven in the search for the real Buddhist scriptures. Besides Sun Wu-kong, Tripitaka is accompanied by three more disciples: Zhu Bajie (the pig), Sha Wujing (the monster), and a dragon horse. The novel starts with Sun Wukong's miraculous birth out of a stone, describes his career as Monkey King at Flower-Fruit Mountain, and tells how Patriarch Subhūti teaches him supernatural abilities. He defeats every antagonist with the help of the Compliant Rod. Sun Wukong's battle culminates in his fight against all heavenly authorities including Laozi, known as the first philosopher of Daoism. When even the Jade Emperor, who reigns in Heaven, sees no way to defeat Sun Wukong, Buddha comes to help and makes a bet with Sun Wukong. He promises to yield to Sun Wukong if the monkey manages to jump out of his palm. Sun Wukong fails and is, thus, imprisoned beneath the Five-Phases Mountain for the next 500 years.

In the meantime, Bodhisattva Guanyin begins to search for a pilgrim who can find the real Buddhist scriptures in the West, and he settles on the monk Tripitaka. Tripitaka can free Sun Wukong from the Five-Phases Mountain, and he offers to do so on the condition that Sun Wukong accom-panies and protects him on his journey to the West. He controls the monkey by means of a cap or headband Sun Wukong wears on his head that hurts whenever he is not obedient. After he encounters and accepts the other dis-ciples, Tripitaka's actual odyssey begins.

Following this, there are approximately 30 episodes that repeat a pattern:

1   The pilgrims encounter hindrances on their journey, mostly in the form of monsters and demons from a variety of religious backgrounds.
2   Sun Wukong contrives a plan to overcome the hindrances, which often involves use of his supernatural abilities and the help of Buddhist advisors.
3   The monsters and demons are defeated.
4   The pilgrims happily continue the journey.

This simple repetitive pattern lends itself particularly to intertextual bor-rowing and creative variations. Elements of *The Journey* have appeared in endless variations and recombinations both inside and outside Asian cul-tures, so that *The Journey* cannot be considered a singular, static work, nor can it be considered a set of variations on an "original" text. The idea of the original is an illusion that is inextricably linked to the Romantic cult of originality, but it does not play a role in transmedia storytelling. I explicitly focus here on variations that put *The Journey* into a new context. Similar to the Marvel cinematic universe, *The Journey* is a radically intertextual story world that appears in forms as diverse as TV series, comics, novels, animated cartoons, plays, roof ornaments, pagoda reliefs, and a mask dance.

The following review of a print cartoon or *manhwa* variation of *The Journey* (Ko, 2006) shows how important the role of additive comprehension is for creating the story universe of *The Journey*. Here, one reader uses different variations of *The Journey* in different media to expand his familiarity with the story world of *The Journey*. Obviously, every new variation adds to the reviewer's understanding of the whole.

> As a student I read *The Journey* more than five times. First I read a story titled *Son Ogong* [Chinese: Sun Wukong] in a collection of fairy tales. Later I came across a story titled *Sŏyugi* [*Journey to the West*] as part of a series for world classics. And then I read a *Sŏyugi* that was thick and really close to the original. I can say that I have enough background knowledge to feel familiar with the contents of *The Journey* ... I think this work [Ko Uyŏng's *manhwa*] is ideal. It's faithful to the original while still including the interpretation of the author ... But strictly speaking it's not really faithful to the original ... Many episodes are left out. But who needs to know all episodes?
>
> (Mogyŏn, 2010, paras. 2–4)

The reviewer expresses concern about the faithfulness of Ko Uyŏng's *manhwa* to the "original." However, he does not specify what he considers the "original" of *The Journey*. Still, he emphasizes the knowledge he has about *The Journey* and proves this knowledge by referring to three variations he has read: a fairy tale, an adaptation as part of a series for world classics (probably a book for children), and a "thick book." He concludes by praising Ko Uyŏng's *manhwa* as being faithful to the "original," while admitting that many episodes are left out and then minimizing that fact: "But who needs to know all episodes?" Obviously, we do not need to read all episodes to be able to say that we know *The Journey to the West*.

Roland Barthes' theory of dynamic texts as a means to approach transmedia stories

Jenkins calls *The Matrix* universe (of the 1999 film) a "bottomless text" that is impossible to be grasped by any one consumer. This also rings true in the case of *The Journey*. Each variation expands our understanding of *The Journey*, but it seems to be impossible to grasp the whole infinite universe of the story. To find a way through transmedia stories, I put forward Roland Barthes' concept of dynamic texts as a means to approach story worlds.

Barthes' (2009) reflections in his manifesto "From Work to Text" are relatively vague, but they can help us get an idea of how to understand transmedia stories such as *The Journey* as dynamic texts rather than static works. Barthes does not mention transmedia stories in his manifesto at all; he does, however, develop the concept of dynamic texts by questioning the conventional preference for stable literary works. Barthes' concept of a dynamic text has much in common with Jenkins' understanding of transmedia stories. Thus, Barthes' concept of dynamic texts can offer us tools for working with transmedia stories. His ideas are particularly helpful for this case study as I attempt to move away from thinking of *The Journey* as a static work in the form of a Chinese novel and toward thinking of *The Journey* as a transmedia story, or as a dynamic text in the form of many variations. In the following, I sum up the main points of Barthes' manifesto.

For Barthes (2009), a "work," or static work, "can be seen" (p. 157) because it is an "object that can be computed" (p. 156), whereas a "text," or dynamic text, "is a process of demonstration" (p. 157). A static work can be "held in the hand," whereas a dynamic "text is held in language" (p. 157). Although we can understand the 16th-century Chinese novel of *The Journey to the West* as a static work that can be seen and held in hand, *The Journey* in all its variations is a dynamic text that can be understood as a process of demonstration, or as a "dynamic experience" (White, 2012, p. 130). We cannot hold *The Journey* in our hands, because as a dynamic text it "cannot stop; ... its constitutive movement is that of cutting across (in particular, it can cut across the work, several works)" (p. 157). Because *The Journey* as a dynamic text cuts across its variations and lives through them, it cannot be reduced to one variation or one edition. While cutting across several works, *The Journey* also cuts across different media and by doing so adopts multiple modalities, as Jenkins would say. *The Journey* cannot be reduced to one single work; as the literary theorist Jonathan Culler (2011) explains, "The idea of the original is created by the copies" and "the original is always deferred—never to be grasped," because it is "produced as an effect of signs, of supplements" (p. 12). Thus, I understand *The Journey* as story universe, and the variations as equal, multifaceted variations of *The Journey*, each adding to our understanding of *The Journey* universe.

Creative recombinations of integral elements as building blocks for transmedia stories

Although Barthes' theory of dynamic texts as opposed to static works can easily be applied to transmedia stories and helps our understanding of story worlds, there is still an urgent need to develop a new terminology for such dynamic texts as *The Journey*. Barthes makes very clear that what Jenkins would call transmedia storytelling can also be found in the past, but the strong preference for stable literary works has controlled our perception for such a long time—at least since the Romantic cult of originality (Broich, 2007, p. 178)—that dynamic texts or transmedia stories seem to be a new phenomenon. Transmedia storytelling seems to open our eyes to a phenomenon that has existed for hundreds of years that we have not been able to perceive because of our focus on stable works. Although we have become aware of story worlds like *The Journey*, we still lack the tools to grasp them. In the next section, I bring the ideas of several scholars from various backgrounds into the dialogue, including Wilt L. Idema from Chinese literature, Michael Emmerich from Japanese literature, and Henry Jenkins, to sketch out some ideas for how we might grasp transmedia stories—if not their whole story universes, at least their skeletons.

Among scholars of Chinese literature and history, one of the most prolific authors in the field of dynamic texts is without doubt Wilt L. Idema. Idema's books (Idema, 2008, 2010, 2014; Idema & Grant, 2008; Idema & Kwa, 2010; Idema & West, 2013) present English translations of radically intertextual dynamic texts whose "original" sources cannot be clearly defined. For example, in the case of the legend of *Meng Jiangnü*, Idema stresses that "there is no single essential tale of Meng Jiangnü; there are only many versions, each with its own idiosyncrasies" (Idema, 2008, p. 22). Although the tale of Meng Jiangnü lives through its many variations, people still tend to perceive it as a stable work. Idema adds, "While almost every Chinese knows about the legend nowadays, few except specialists are aware of the immense richness and variety of its many versions in late-imperial times and in the popular traditions of the twentieth century" (Idema, 2008, p. 5).

Like *The Journey*, the texts Idema presents can all be understood as dynamic story worlds in that they circulate as variations without any precisely definable origin. Idema does not devote much space to the question of what these texts actually are, but he leaves random notes in the introductions that might help us to develop a new terminology. On *Mulan*, for example, he states that over the centuries "Mulan has been reiterated," but "a few basic elements have remained constant" (Idema, 2010, p. xi) in the variations. Although Idema does not specify how these "basic elements" appear in the variations, he nevertheless acknowledges that some elements remain constant even as the context varies.

It is an expert of Japanese literature who most clearly articulates the need to overcome our scholarly dependence on allegedly stable texts. In The Tale of Genji: *Translation, Canonization, and World Literature*, Michael Emmerich (2013) makes the argument that the reception of *The Tale of Genji* was actually a "replacement" of it. Given the immense popularity of the story, Japan is sometimes even referred to as "the country of *The Tale of Genji*" (Emmerich, 2013, p. 3). Emmerich, however, clarifies that it is actually not the "(unknown and unknowable) original" (p. 14) that is responsible for this popularity, but "replacements" of it in the form of translations, adaptations, *manga* versions, a 2,000-yen banknote that features a scene from the tale, or the *Genji monogatari* Millennial Anniversary Matcha Baumkuchen. In his introduction he argues that

> there is a need for a new terminology more in tune with the shift that has already occurred, away from a focus on supposedly stable classic texts themselves and toward an interest in the mutable history of books and other material forms, in the processes by which new *images* of texts are produced. I propose that we think in terms not of reception, but of a more engaged notion of *replacement*.
>
> (p. 10)

Emmerich chooses the term *replacement* instead of *reception* to emphasize the creativity that is involved when the author of a variation creates a new place in the present for a dynamic literary narrative. He emphasizes that the idea of the "original" is illusory in the case of *The Tale of Genji* and that it is not any "original" that made the story popular in the world. This is also true of *The Journey*. As a dynamic story world, *The Journey* has no original and has become popular through its variations. This also means that the search for the "original" is futile for both *The Tale of Genji* and *The Journey*. It is not the case that the "original" of both stories has not been discovered yet; in the case of transmedia stories, the "original" simply does not exist.

If Idema notes the continuity among variations of a dynamic text and calls our attention to "the elements" that "have remained constant," Emmerich makes us aware of the radical breaks and creative changes that happen in replacements or variations of *The Tale of Genji*. Jenkins calls the elements of a fiction that are dispersed across media "central" (2006, p. 111) or "integral" (Jenkins, 2011). He explains, "No given work will reproduce every element, but each must use enough that we recognize at a glance that these works belong to the same fictional realm" (Jenkins, 2006, p. 112). I suggest taking account of both continuity and breaks, analyzing variations as creative "recombinations" of integral elements that appear in the variations of *The Journey*. It is, of course, not possible and not my aim to define the exact number of elements that are affiliated with *The Journey*; instead, I want to be able to visualize *The Journey* as a dynamic story world and to get an idea of the variability of *The Journey*. I focus on a selection of 67 basic elements that recur in the variations in ever-new combinations. Table 2.1 shows the heuristic element pool for *The Journey* used in this article, which includes 12 characters, three objects, six places, six motifs, the title (*The Journey*), the author (Wu Cheng'en), and 38 episodes.[1]

The episodes are listed in Table 2.1 in the order they appear in Antony Yu's (2012) translation of the 16th-century (Shidetang) novel *The Journey to the West*. Because every episode can be understood as an independent story, many authors select some of them, mix parts of them, or recombine the episodes in a different order. The 67 integral elements of *The Journey* are shown as a radial tree diagram[2] in Figure 2.1.

Table 2.1 Element Pool for *The Journey*

12 Characters	3 Objects	6 Places	6 Motifs
Monkey	Compliant weapon	Flower-Fruit Mountain	Transformation
Monk	Headband	Five-Phases Mountain	Cloud soaring
Pig	Scriptures	Heaven	Magic of shortening the ground
Sand Monster		West	Supernatural abilities
Horse		Thunderclap Monastery	Travel
Jade Emperor		Tang	Monsters and hindrances
Subhūti			
Buddha			
Taizong			
Guanyin			
Bull Demon King			
Laozi			

38 Episodes

1 Havoc in Heaven	14 Dragon King in Black River	27 Lion-Camel Mountain
2 Search for Scripture Pilgrim	15 Cart Slow Kingdom	28 Bhiksu Kingdom
3 Tripitaka's Childhood	16 Heaven-Reaching River	29 Bottomless Cave
4 Taizong in Underworld	17 Great King One-Horn	30 Dharma Destroying Kingdom
5 Grand Mass	18 Women State	31 Phoenix-Immortal Prefecture
6 Recruitment of Disciples	19 Two Sun Wukongs	32 Jade-Flower District
7 Widow and Three Daughters	20 Mountain of Flames	33 Gold-Level Prefecture
8 Ginseng	21 Golden Light Monastery	34 Kingdom of India
9 White-Bone Lady	22 Poetry at Brimble Ridge	35 Squire Kou
10 Scarlet Purple Kingdom	23 Small Thunderclap	36 Obtaining the Scriptures
11 Silver Horn & Golden Horn	24 Tuluo Village	37 Last Ordeal
12 Black Rooster Country	25 Scarlet-Purple Kingdom	38 Return to the East
13 Red Boy	26 Cobweb Cave	

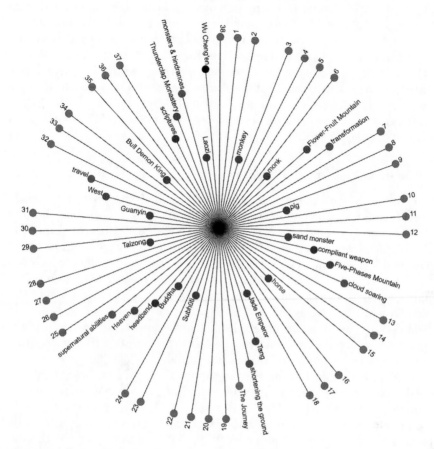

Figure 2.1 Tree diagram of integral elements of *The Journey*.

Each of the episodes (see Table 2.1) has a number that appears at the node that symbolizes the episode in the radial tree diagram. The nodes in the diagrams appear in seven colors according to the category the elements belong to. Each class of nodes is at a fixed distance from the center. Characters can be found closest to the center, followed by objects, places, motives, title, author, and episodes. To help visualize which of the elements of *The Journey* can be found in the variations, each variation described in the next section is accompanied by a radial tree diagram.

Mapping *The Journey* universe from the 14th century to today

In the final part of this article, I present a selection of six Korean variations of *The Journey* universe, including a webtoon, a K-drama, reliefs on a pagoda, a lantern festival, a mask dance, and roof decorations. Although an investigation of all variations of *The Journey* around the world would be an interesting project, the time and resources required for such a project are prohibitive. Here, I exclusively focus on Korean variations of *The Journey*. The variety and richness of variations of *The Journey* in Korea legitimize my rhetorical stance that the Korean variations may be considered a representative subset of all variations around the world. Among the Korean variations, I specifically chose a set whose interaction could be experienced during one day in Seoul.

Yi Mallyŏn's webtoon *The Journey*

Popular webtoon author Yi Mallyŏn published *The Journey*, or *Sŏyugi*, weekly as a webtoon in 135 episodes on the South Korean online platform Naver from December 4, 2013, through September 4, 2016 (M. Yi, 2013–2016). He recombines integral elements of *The Journey* universe and mixes them with humorous references. For example, the headband by which Sun Wukong is tamed, in this case a hair band that looks like a crown, only hurts when Tripitaka sings Pak Sangch'ŏl's old-fashioned trot song "Unconditionally" ("Mujogŏn"), which is widely known in South Korea. In addition, the Buddhist scriptures the pilgrims receive at the end are actually *manhwa*, which Buddha is said to have especially created to make it easier for everybody to attain Buddhahood.

Although we can find most of the integral characters, objects, places, and motifs of *The Journey* in this variation, Yi Mallyŏn selects only a couple of the basic episodes (see Figure 2.2). He uses 43 of the 135 webtoon episodes to depict the Havoc in Heaven episode, which ends with Sun Wukong's imprisonment under the Five-Phases Mountain. So, this one episode element alone takes up more than one third of the plot in the webtoon. After this, Yi Mallyŏn seems to jump back and forth in the universe of *The Journey*. He starts with the Silver Horn and Golden Horn episode (Part 65), continues with the Red Boy episode (Part 68), and then jumps back again to the Ginseng episode (Part 75). Based on the element pool in Table 2.1, the webtoon jumps from Episode 11 to 13 and then back to Episode 8. Yi Mallyŏn explicitly mentions the names of the episodes as they are generally known; for example, he announces that the pilgrims are in Cart Slow Kingdom (Part 106) or in Scarlet Purple Kingdom (Part 122), but he does not follow the order of the episodes as they appear in the Chinese novel. More important, he frequently mixes several episodes. Red Boy, for example, appears in several episodes. In short, Yi Mallyŏn's webtoon variation of *The Journey* is a good example of how elements of *The Journey* can be mixed in a range of combinations. Yi Mallyŏn does not necessarily retell the Chinese novel; he might just as well have "retold" any other variation of *The Journey*.

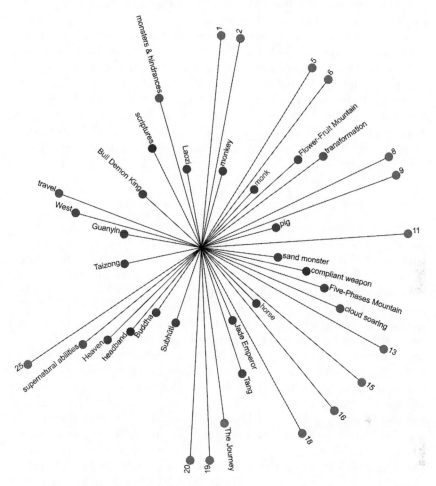

Figure 2.2 Radial tree: Yi Mallyŏn's journey.

In fact, it is very clear that Yi Mallyŏn is aware of other variations. The radical intertextuality of *The Journey* becomes evident when in Part 42 of the webtoon, just before Sun Wukong is defeated by Buddha, we can see Sun Wukong reading *Dragon Ball* to find out how he can become stronger. *Dragon Ball* is one of the most popular variations of *The Journey* and was created by Akira Toriyama. Yi Mallyŏn does not follow the story line of *Dragon Ball*, although he is clearly aware of it and may have been inspired by it. Transmedia stories seem to encourage the recipients to become part of the story universe themselves and to complement it with their own thoughts. The line between the production side and the audience thus becomes blurred. Each variation can be understood as verifiable traces of productive reception.

Also, the title of this variation suggests that the author wants his readers to understand *The Journey* as a dynamic text that lives through its variations. He called his webtoon *Yi Mallyŏn Sŏyugi*, which means *Yi Mallyŏn's Journey to the West*. The fact that the author's name is incorporated into the title emphasizes that what we read is *The Journey*, but *The Journey* told from the perspective of Yi Mallyŏn. His title draws attention to the idea that there is not one single *Journey*, but many variations of it. In total, Yi Mallyŏn recombines 40 of the integral elements of *The Journey* universe.

The K-Drama *Hwayugi*

The Journey universe also includes a K-drama that is not called *Journey to the West*, but instead *Journey to Harmony*, or *Hwayugi* 和遊記 (J. Yi & Park, 2017–2018). It was aired from December 23 in 2017 to March 4 in 2018 on tvN and tells the story of Chin Sŏnmi, a beautiful and successful realtor. Chin Sŏnmi, who is also Tripitaka in the show because she is said to be a reincarnation of the monk, works with Sun Wukong, a monkey spirit, and the spirit of the Bull Demon King to bring light into the dark world ruled by bad spirits in today's South Korean society. In addition to her career as a real estate agent, Tripitaka also has the ability to see ghosts and expel evil spirits. In this variation, Sun Wukong had once been an immortal in the heavenly realm; however, after committing a serious crime in heaven he was imprisoned in the Five-Phases Mountain. Here, the Five-Phases Mountain is symbolized by five candles that hold Sun Wukong captive that cannot be put out by Sun Wukong himself. When as a young girl Tripitaka first meets the imprisoned Sun Wukong, he asks her to put out the candles and offers in return to serve as her guardian. She only has to call his name, he promises, and he will appear in front of her. Chin Sŏnmi or Tripitaka frees Sun Wukong, but once freed he uses a trick to make her forget his name. Twenty-five years later he meets Tripitaka again. She remembers him and with the help of heavenly powers she attaches an armband—a variation of the more common headband—to Sun Wukong's wrist. In other variations, the headband hurts whenever Sun Wukong is not obedient to Tripitaka, but in the drama the armband makes Sun Wukong fall in love with her. The armband in combination with the fact that Tripitaka appears as a woman in this drama give *The Journey* universe the chance to develop a romantic plot that cannot be found in many variations.

Hwayugi demonstrates how *The Journey* persists through its variations in which a selection of its integral elements are recombined and put into ever-new contexts. We can find 21 integral elements in this variation in Figure 2.3.

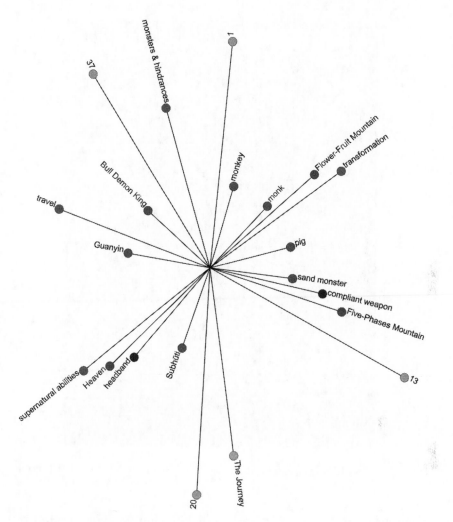

Figure 2.3 Radial tree: *Hwayugi.*

The Journey as reliefs on Pagodas

The oldest Korean variation of *The Journey* can be found in form of reliefs on the 10-story pagoda of the Kyŏngch'ŏn Temple (1348), which is
now preserved in the National Museum of Korea in Seoul (see Figure 2.4).
It depicts 12 episodes of *The Journey* in 22 scenes. Given that the pagoda
was built more than 200 years before the 16th-century Chinese novel, it
has not been mentioned in any studies on the "reception" of *The Journey*
in Korea.

Figure 2.4 The 10-story pagoda of Kyŏngch'ŏn Temple at the National Museum of Korea.

On the pagoda's ten stories are depicted Buddhist symbols or narratives often derived from Buddhist scriptures. Most of them do not allude to *The Journey*. Twenty-two panels depicting scenes of *The Journey*, however, can be found in the second story of the stylobate, the place that visitors notice first (Sin, 2006, p. 79). It is significant, then, that this very central place of the pagoda features not scenes from Buddhist scriptures, but rather a variation of *The Journey*. Furthermore, this variation embeds *The Journey* in a religious context.

With regard to the characters, on the pagoda we can find all of the pilgrims, Emperor Taizong, and Guanyin. Sun Wukong the monkey is shown with his compliant rod, and we can easily identify scriptures on the back of a horse. The 12 episodes that are depicted on the pagoda also include the Red Boy episode. In Figure 2.5, we see Guanyin slightly to the left of the middle, with a halo and riding a wave. On the right is Tripitaka on the shoulders of one of his disciples. And in the middle, we see the Red Boy

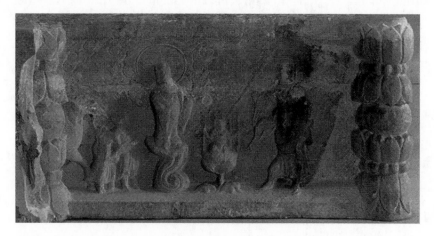

Figure 2.5 The Red Boy episode on the Pagoda of the Kyŏngch'ŏn temple.

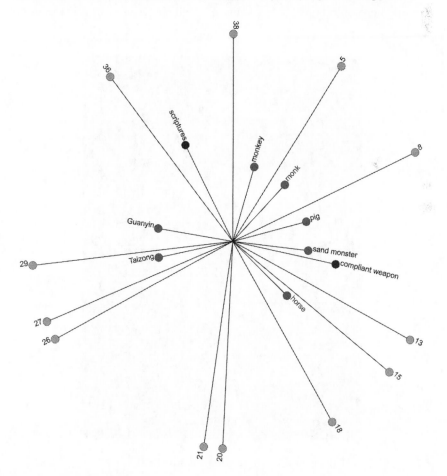

Figure 2.6 Radial tree: Pagoda.

sitting in a flower. In the Red Boy episode, Guanyin transforms everything into an ocean as part of his strategy to block Red Boy's attacks and finally capture him. The scenes on the Kyŏngch'ŏn Pagoda suggest that many of the episodes of *The Journey* universe were known more than 200 years before the traditional novel. Visitors were expected to be familiar with the story to recognize them on the pagoda in a Buddhist context.

At least 21 of the integral elements of *The Journey* can be found on the reliefs (see Figure 2.6).

Seoul Lantern Festival 2017

The Seoul Lantern Festival 2017 primarily used the characters and their weapons, as well as one of the motifs of *The Journey* universe. Besides Sun Wukong (see Figure 2.7), the festival included lanterns portraying Zhu Bajie, Sha Wujing, and Tripitaka—or, at least, the horse that was supposed to accompany Tripitaka.

When I visited the Seoul Lantern Festival on November 19, 2017, the lantern of the monk Tripitaka was missing, which resulted in a commotion

Figure 2.7 Sun Wukong at the Seoul Lantern Festival 2017.

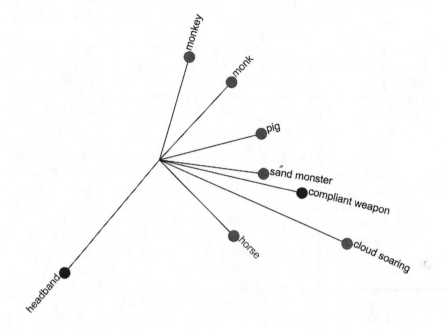

Figure 2.8 Radial tree: lantern.

among visitors who wanted to take a picture with Tripitaka, shouting, "Trip-itaka, where have you gone?" This incident shows how familiar many people are with *The Journey* universe and how each of the variations interacts with other variations of *The Journey*. This familiarity, however, does not reduce the spectators' or readers' openness to experiencing new variations of *The Journey* and to learning more about the story world in new contexts.

The lanterns were supposed to show Zhu Bajie and his rake, Sha Wujing, the horse, the monk, and Sun Wukong and his Compliant Rod. A close inspection of the picture of Sun Wukong in Figure 2.7 reveals that he is actually riding a cloud, which alludes to his ability of cloud soaring. In addition, he is wearing his headband, which is depicted as a ring around his head. The lanterns recombine eight integral elements of *The Journey* universe (see Figure 2.8).

Pongsan mask dance

The Pongsan Mask Dance also contributes to *The Journey* universe. Pong-san is now a county in North Hwanghae Province of North Korea. Located along the route from the Korean capital to China, during the Chosŏn Dynasty, Pongsan not only served as a trade center for agricultural products, but also as a place for merchants and envoys who passed through the region to find entertainment. It is not clear when the Pongsan Mask Dance was performed for the first time. The part of the lion dance that is relevant to my study of *The Journey* universe was probably added in the late 19th century or even later (Im, 1957, p. 222).

Generally speaking, the Pongsan Mask Dance tells the following story. It begins with a Buddha-like monk who is reading the Diamond Sutra, and who is visited by a Mephisto-like friend in a temple. What follows is the whole temple's descent into corruption. This process can only be stopped by the appearance of a white lion that is not willing to reveal its identity until one monk realizes who the lion is.

> Now, I think, I know who you are! During the Tang-period when the weather was dry in Black Rooster Kingdom and all people complained about it, the king invited you. With supernatural power you made it rain and, thus, won the king's favor. You could live in the palace as you pleased and enjoyed great honor. However, then you buried the king alive in the marble well of the imperial garden, transformed instead yourself into the king and lived in wealth and honor for three years. When Tripitaka, who was on the way to the Western Heaven to find the Buddhist teachings, stayed at the Baolin Temple, the King of the Black Rooster Kingdom whom you had buried alive appeared in the monk's dream. Afterwards, Tripitaka's best disciple, pilgrim Sun, the Great Sage, Equal to Heaven, who had caused uproar in Tuṣita Heaven, finally realized your real nature and you had escaped by only a hairbreadth. Thanks to the bodhisattva Mañjuśrī's help you barely survived, and you became the lion he used to ride on. That's you, isn't it?
>
> (O, 2002, p. 41)[3]

When the lion nods his head, the corrupt monks ask why he has come and starts to whip him (see Figure 2.9). However, after the lion has killed one of them, the others are filled with remorse and promise to return to the Buddhist teachings. This passage references the Black Rooster Kingdom episode of *The Journey*. In the Black Rooster Kingdom episode, it is the Bodhisattva Mañjuśrī himself who sends the lion to the Black Rooster Kingdom to punish the king because at some previous point the king had not recognized Mañjuśrī and mistreated him when Mañjuśrī had appeared in front of the king in the form of an ordinary monk. In both *The Journey* and the Pongsan Mask Dance, the lion is sent by Mañjuśrī to punish someone who had violated Buddhist concepts.

Although performances of the Pongsan Mask Dance today vary, this version uses seven integral elements of *The Journey*: the monk, the monkey, Heaven, the West, Buddhist scriptures, the Havoc in Heaven episode, and the Black Rooster Kingdom episode (see Figure 2.10).

The Journey on the top of royal palaces

The Journey has also been visible on the rooftop of Korean royal palaces for the last 350 years in the form of roof ornaments (see Figure 2.11).

Figure 2.9 The lion dance.
Source: CedarBough T. Saeji, The Lion in the Pongsan Mask Dance.

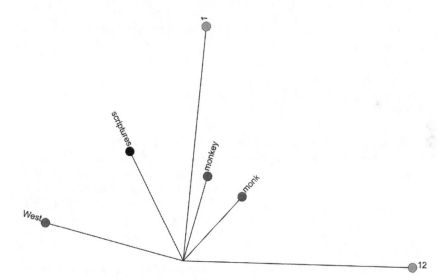

Figure 2.10 Radial tree: Pongsan mask dance.

The Royal Palaces are among the most popular sightseeing destinations in Seoul today, and the roof ornaments on the palaces catch the eye of many visitors. What many do not realize is that some key palace roof ornaments also tell the story of *The Journey*. At the time, *The Journey* appeared as roof ornaments in the 17th century, a strong Confucian—and at the same

Figure 2.11 Kyŏngbok Palace, Kŭnjŏng Hall.
Source: Author, Roof Ornaments on Kŭnjŏng Hall.

time anti-Buddhist—atmosphere pervaded Korean royal palaces. How did *The Journey*, whose Buddhist background can hardly be denied, rise to the top of these centers of Confucianism?

The first mention of the names of these common roof figures appears in Yu Mongin's (2004; 柳夢寅, 1559–1623) miscellaneous tales *Ŏu yadam* 於于野譚.:

> When newly appointed officials meet their predecessors for the first time, they have to be able to tell the names of the ten divine figures on top of the palace gates for ten times... The names are Master of Great Tang (Taedang sabu, 大唐師傅 [Tripitaka]), Pilgrim Sun (Son haengja, 孫行者 [Sun Wukong]), Zhu Bajie (猪八戒), [and] Monk Sha (Sa Hwasang, 沙和尙 [Sha Wujing]).
>
> (M. Yu, 2004, p. 132)

On Yu Mongin's list of roof ornaments, four of the main characters of *The Journey* are included. By his account, the roof ornaments as variation of *The Journey* can be visualized as shown in Figure 2.12.

Interestingly, there are also nonfictional records of these roof ornaments that are part of *The Journey* universe. The *Ch'angdŏkkung suri togam ŭigwe* 昌德宮修理圖監儀軌, an official record of repair works of the Ch'angdŏk Palace in 1647, explicitly mentions "Sun Wukong" to identify a roof ornament. From this, "Sun Wukong" also became associated with the nails by which the roof ornaments were fixed (Chang, 2004, p. 8), which came

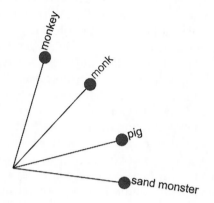

Figure 2.12 Radial tree: roof ornaments.

to be called "(Son) haengja taech' ŏl" (孫)行者帶鐵, or Pilgrim Sun-nails).[4] This suggests that Sun Wukong was at some point considered representative of all roof ornaments—and this was not a custom that was imported from China. Roof ornaments in China were arranged so that one immortal occupied the first position, and animals (e.g., dragons, phoenixes, lions, etc.) were behind it (Li, 1990, p. 277). In Korea, however, all of the main characters of Korean roof ornaments were based on *The Journey*, which is surprising because Confucianism was the official state ideology during the time these roof ornaments were installed, and the general atmosphere was anti-Buddhist. Moreover, Chinese novels were officially disrespected. Yi Tŏngmu's (李德懋, 1741–1793) critique of *The Journey* reflects the official opinion about novels in general at that time:

> I have already read *The Journey* and *The Three Kingdoms* long ago. But when my father learned about it, he scolded me: "These literary excrescences tarnish the official history and ruin the minds of their readers. How could I, as strict teacher and good father, let you indulge in such books?" I took his words to heart and never read historical or popular novels again.
>
> (Yi Tŏng-mu, n.d., p. 87))[5]

At the time, *The Journey* was widely criticized by scholars, which suggests that *The Journey* universe must have enjoyed a huge popularity. Surprisingly, its Buddhist background was generally not the target of this criticism. Thus, it is conceivable that Sun Wukong as a roof ornament might also not have been primarily associated with Buddhist ideas. It is important to remember that it was not the monk Tripitaka, but the monkey Sun Wukong who became the main character among the roof ornaments in Korea, perhaps because it was just too much to have a Buddhist monk on the roof of a grand building at the center of Confucianism. Because Sun Wukong was seen not as a Buddhist disciple, but rather as a fighter who defeats all evil demons, the Sun Wukong roof ornament thus embodies the traditional function of roof figures as guardians against fire and evil spirits (Li, 1990, p. 276).

The fact that Sun Wukong was mentioned in nonfictional records as a roof ornament in the first half of the 17th century suggests that Sun Wukong was not only widely known by this time, but that his image as a guard or fighter against evil spirits was strong enough that most people overlooked or did not know of the character's roots in a Chinese novel with a Buddhist background. As the use of the term "Pilgrim-Sun nails" shows, Sun Wukong was so common as a roof ornament that it was representational of them in general. Like written and oral texts, the roof ornaments as variation of *The Journey* show the variability of the narrative. Although *The Journey* is strongly influenced by Buddhist ideas in other variations, as roof ornaments in the late Chosŏn Dynasty, its association with Buddhism was so downplayed that it was used to decorate the very centers of Confucianism. Thus, like a chameleon, *The Journey* succeeds in adapting to ever new and often contradictory contexts, unfolding its radical intertextuality across multiple media.

Conclusion

In this article, I have traveled through one part of the universe of *The Journey*—six variations that span centuries and yet could, in theory, all be experienced today in a one-day visit to Seoul, Korea—to show that transmedia storytelling is not only the future of storytelling, but also part of its history. On the way, I have suggested that our preference for static works has obscured our awareness of dynamic story worlds, which in turn has made the concept of transmedia storytelling seem like a new phenomenon. In addition, I have offered Roland Barthes' theory of dynamic texts as a possible method for approaching and grasping story universes like *The Journey*. Drawing from the ideas of various scholars from media and literature studies, I propose thinking of a story's "variations" as the building blocks for transmedia stories, and I define "variations" as creative recombinations of integral elements that recur in the dynamic text.

To demonstrate how this might work, I have applied this approach to six Korean variations of *The Journey*, including a webtoon, a K-drama, reliefs on a pagoda, a lantern festival, a mask dance, and roof ornaments. This case study illuminates the radical intertextuality as well as the multimodality of *The Journey* universe. Each variation is accompanied by a radial tree diagram, and all six diagrams taken together give an idea of how dynamic and variable *The Journey* universe is. I would suggest that it is exactly the variability of dynamic texts that makes them ideal for transmedia storytelling.

Let us come back once more to Henry Jenkins' argument that the universes of transmedia stories are too broad and deep to be grasped. The tree diagrams in the article are a way to visualize each variation, but how could the whole story universe be grasped?

This animation in Figure 2.13 is based on the six variations that I examined in this article, and it shows how, with a dynamic text such as *The*

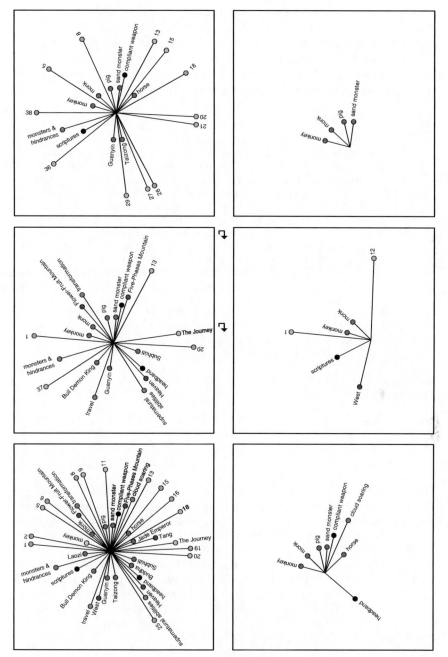

Figure 2.13 The journey to the West universe in motion. https://youtu.be/7y42lvkNLqc.

Journey, the universe "text" can start to be grasped in the similarities, differences, overlap, and interactions among several variations. Additional variations, presented in the same manner of the radial trees, fill in the open spaces in the center of the tree and confirm or expand the outer "boundary" of the story's universe. Although the radial tree diagrams and the animation serve as relatively simplistic heuristics, they make the dynamic nature of transmedia stories visible. I hope that these methods will also be helpful to grasp other story universes in the broader world of transmedia storytelling.

Notes

1　Tim Tangherlini (2018) develops a similar model to visualize narratives that takes into account not only actants (people, places, things), but also relationships and sequencing. The actant–relationship model can definitely be applied to *The Journey,* but because the main aim of this study is the visualization of the dynamic nature of the story universe, I use the simpler radial tree diagrams and combine them as animation in the Conclusion.

2　All tree diagrams in this article are based on a PHP/JavaScript application.

3　English translation by the author. Three scripts exist of the Pongsan Mask Dance performance in 1936—one each by O Ch'ŏng, Song Sŏkha, and Im Sŏkchae. Although O, Song, and Im recorded the same performance, their scripts differ from each other. However, the passage quoted here remains consistent in all three versions.

4　See, for example, *[Sunhoe seja] Sangsi pong'wŏn togam ŭigwe* [順懷世子]上謚封園都監儀軌, 1755 in e-kyujanggak. http://kyujanggak.snu.ac.kr/home/index.do?idx=06&siteCd=KYU&topMenuId=206&targetId=379.

5　English translation by the author.

References

Barthes, R. (2009). From work to text. In S. Heath (Ed. & Trans.), *Image, music, text* (pp. 155–164). New York, NY: Hill & Wang.

Broich, U. (2007). Intertextualität [Intertextuality]. In H. Fricke (Ed.), *Reallexikon der deutschen Literaturwissenschaft* (Vol. 2, pp. 175–179). Berlin, Germany: De Gruyter.

Chang, Y. (2004). *Chosŏn sidae kunggwŏl changsikki wa chapsang ŭi kiwŏn kwa ŭimi* [Origin and meaning of decoration tiles and roof ornaments of Chosŏn palaces] (Master's thesis, Kookmin University, Seoul, South Korea). Retrieved from http://www.riss.kr/search/download/FullTextDownload.do?control_no=15fe0d6aab2c9609&p_mat_type=be54d9b8bc7cdb09&p_submat_type=f1a8c7a1de0e08b8&fulltext_kind=dbbea9ba84e4b1bc&t_gubun=undefined&DDODFlag=&redirectURL=%2Fsearch%2Fdownload%2FFullTextDownload.do&loginFlag=1&url_type=&query=%EC%A1%B0%EC%84%A0%EC%8B%9C%EB%8C%80+%EA%B6%81%EA%B6%90+%EC%9E%A5%EC%8B%9D%EA%B8%B0%EC%99%80&content_page=&mingan_org_storage=

Costa-Zahn, K., Kokoska, K., Sedlag, G., Martin, D., Zimmerman, P., Moller, P., … Coelle, M. (2011). *Transmedia manifest.* Retrieved from https://transmedia-manifest.com/

Culler, J. (2011). *Literary theory: A very short introduction.* New York, NY: Oxford University Press.

Emmerich, M. (2013). *The tale of Genji: Translation, canonization, and world literature.* New York, NY: Columbia University Press.

Idema, W. L. (Trans.). (2008). *Meng Jiangnü brings down the Great Wall: Ten versions of a Chinese legend.* Seattle, WA: University of Washington Press.

Idema, W. L. (Trans.). (2010). *Judge Bao and the rule of law: Eight ballad-stories from the period 1250–1450.* Singapore: World Scientific.

Idema, W. L. (Trans.). (2014). *The resurrected skeleton: From Zhuangzi to Lu Xun.* New York, NY: Columbia University Press.

Idema, W. L., & Grant, B. (Trans.). (2008). *Escape from blood pond hell: The tales of Mulian and Woman Huang.* Seattle, WA: University of Washington Press.

Idema, W. L., & Kwa, S. (Eds. & Trans.). (2010). *Mulan: Five versions of a classic Chinese legend with related texts.* Indianapolis, IN: Hackett Publishing.

Idema, W. L., & West, S. H. (2013). *The generals of the Yang family: Four early plays.* Hackensack, NJ: World Century.

Im, S. (1957). Pongsan t'alch'um taesa [The lines of Pongsan Mask Dance]. *Kug'ŏ kungmunhak, 18,* 188–222.

Jenkins, H. (2006). *Convergence culture: Where old and new media collide.* New York, NY: New York University Press.

Jenkins, H. (2011, July 31). Transmedia 202: Further reflections [Web log post]. Retrieved from http://henryjenkins.org/2011/08/defining_transmedia_further_re.html

Ko, U. (2006). *Sŏyugi* [The journey to the West]. Seoul, South Korea: Chaŭm kwa moŭm.

Li, Y. (1990). *Huaxia yiiang: Zhongguo gudian jianzhu sheji yuanli fenxi* 華夏意匠:中國古典建築設計原理分析 [Cathay's idea-design theory of Chinese classical architecture]. Taibei, Taiwan: Mingwen shuju.

Mogyŏn. (2010, November 21). Sŏyugi 3 [The Journey 3] [Web log post]. Retrieved from http://blog.yes24.com/blog/blogMain.aspx?blogid=yyhome53&artSeqNo=2791966

O, C. (2002). Ka'myŏn muyong Pongsan t'al kakpon [The script of Pongsan Mask Dance]. *Minjok munhwa yŏn'gu, 36,* 12–40.

Sin, S. (2006). Wŏngaksaji sipch'ŭng sŏkt'ap ŏkt'ap ŭi Sŏyugi pugak yŏn'gu [Reliefs of *The Journey* on the 10 story pagoda of the Wŏngak Temple site]. *Misulsahak yŏn'gu,* 79–112.

Tangherlini, T. R. (2018). Toward a generative model of legend: Pizzas, bridges, vaccines, and witches. *Humanities, 7*(1), 1. doi:10.3390/h7010001

White, E. (2012). *How to read Barthes' image-music-text.* London, UK: Pluto Press.

Yi, J. (Producer), & Park, H. (Director). (December 23, 2017–March 4, 2018). *Hwayugi [Journey to harmony]* [Television series]. Seoul, South Korea: tvN.

Yi, M. (2013–2016). *Yi Mallyŏn Sŏyugi [Yi Mallyŏn's Journey to the West].* Naver Webtoon. Retrieved from http://nstore.naver.com/comic/detail.nhn?productNo=2534899

Yi, T. (n.d.) Sŏngo pugun yusa [The heritage of my late father]. *Ch'ŏngjanggwan chŏnsŏ* [Collection of works by Yi Tŏngmu]. Retrieved from http://db.itkc.or.kr/inLink?DCI=ITKC_BT_0577A_V004_0657_IMG

Yu, A. C. (Trans. & Ed.). (2012). *The journey to the west* (Rev. ed.). Chicago, IL: University of Chicago Press.

Yu, M. (2004). *Ŏu yadam* [Ŏu miscellaneous tales]. (K. Cha & W. Yi, Trans.). Seoul, South Korea: Hanguk munhwasa.

3 The storyteller who crosses boundaries in Korean reality television

Transmedia storytelling in *New Journey to the West*

Ju Oak Kim

On September 4, 2015, Korea's cable television provider, tvN, exclusively released its new reality show, *New Journey to the West* (*NJW*; Lee & Na, 2015), via the Web broadcast network Naver TVCast and the mobile application, tvNgo. The five clips of the first episode reached 6.1 million views within a day of its initial release (M. J. Jin, 2015). The domestic audience's immediate reaction to the Web-based media content was quite unprecedented. The *NJW* series has suggested two focal points in the transformation of the Korean media industry. First, with the recognition that media convergence has liberated audiences from remaining loyal to a specific network in the consumption of media content (Jenkins, 2006), Korea's leading cable television channel attempted to form an unconventional collaboration with an online platform provider. Second, the inroads of media professionals, who had only worked in network television, into the online media world have resulted in the creation of a locally bounded transmedia entertainment brand, breaking conventional rituals in reality-based storytelling.[1]

The market success of *NJW*'s first season has come into the spotlight with respect to the television director, Young-seok Na, who took the lead in the production of the reality show franchise. Since directing the Korean Broadcasting System's (KBS's) primetime travel reality show, *2Days and 1Night* (*2D1N*; Lee & Na, 2007–2012),[2] he has received critical and public acclaim with several reality TV shows, including *Grandpas Over Flowers* (Lee & Na, 2013–2018), *Sisters Over Flowers* (Lee & Na, 2013–2014), *Youth Over Flowers* (Lee & Na, 2014–2016), *Three Meals a Day* (Lee & Na, 2014–2017), and *Youn's Kitchen* (Lee & Na, 2017–2018). The continued achievement of these television programs has given Na an unchallenged position in the Korean reality television business. He then became the first reality show director who received the Grand Prize in the Television category at the 2015 Baeksang Arts Awards.[3]

Acknowledging that the show director is an essential force in creating the transmedia and intraregional connectivity of storytelling in the form of reality-based television programming, this study attempts to answer two important questions: How is the culturally bounded construction of reality embedded in the creation of characters and narratives in the *NJW* series? In what ways is the aura of a local television director involved in the development of an intraregional transmedia reality show franchise? This study starts from Jenkins' (2006) notion of transmedia storytelling as the impetus of a cross-platform franchise. Benjamin's (1955/1968) articulation of the storyteller is also revisited to better comprehend how the television director guides readers to follow a journey to a transmedia world. By integrating Jenkins' concept of transmedia storytelling into Benjamin's (1955/1968) articulation of the storyteller, this study aims to resonate with the aura that the Korean reality show director has shaped in producing and expanding transmedia storytelling in the East Asian context.

Media convergence, storyteller, and transmedia storytelling

For better or worse, as Jenkins (2006) pointed out, contemporary societies are passing through an era of convergence culture, where traditional and new media merge, corporate and individual media intersect, and producers and consumers collaborate (p. 2). By this convergence, we have witnessed fundamental transformations in media production, circulation, and consumption: the flow of media products across media platforms, the coproduction between traditional and online media companies, and the evolution of participatory consumer culture (Jenkins, 2006). As many media players have admitted, in the contemporary media business world, the exploration of potential markets, the discovery of economic opportunities, and the promotion of media franchises across multiple delivery systems are almost impossible without the nomadic consumer's collaboration (Jenkins, 2006, p. 19).

Although fully admitting the empowerment of active audiences (Jenkins, 1992/2013, 2006, 2010), he did not disregard the notion that corporations and media producers have maintained their initiatives to decide on story continuity and to control consumers' association with a franchise on any media platform and also their loyalty across all different media sectors (Jenkins, 2006, p. 98). As indicated in his analysis of *The Matrix*, a transmedia entertainment franchise, "integrating multiple texts to create a narrative so large" (p. 97) is pivotal in initiating the audience's curiosity and in stimulating their desire for more information about the story world. In other words, the authorship of a transmedia world sustains the media producer's subjectivity in the relationship with the audience because it is impossible for a consumer to "master the franchise totally" by discovering the hidden meanings through connecting all of the characters and narratives across numerous media texts (Jenkins, 2006, p. 101).

The characteristics of storytelling that Benjamin (1955/1968) articulated, based on an analysis of the Russian writer Nikolai Leskov's works—orality, the value of everyday life, the gravity of space and time, and the shared experience between storytellers and audiences—unveil the importance of investigating the locality of storytelling (see J. Kang, 2014, pp. 28–29). In his view, the longevity of a story depends considerably on the storyteller's capacity to implant a story into the memory of the listener (Benjamin, 1955/1968, p. 91). In other words, storytelling as an art of repetition maintains its vitality only when the listeners of a community retell the storyteller's experiences. Therefore, the circumstances in which the storyteller and listener collectively live are the key to shaping a boundary of retelling a story (p. 92). In this regard, the gravity of geographic and cultural belongings should be more carefully addressed, even when media convergence has fundamentally extended a story world across platforms on a global scale.

Benjamin's (1955/1968) other point—that the storyteller's consultation functions as a compass—helps us understand storyteller–audience companionship (p. 86). In his view, the counsel of the storyteller is key in retaining the power of storytelling among audiences (Benjamin, 1955/1968, p. 87). By doing so, storytellers ultimately obtain the status of mentors, who have the ability to situate their lives in storytelling, and their ability serves as the foundation of "the incomparable aura about the storyteller" (Benjamin, 1955/1968, p. 109). His emphasis on the aura of the storyteller in retaining the power of storytelling coincides with Jenkins' (2006) articulation of storytellers who serve as "oracles" (p. 101) in the audience's construction of the whole story in the transmedia world. The puzzles of transmedia storytelling, which are strategically fragmented by the storyteller, makes the audience's journey irresistible, and their participatory actions to complete the whole story finally solidify the storyteller's symbolic power in their relationship.

The transmediated construction of reality

The contributions of media and communications in constructing social reality have become a major subject of analysis in media sociology. From the phenomenology of the social world, Couldry and Hepp (2017) claimed that everyday reality as "the foundation of the social world" (p. 19) is constructed through human beings' actions and interactions. They further pointed out that the contemporary social world is interwoven with media and, therefore, it is salient to recognize that our understanding of everyday reality is deeply intersected with "the constraints, affordances and power-relations" that the media have engendered (Couldry & Hepp, 2017, p. 7). The social construction of reality, therefore, should also be discussed in connection with the media's structures and practices (Couldry & Hepp, 2017).

Reality television, as one of the central spaces where the media construct everyday reality, has been rigorously explored by media and communication scholars (Andrejevic, 2004; Friedman, 2002; Murray & Ouellette, 2009). One of their major concerns involves examining how television has addressed viewers' desire to experience a sense of everyday reality (Andrejevic,

2004; Bonner, 2003; Caldwell, 2002; Fetveit, 2002; Friedman, 2002; Murray & Ouellette, 2009). For Friedman (2002), viewers consume reality-based television "as a form of televisual neorealism" (pp. 7–8). What he would state here is that, despite the appearance of ordinary people and the minimization of directing, scripting, and editing in the production process, no reality-based show represents reality as it occurs. Rather, these programs provide audiences with the opportunity to consume "reality conventions with dramatic structure" (Friedman, 2002, p. 8).

Ouellette and Murray (2009) took a critical standpoint with respect to the visibility of "entertaining real" on television (p. 5). In their view, reality television's "self-conscious claim to the discourse of the real" (Ouellette & Murray, 2009, p. 3) is problematic because reality programming "celebrates the real as a selling point" (p. 5) and liberates itself from ethical considerations on human subjects, unlike other reality-based television genres—news programming and television documentaries (Ouellette & Murray, 2009, p. 4). Relatedly, they argued that reality television's devotion to authenticity has become a significant topic of investigation in which the miniaturization of handheld cameras and the absence of narrations have rapidly collided with the boundary of reality television and observational documentaries (p. 7). Andrejevic (2004) focused on technological innovations in the proliferation of reality formats, stating that digital media enable ordinary people to produce their own "reality shows" (p. 61). He further stated that network television and show directors have recognized the potential of this genre in media convergence and have actively used the interactivity of online media in reality show production to deconstruct the barriers "between audience and spectacle, consumer and producer, passive viewing and active participation" (Andrejevic, 2004, p. 89).

The penetration of reality-based programming in primetime television has inspired Korean media and communication scholars to discuss the local specificity of reality television (J. Kim, 2018; Kim & Huang, 2017; S. Kim, 2011; Ryoo & Park, 2012; Yoon, 2011). Yoon (2011) commented on the social construction of reality and the audience's emotional engagement in discussing reality television in the local context. According to Yoon's (2011) argument, Korean viewers care about the authenticity of the process in representing reality (p. 19). Therefore, Korean show directors actively use storytelling, voyeurism, and the producer–entertainer friendship to heighten the audience's emotional immersion (pp. 25–26). The proliferation of competition-based reality shows is thoroughly explored, either as an attachment of neoliberalism to Korean viewers' daily lives (Ryoo & Park, 2012), or as a reflection of collectivism, familism, and affective egalitarianism (S. Kim, 2011). Although previous studies have offered an in-depth understanding of Korean television culture in "the *mediated* construction of reality" (Couldry & Hepp, 2017, p. 8), a national focus has failed to address the recent influence of the regional media market in the narratives and characters of Korean reality franchises.

In the early 2010s, the exportation of Korean unscripted formats has engendered additional scholarly investigation in the expansion of an imagined boundary in constructing reality on television. Many media scholars have claimed that the similarity and dissimilarity of the cultural traditions between Korea and China have been immersed in the Chinese localization of Korean reality show formats (Cho & Zhu, 2017; J. Kim, 2018; Kim & Huang, 2017; Zeng & Sparks, 2017). The transnational expansion of Korean reality television has also been discussed in the context of the Korean Wave phenomenon. D. Y. Jin (2017) claimed that the reality format trade with China and the U.S. has opened up a new phase of media flows, making Korean reality shows a global commodity. Certainly, recent publications have enlightened the visibility of Korean unscripted formats on a global scale. However, the geographic gravity of cultural sensibility needs to be more carefully considered in the transaction of media products and practices.

This study is conducted based on two major considerations. First, because of the domination of U.S./European cases in English-based publications, the transmedia storytelling scholarship has remained uncharted territory with respect to Korea's transmedia franchise. Second, television scholars have rarely paid attention to the authorship of reality television. This tendency can possibly be attributed to the production culture of U.S./ European reality television. By addressing the regionality of Korean reality show production, this study spotlights a Korean show director who has shaped the perceptual closeness between show casts and audiences by blurring the line between reality and fiction, and by promoting the regionalization of transmediated reality in an East Asian context. This study not only fills a gap in the discussion of reality television within the local context but also proposes the intersection of reality-based programming and transmedia storytelling in general.

A Korean transmedia reality show: *New Journey to the West*

The emergence of digitally converged media culture has resulted in the celebration of the real in the media industry; primetime television is filled with reality show formats, whereas online media providers have offered the ordinary individual a revolutionary domain for displaying the self (Andrejevic, 2004). Relatedly, the proliferation of *meokbang* and makeup tutorial videos shows that digital media environments have reshaped the audience's preference for consuming everyday reality (Andrejevic, 2004, p. 38). Nicholas Negroponte and Bill Gates' expectation that online media would take the lead in deconstructing "the top-down model of information delivery" turns out to be right: the potential of Web-based reality shows increasingly drew attention from conventional media sectors (as cited in Andrejevic, 2004, p. 38). Korean media conglomerates then sought out new revenue sources in the convergence of media culture across traditional and online platforms, developing their own multichannel network business models.[4]

In these newly shaped infrastructures of media and communications, reality show directors who had been working in network television have experienced mixed feelings with respect to crises and opportunities. At a public lecture in January 2018, Na described *NJW* as the byproduct of pressures to survive from profoundly reformulated media environments. At the preproduction stage, he established three personal goals to achieve from the *NJW* experiment: (1) checking the potential of Internet content; (2) penetrating the Chinese media market; and (3) positioning entertainers at the center of storytelling (Yoo, 2018). He also mentioned that, by taking an alternative approach to producing and distributing his new reality series, he wanted to attract younger audiences, who prefer to watch short clips of the television series on YouTube rather than watch its full episodes on television (Yoo, 2018).

His testimonies echo recent scholarly discussions regarding the transformations that technological innovation has largely generated in television production. As Clarke (2013) pointed out, major networks have no longer sustained their position within the media market; indeed, they are being forced to work with "alternative organizational and creative forms" (p. 1) in experimental ways. Hence, the creation of a transmedia entertainment brand is a destined direction by which the media industry seeks to expand its properties in the era of media convergence (Bernardo, 2014; Clarke, 2013; Jenkins, 2006; McErlean, 2018). The emergence of "a lean-forward audience" (Staffans, 2014, p. xv), who uses mobile phones, puts tablets on the table, and listens to the television in a room, has also transitioned the media industry's main task, from alluding to the active audience to providing them with "engaging and immersive content" (Staffans, 2014, p. xv).

The reconfiguration of the audience was well reflected in the first season of the *NJW* series. All clips of each episode did not last longer than ten minutes. Na explained that this reality show franchise aimed to "provide joy to people for at least five minutes per day when commuting on buses and subways" (as quoted in E. S. Jin, 2015, para. 4). Na's comments resonate "a shift from an appointment-based model of television viewing toward an engagement-based paradigm" (Jenkins et al., 2013, p. 116). Such transformations were, as mentioned by Jenkins et al. (2013), happening in the contemporary televisual sphere: Instead of bringing the audience in the living room at a certain time, television directors offer audiences more channels to consume media content according to their own schedules (Jenkins et al., 2013).

Na's other experiment through the second season of *NJW* series, however, suggests that audiences' loyalty to the specific media franchise can be more complicated in the post-television era (Cho, 2015). Put simply, the promise of spreadability does not guarantee audiences' adherence to a specific media brand. For example, CJ E&M chose a windowing strategy for the second season of *NJW* instead of holding its exclusive distribution through the online platform. A new episode was first released on the Internet; two days later, that episode was broadcast on the cable network tvN. The company not only released clips of each episode broadcast on cable television but also uploaded unabridged editions to the Web-based media platform, Naver TV Cast. Although the media company expected this combined distribution strategy to attract more consumers, it ended up distracting the audience, as was reflected in lower viewership compared with its first season (Yoo, 2018). Na admitted the failure of the strategy in a statement outlining that

> the viewers who had missed the Internet broadcasting thought that they would watch the episode on television two days later, while others did not watch the show on television due to the fact that they could watch the episode on the Internet anytime later.
>
> (as quoted in Yoo, 2018, para. 2)

As he pointed out, the increasing availability of the reality series on multiple platforms discouraged viewers from prioritizing viewership of the show.

In addition, the *NJW* case proposes the possibility that the imagined boundary of everyday reality can be regionally constructed in an era of media convergence. What to point out is that *NJW* contains the Chinese folktale's basic storyline and characters: the main protagonist, Tang Sanzang (a monk), who was assigned by Gautama Buddha to the Western regions (such as Central Asia and India) to obtain sacred Buddhist texts (sutras), and three companions—Sun Wukong (a monkey), Sha Wusing (a celestial), and Zhu Bajie (a pig)—who supported the monk to atone for their sins (Wu, Jenner, & Shi, 2003). Each season of *NJW* begins with a game that assigns the fictional characters to the show hosts. In *NJW*'s earlier seasons, any celebrity who had won the game became the monk, Tang Sanzang, and assigned other roles to his colleagues. By revitalizing the classic Chinese story, the director attempted to heighten a sense of intimacy about the show among Chinese audiences (Yoo, 2018). Moreover, by adding the main plot of a Japanese manga, *Dragon Ball*, to the show, gathering the seven wish-granting balls to make a wish, Na raised affinity among audiences who have consumed the Japanese transmedia franchise. The deployment of regionally renowned storylines and characters yielded a meaningful outcome from the neighboring market.[5] For instance, an official of the company viewed the success of its second season as attributable to the active application of Chinese folklore and the employment of Chengdu, a historical city in China, as the main production site in the episodes (Jeong, 2016).[6]

The adaptation of *JW* and *Dragon Ball* led the show directors to film the series in multiple cities in China and Japan; the main hosts and the production crew traveled to major cities in the East and Southeast Asian region, including Xian, Chengdu, Lijiang, Guilin, Xiamen, and Hong Kong in China; Hanoi, Cat Ba, Hai Phong, and Sa Pa in Vietnam; and Hokkaido in Japan. By visiting these locations, the transmedia reality franchise embodied the story world on a regional scale; more importantly, the mediated spectacle of the regionally constructed stories and characters allows the audience to experience the regional specificity of a constructed reality world across media platforms. The mixture of reality and constructed reality in the *NJW* franchise resonates with Jenkins' (2007) notion of world building, in which transmedia stories are "based not on individual characters or specific plots but rather a complex fictional world that can sustain multiple interrelated characters and their stories" (Jenkins, 2007, para. 3).

Finally, the director centralized the entertainers and production crew in the storytelling, which was key to making the show's storyline interactive, unpredictable, and expandable. During the show, viewers have often seen the director break his planned storylines and ignore preset events.[7] The reactions of the celebrities and the production crew convinced audiences that the situations were "real" rather than scripted or planned. Similarly, in the first and last episodes of the *NJW* series, viewers were watching scenes where the director, writer, and celebrity went to have dinner and drink beer in private settings. The assistant directors and production associates either used their mobile phones or set up camcorders on the wall to film their ad hoc gatherings. The director actively used the footage of conversations among the entertainers and production staff behind the scenes as a source of presenting "the real" in the reality show franchise. In other words, the unexpected situations, shot by handheld camcorders and mobile phones, guide the audience to experience "relatively authentic" reality in the trans-mediated story world.

Reality show director as a storyteller

Before the release of the *NJW* series, at the media conference, show hosts collectively described their trips as amazing experiences of reuniting with former colleagues (E. S. Jin, 2015). Such emotions were developed because the four members of *2D1N*'s first season—Seung-gi Lee, Ho-dong Kang, Ji-won Eun, and Su-geun Lee—appeared on the first season of *NJW* (Cho, 2015). Their comeback was possible because the director and main writer of *2D1N Season 1* created the *NJW* series. At the media conference, Na also confessed that he had decided to produce *NJW* when the youngest host, Seung-gi Lee, had talked about another trip with the old members (as quoted in E. S. Jin, 2015).

In fact, the reunion of the old members had little chance of success, given that some of them—Ho-dong Kang and Su-geun Lee—had been left out of television shows because of scandals.[8] Despite their damaged reputation, Na invited them to the *NJW* franchise. At a certain level, Na's decision gave these controversial figures a chance to resume their professional careers in the entertainment industry. Their joining the reality show reiterates Andrejevic's (2004) argument that reality television provides faded stars with space for a comeback (p. 3). It is important to mention, though, that their return to show business is possible only when the show director not only gives them an opportunity to appear on television but also shapes their images in a positive way. According to Benjamin (1955/1968), the storyteller has the capacity to employ his life as the basis for creating a story. This view assists us in understanding why Na employed his unscripted interactions with the celebrities in the narrative of the *NJW* series. By doing so, he built up his position as a storyteller who talks to reality show viewers about his long-standing friendships. That approach seemed to be successful in reducing the audiences' complaints about Na's decision to bring the controversial individuals back to the televisual sphere. By taking the role of the storyteller in the show, Na guided the audience to experience Kang and Lee's regret and repentance as seen in his eyes. Because the intimate relationship between celebrities and audiences is key to producing a successful reality show, Na wisely employed his social credibility to restore the audience's fondness for the celebrities. As a result, the success of this reality franchise has been ongoing after its migration from online broadcasts to a cable channel; according to AGB Nielsen Korea, the show's viewership had gradually increased from the first episode of its second season (2.7%) to the eighth episode of its sixth season (6.6%)[9]; moreover, *NJW* ranked at the top of Gallup's survey of favorite Korean television shows in November 2018 (Gallup Report, 2018).

It is notable that Na never explicitly mentioned on the program that *NJW* is a sequel to *2D1N*. Instead, he let the show hosts and production crew members talk about their memories of *2D1N* in a natural setting. This strategy echoes Benjamin's (1955/1968) understanding of the storyteller as a counselor: "Counsel is less an answer to a question than a proposal concerning the continuation of a story which is just unfolding" (p. 86). A particular example is a relatively flattering relationship between the oldest and the youngest hosts. Many Korean viewers observed how Ho-dong Kang strictly taught Seung-gi Lee about his reaction techniques during the first season of *2D1N* in the late-2000s. However, in the first season of *NJW*, the tables appear to have turned. Because the show's first season was targeting online users, the youngest host, Seung-gi Lee, played a leading role in meeting the target audience's expectations.[10] The main host, Ho-dong Kang, was frustrated with Lee's bold expressions because such Internet slang terms were not allowed within the realm of reality shows, broadcast on major networks. Indeed, the knowledge gap between Kang and Lee regarding online media cultures became a main source of humor in the first season of the *NJW* series. A symbolic connection between the two franchises was made in the description of the host's continued but changed relationships, which guided viewers to absorb the two franchises as a whole story.

The ways of creating characters and managing unexpected events in *NJW* echo Friedman's (2002) emphasis on postmodernism in constructing reality on television. Importantly, the fundamental deconstruction of the boundaries between realities and constructed realities is made within "the modernist conviction that there is still a reality 'out there'" (p. 2).

He underscored that celebrities have produced intimacy, based on their naturalistic acting skills, in helping audiences experience a different level of reality about the characters and events on television (Friedman, 2002, p. 13). His claim is helpful in understanding what the director has done in the *NJW* series. Na perceived the similarity between the celebrity of *NJW* and the fictional characters of *JW* and adopted the main plot of *NJW*, where the sinners go on a journey to pay for their sins. Then, he invited the audience to observe the celebrity's genuine effort to recover their social reputation. This was only possible in the reality format because people believe that what they watch is real, even though the celebrities were playing fictional characters in the mediated world of everyday reality.

Spin-offs: the longevity of transmedia storytelling

The success of the *NJW* series has led to two spin-off series—*Kang's Kitchen* (KK) (Lee & Na, 2017a) and *Youth Over Flowers—Winner* (*YF–Winner*) (Lee & Na, 2017b). These spin-off series display not only the active application of transmedia storytelling strategies to reality television production but also the aura of media players in the expansion of real stories across program formats, titles, and time slots. The production of supplementary stories was initiated from the director's inside joke during the second episode of *NJW*'s fourth season. In that episode, the television director asked the show's hosts to complete five difficult missions within a limited time frame, granting prizes when they were completed.[11] At the end of the season, Minho finally got his wish by completing the missions. He then used the opportunity to go on *YF* with the remaining members of his boy band, Winner, and the other members of *NJW* decided to shoot their version of *Youn's Kitchen* (Lee & Na, 2017–2018).[12] By actively integrating the two reality show formats that Na had produced, *NJW* demonstrated that Na's filmography had become a foundation of transmedia and intertextual storytelling.

Na's excellent skills in developing transmedia and intertextual characters and stories are apparent in his earlier works. His travel reality show, *YF*, which originally premiered in 2014, is a good example.[13] In this programming, Na strategically extended the fictional characters and relationships to real-life situations by casting some rising and renowned actors who had previously appeared on tvN's original series, such as *Reply 1988* (Lee & Shin, 2015) and *Reply 1994* (Lee & Shin, 2013). Therefore, the loyal viewing communities of these television dramas could discover the symbolic connections between the dramas and reality shows on tvN channels. Notably, these television drama series were directed by Won-ho Shin, a former show director who worked with Na in the division of entertainment program production for KBS. Their comradeship was an important source of intertextual storytelling, in which Na played a cameo role in the television series, *Response 1994,* and Shin appeared in the *YF* series to assist in disguising actors who had worked with him.

YF—Winner, a spin-off of *NJW*, has offered loyal viewers the experience of interconnecting constructed reality with everyday reality across media platforms. The original plot of the *YF* series was to invite rising stars on overseas trips by surprise. However, the production of the *YF—Winner* was already announced in the fourth season of *NJW*, and therefore the production team had difficulties in taking the members of Winner to the airport without recognition. That situation certainly attracted the fans of the *NJW* series, and the show director and hosts actively promoted the spin-off series through the extension of the media narrative to the domain of social media; after the show's director expressed her embarrassment at a media interview, the members of Winner teased the director via Instagram (Park, 2017). The interactions between the celebrities and the production crew were later included in the episode of *YF—Winner*.

Another spinoff series, *KK*, was developed based on the reality cooking show, *Youn's Kitchen*. The main narrative of the reality show was to open a Korean restaurant in foreign countries. The show's franchise has become one of the most successful programs that Na has produced for tvN (Woo, 2018). Similarly, in *KK*, Na gave Ho-dong Kang the mission of being a rookie who served pork cutlets and omelet rice to the guests of ten teams during the day. The marriage of *NJW* with *Youn's Kitchen* drew the public's attention, and *KK* received high viewer ratings. During an interesting moment in *KK*'s promotional video, Kang filmed himself and other guests in a car using his mobile phone, saying that the footage could possibly be used for the show. It seemed natural for the show's hosts to play any role behind the scenes, as well as the director, who shot the gathering scene with the show's hosts of *NJW*, in which he had called Kang an older brother (*hyeong*) informally. Kang and Na's actions showed that the boundary between hosts and production associates, and onstage and offstage were often deconstructed in the programs, which ultimately guided viewers to immerse themselves in the transmediated reality world that Na had created.

Notably, the addition of storylines and characters through the production of the spin-off series did not ruin the singularity of the transmedia brand. *YF—Winner* offers the audience a context in which it is a part of the *NJW* series by inserting shots of the *NJW* members gathering in the first episode, and by releasing a promotional video for *KK* in the finale of the series. Similarly, the narratives of these two spin-off series were combined, in which the four members of Winner abruptly appeared in the ending scene of *KK*. After closing the restaurant, all the hosts of *KK* went to karaoke with the production crew, and Winner entered the room by singing a song. The encounter of these two spin-off series helped the director promote another season of *NJW*.

Na's remarks in a public lecture resonate with the different contributions of the two spin-off series in developing his transmedia entertainment franchise. In his view, there are two ways of guaranteeing the survival of a new show from the stiff competition at large: attract a mass audience, or draw solid support from targeted audiences (Yoo, 2018). The latter was helpful in explaining why he could continue to produce six seasons of *NJW*, as well as extend the original series in the past three years. Certainly, the construction of media fandom is not the primary objective for traditional television production. Therefore, he attempted to produce the spin-off series, *KK* and *YK* (Yoo, 2018). He claimed that although media fandom can prevent the early termination of a television show, the show's longevity still depends on the mass audience's attention (Yoo, 2018). This market logic is greatly influential in the creation of reality television storytelling as well as in the temporal connection between media platforms. At the same time, he fully admitted that media fandom was necessary to bring television programming to life in the era of multimedia environments. This recognition was reflected in another spinoff series, *YF—Winner*. This spin-off series had relatively low viewership compared with other *YF* series, as well as *NJW*'s spin-off series *KK*. However, this spin-off series is clearly helpful in strengthening the *NJW* series as a transmedia entertainment franchise.

Conclusion: an East Asian context

Jenkins' (2006) articulation of transmedia storytelling raises a fundamental question regarding the mission of media industries in creating a new type of storytelling in the interactive and interconnected condition of media and communication. As he pointed out, the spread-out media culture complicates the flow of media content, and therefore the circuit of media products and services is hardly predictable or regulated. In these new media circumstances, consumers' empowerment has been increasingly acknowledged in media production, and the media industry attempts to improve consumer engagement at a deeper level through the fragmentation of media content across platforms (Jenkins, 2006, p. 17). More to the point, although media fandom has been deeply involved in the proliferation of transmedia contexts, media producers have never lost their prestigious position in the game of transmedia storytelling (Jenkins, 2006).

This study applies Jenkins' notion of transmedia storytelling to the realm of Korean reality television, examining how a Korean show director has shaped the audience's consumption of everyday reality through the deployment of transmedia storytelling strategies. Jenkins (2006) focused on how transmedia storytelling encourages audiences to play "the role of hunters" (p. 21), collecting parts of a whole story across media platforms in the fictional world. This study, instead, applies his conception of transmedia storytelling to exploring the Korean media industry's production of a transmedia reality show franchise, *NJW*, by illuminating the role of storytellers who spread pieces of the entire story on multiple media texts and channels. By doing so, this study identified the following characteristics of the East Asian-based transmedia reality franchise. First, *NJW* takes viewers into a space where the boundary between reality and constructed reality is consistently shrinking, and where celebrities' genuine personalities and their characters in the original story, *JW* and *Dragon Ball*, and its prequel, *2D1N*, are consistently intermixed. The mobility and continuity of storylines and characters across space and time motivate viewers to immerse themselves in grasping the transmedia franchise as a whole. Their knowledge about the original stories and their memories of regularly watching the show's prequel then becomes the major engine of mapping out fragmented stories as a whole world. Second, the third season of *NJW* contains a cast of new characters, expanding its storytelling and moving beyond its image as a sequel of the reality show *2D1N*. It brings the original cast members back to the show in the next season, and it also extends the storytelling without a recap. In its fifth season, *NJW* broke the audiences' perception that the series was limited to the realm of *NJW* and *Dragon Ball* by borrowing new characters from horror movies. Third, the show's director also dissolves the conventional boundary between onscreen and offscreen. When the show director negotiates with celebrities about the direction of upcoming episodes, it helps audiences believe the authenticity of the reality, but also helps them stay tuned to the expansion of the franchise with another spin-off series. Fourth, the director adopted the classic Chinese novel and Japanese manga because of the familiarity of these regional stories to Korean audiences. This transmedia storytelling strategy echoes Benjamin's (1955/1968) view on the impetus of a local community's traditions in the story world. Finally, it is necessary to mention that *NJW*'s show director, employing his personal relationships with entertainers, established his own transmedia storytelling. By deconstructing the line between objective reality and the subjective consumption of reality, he has developed his aura as the storyteller in the realm of reality television, revealing the regional gravity of cultural experiences and arousing the regional audience's sense of belonging in the transmedia story-craft world.

Notes

1 Changes in the narratives and characters of reality television can be made because of the different regulations between the two media channels. Unlike network and cable television, specific brand names can be mentioned in Web-based television series in the Korean media industry. When the show host, Ho-dong Kang, who was accustomed to the production culture of network television, revealed his concerns about mentioning the brand names of investing companies, the director Na responded to him that "you should" instead of "you can" (Cho, 2015, para. 3).

2 *2D1N* increased the nationwide popularity of its hosts and production crews, including the director, Na, and the main writer, Woo-jeong Lee, who have often appeared onscreen (Pyo, 2012).

3 The Baeksang Arts Awards is one of the major awards ceremonies in the Korean entertainment industry. This annual event is organized by the IS Plus Corporation. The Grand Prize is awarded to the individual who has had outstanding achievements in film and television production.

4 As an example, MBC, one of the major networks in Korea, initiated an attempt to integrate webcam-based, single-handed, live performances into television

programming in the early 2010s. The cable television provider tvN later advanced that tendency by producing online-exclusive content in the first season of *NJW*.

5 When Tencent—a major provider of value-added Internet services in China—released the latest episode of *NJW* to Chinese audiences the day after the episode had been broadcast on Korean television, with subtitles, each clip reached approximately 30 to 40 million views (Yoo, 2018). According to the company, tvNgo, the show's second season had significantly increased its popularity in China, surpassing a total of 120 million hits with the season's first four episodes (Jeong, 2016).

6 The intra-regional expansion of Korean reality franchises can be discussed in "the market logic of territoriality" (Zhao, 2018, para. 22). Although the Chinese government has actively employed its sovereignty in regulating the online media world, market players have established their own logic of territorialization to boost revenue (Zhao, 2018).

7 On the shooting day of the show's Season 2.5, after having lunch, the director and writer had friendly chats with the show's hosts. Then, the director made an impromptu suggestion about whether the three younger hosts—Kyuhyun, Jae-hyun Ahn, and Minho—could bounce a ball with a bat more than 20 times without it dropping on the ground; if they could do so, the director would cancel the shooting schedule for the day. When the three hosts successfully completed this suggested mission, the director ordered the assistant directors to leave the production location.

8 Ho-dong Kang announced his temporary leave from the entertainment industry because of his involvement in a tax evasion scandal on September 9, 2011. At a media conference, he stated, "I am sorry for causing the public to worry. From this moment, I will temporarily retire from the entertainment industry" ("Kang Ho Dong," 2011, para. 1). Soo-geun Lee was investigated for online gambling in 2013, which is (with some exceptions) illegal in Korea. That scandal prevented him from appearing on television programs for years ("Why Celebrities," 2013).

9 The data were retrieved from AGB Nielson Korea (https://www.nielsenkorea.co.kr).

10 Seung-gi Lee directly mentioned the legal and socially problematic behaviors in which the other older hosts had been previously involved; he referred to Su-geun Lee as "a betting man who lives in Sangam-dong" (*Sangam-dong betingnam*) and Ji-won Eun as "a divorced man who lives in Yeoido" (*Yeoido singlenam*) (Lee & Na, 2015, ep. 1, as cited in Kwon, 2015, para. 4).

11 After completing the missions successfully, the show hosts would spin on the spot for 15 rounds, and then touch a dart board with their fingers, which showed various gifts and benefits. The outcome of that game went against the director and writer's expectations: Minho, the youngest member of *NJW's* Season 4, touched very tiny areas for a Porsche and a Lamborghini with his forefinger. The director and the writer, who could not afford to give the hosts such expensive presents, tried negotiating with them.

12 Another spinoff series, *KK* (Lee & Na, 2017a), was developed based on the reality cooking show, *Youn's Kitchen* (Lee & Na, 2017–2018). The main narrative of the reality show was to open a Korean restaurant in foreign countries. The veteran actress Yuh-jung Youn played the role of the rookie cook who offered foreign guests Korean dishes, such as bulgogi rice and bibimbap. Some actors and actresses—Seo-jin Lee, Yu-mi Jung, Gu Shin, and Seo-joon Park—participated in the show's production, playing the role of the cook's assistant. The show's franchise has become one of the most successful programs that Na has produced for tvN.

13 In the programming, three singer-songwriters—Sang Yoon, Hee-yeol You, and Juck Lee—went to Peru. As a surprise, they were informed that they would be taking the trip in a couple of hours before the flight, and they had to get

on board without their personal items. Their unprepared travel with lifelong colleagues and friends gave viewers an escape from daily life. Since then, three more seasons were produced, making it another hit franchise for tvN.

References

AKP STAFF. (2011, September 11). Kang Ho Dong to temporarily leave the industry to reflect on his actions. *AllKpop.com*. Retrieved from https://www.allkpop.com/article/2011/09/kang-ho-dong-to-temporarily-leave-the-industry-to-reflect-on-his-actions

Andrejevic, M. (2004). *Reality TV: The work of being watched*. Lanham, MD: Rowman & Littlefield.

Benjamin, W. (1968). The storyteller: Reflections on the works of Nikolai Leskov. In H. Arendt (Ed.), & H. B. Jovanovich (Trans.), *Illuminations: Essays and reflections* (pp. 83–110). New York, NY: Schocken Books. (Original work published 1955).

Bernardo, N. (2014). *Transmedia 2.0: How to create an entertainment brand using a transmedial approach to storytelling*. Lisboa, Portual: beActive books.

Bonner, F. (2003). *Ordinary television: Analyzing popular TV*. London, UK: SAGE Publications.

Caldwell, J. (2002). Prime-time fiction theorizes the docu-real. In J. Friedman (Ed.), *Reality squared: Televisual discourse on the real* (pp. 259–292). New Brunswick, NJ: Rutgers University Press.

Cho, Y. (2015, October 6). Sinseoyugi, poseuteu TV sinhotan doelkka [*New Journey to the West*, would it be the sign of the post-TV era?]. *Joongang Ilbo*. Retrieved from https://news.joins.com/article/18803825

Cho, Y., & Zhu, H. (2017). Interpreting the television format phenomenon between South Korea and China through inter-Asian frameworks. *International Journal of Communication, 11*, 2332–2349.

Clarke, M. (2013). *Transmedia television: New trends in network serial production*. New York, NY: Bloomsbury.

Couldry, N., & Hepp, A. (2017). *The mediated construction of reality*. Cambridge, UK: Polity Press.

Fetveit, A. (2002). Reality TV in the digital era: A paradox in visual culture? In J. Friedman (Ed.), *Reality squared: Televisual discourse on the real* (pp. 119–137). New Brunswick, NJ: Rutgers University Press.

Friedman, J. (Ed.). (2002). Introduction. In J. Friedman (Ed.), *Realty squared: Televisual discourse on the real* (pp. 1–24). New Brunswick, NJ: Rutgers University Press.

Gallup Report. (2018, November 21). Yojeum gajang joahaneun peuloglaemeun? [What are your favorite television programs these days?] *Gallup Korea*. Retrieved from http://www.gallup.co.kr/gallupdb/reportDownload.asp?seqNo=965

Jenkins, H. (1992/2013). *Textual poachers: Television fans and participatory culture*. New York, NY: Routledge.

Jenkins, H. (2006). *Convergence culture: Where old and new media collide*. New York, NY: New York University Press.

Jenkins, H. (2007, March 21). Transmedia storytelling 101 [Blog post]. Retrieved from http://henryjenkins.org/blog/2007/03/transmedia_storytelling_101.html

Jenkins, H. (2010). Transmedia storytelling and entertainment: An annotated syllabus. *Continuum: Journal of Media & Cultural Studies, 24*(6), 943–958. doi: 10.1080/10304312.2010.510599

Jenkins, H., Ford, S., & Green, J. (2013). *Spreadable media: Creating value and meaning in a networked culture.* New York, NY: New York University Press.

Jeong, B. K. (2016, May 12). "New Journey to the West" is a hit in China. *Korea Joongang Daily.* Retrieved from http://koreajoongangdaily.joins.com/news/article/article.aspx?aid=3018610

Jin, D. Y. (2017). *New Korean Wave: Transnational cultural power in the age of social media.* Chicago: University of Illinois Press.

Jin, E. S. (2015, September 3). Exploring a new frontier in content. *Korea Joongang Daily.* Retrieved from http://koreajoongangdaily.joins.com/news/article/article.aspx?aid=3008710

Jin, M. J. (2015, September 7). "New Journey" hits 6.1M viewers. *Korea Joongang Daily.* Retrieved from http://koreajoongangdaily.joins.com/news/article/Article.aspx?aid=3008831

Kang, J. (2014). *Walter Benjamin and the media: The spectacle of modernity.* Cambridge, UK: Polity.

Kim, J. (2018). Regionalizing reality: The rise of East Asian collaborations in television production. In M. Keane, B. Yecies, & T. Flew (Eds.), *Willing collaborators: Refashioning content for the Chinese media market* (pp. 155–170). London, UK: Rowman & Littlefield.

Kim, J., & Huang, L. (2017). *The unscripted format trade in a new era of the Korean Wave: The Chinese remaking of Korean reality TV, Dad! Where Are You Going?* In T. Yoon & D. Jin (Eds.), *The Korean Wave: Retrospect and prospect* (pp. 209–224). London, UK: Lexington Books.

Kim, S. (2011). Hangug lieoliti peulogeulaemui jeongseogujowa munhwajeongchi-hag [The structure of feelings and cultural politics in Korean TV reality shows]. *Broadcasting Culture Research, 23*(2), 37–72.

Kwon, M. (2015, September 4). Singseoyugi ganghodong, inteones bujeonge-ungja hudeoldeolt eige inteoneseulo hamyeon yogeul an deuleomeogneundago? [New journey to the west, Ho-dong Kang, a novice Internet user showed his surprise. "If you do this on the Internet, you do not take criticism?] *News Inside.* Retrieved from http://www.newsinside.kr/news/articleView.html?idxno=343233

Lee, W. (Writer), & Na, Y. (Director). (2007–2012). *2Days and 1Night* [Television series, Season 1]. Seoul, Korea: KBS2.

Lee, W. (Writer), & Na, Y. (Director). (2013–2014). *Sisters over flowers* [Television series]. Seoul, Korea: tvN.

Lee, W. (Writer), & Na, Y. (Director). (2013–2018). *Grandpas over flowers* [Television series]. Seoul, Korea: tvN.

Lee, W. (Writer), & Na, Y. (Director). (2014–2016). *Youth over flowers* [Television series]. Seoul, Korea: tvN.

Lee, W. (Writer), & Na, Y. (Directors). (2014–2017). *Three meals a day* [Television series]. Seoul, Korea: tvN.

Lee, W. (Writer), & Na, Y. (Director). (2015–2018). *New journey to the west* [Television series]. Seoul, Korea: tvN.

Lee, W. (Writer), & Na, Y. (Director). (2017–2018). *Youn's kitchen* [Television series]. Seoul, Korea: tvN.

Lee, W. (Writer), & Na, Y (Director). (2017a). *Kang's kitchen* [Television series]. Seoul, Korea: tvN.

Lee, W. (Writer), & Na, Y. (Director). (2017b). *Youth over flowers—Winner* [Television series]. Seoul, Korea: tvN.

Lee, W. (Writer), & Shin, W. (Director). (2013). *Reply 1994* [Television series]. Seoul, Korea: CJ E&M.

Lee, W. (Writer), & Shin, W. (Director). (2015). *Reply 1988* [Television series]. Seoul, Korea: CJ E&M.

McErlean, K. (2018). *Interactive narratives and transmedia storytelling: Creating immersive stories across new media platforms.* New York, NY: Routledge.

Murray, S., & Ouellette, L. (Eds.). (2009). *Reality TV: Remaking television culture.* New York, NY: New York University Press.

Ouellette, L., & Murray, S. (2009). Introduction. In S. Murray & L. Ouellette (Eds.), *Reality TV: Remaking television culture* (pp. 1–20). New York, NY: New York University Press.

Park, E. J. (2017, October 12). "Wineo nabchihalyeogo ..." Gajja inseuta gesimul ollin "Kkochcheongchun" PD [The show director of YF updated a fake post to Instagram in order to disguise members of Winner]. *Wikitree.co.kr.* Retrieved from http://m.wikitree.co.kr/main/news_view.php?id=316234

Pyo, J. M. (2012, February 25). "1bag 2il" 5neyon, sicheonglyul TOP5ui myeongjangmyeondeul [The best scenes of *2Days and 1Night* in the past five years]. Osen. Retrieved from https://news.nate.com/view/20120225n02728

Ryoo, W. J., & Park, J. W. (2012). Seobaibeol pomaes peulogeulaeme chimtuhan sinjayujuui gyeongjaeng damlon: Peulogeulaem chaetaeggwa jejaggwajeonge daehan saengsanja simsheunginteobyuleul jungsimeulo [Neo-liberal discourses on competition permeated in the survival format program: Focusing on an in-depth interview with the producers]. *Broadcasting Culture Reserach,* 24(1), 139–165.

Staffans, S. (2014). Foreword. In N. Bernardo (Ed.), *Transmedia 2.0: How to create an entertainment brand using a transmedial approach to storytelling* (p. xv). Dublin, Ireland: beActive Books.

Why celebrities get hooked on gambling. (2013, November 12). *The Chosun Ilbo.* Retrieved from http://english.chosun.com/site/data/html_dir/2013/11/12/2013111201152.html

Woo, J. Y. (2018, January 24). "Youn's Kitchen 2" continues to grip TV viewers. *The Korea Times.* Retrieved from http://www.koreatimesus.com/youns-kitchen-2-continues-to-grip-tv-viewers/

Wu, C., Jenner, J. F., & Shi, C. (2003). *Journey to the west.* Beijing, China: Foreign Languages Press.

Yoo, Y. S. (2018, January 24). Na-yeong-seog PD "sin-seo-yu-gi, gyeol-gwa-man noh-go bo-myeon sil-pae-jak" [Nah, Young-Seok PD, "New journey to the west is a failure, looking at its results only"]. *Nocut News.* Retrieved from http://www.nocutnews.co.kr/news/4911688#csidxf234c41a0310714b43a8505182d2a68

Yoon, T. J. (2011). Jeongseojeog chamyeowa siljaeui jaeguseong: Hangug lieoliti telebijeonsyoui jagdongbangsige daehan gochal [Affective participations and reconstruction of reality: A study on Korean reality television shows]. *Broadcasting Culture Research,* 23(2), 7–36.

Zeng, W., & Sparks, C. (2017). Localization as negotiation: Producing a Korean format in contemporary China. *International Journal of Digital Television,* 8(1), 81–98.

Zhao, E. J. (2018). Negotiating state and copyright territorialities in overseas expansion: The case of China's online video streaming platforms. *Media Industries,* 5(1). doi:10.3998/mij.15031809.0005.107

4 Snack culture's dream of big screen culture

Korean webtoons' transmedia storytelling

Dal Yong Jin

Introduction

> Snack culture—referring to the quick habit of consuming information and cultural resources rather than engaging in a deeper road—is becoming representative of the Korean cultural scene. It is easy to find Koreans reading news articles or watching films or dramas on their smartphones on a subway. To cater to this increasing number of mobile users whose tastes are changing fast, the web-based cultural content is churning out diverse sub-genres from conventional formats of movies, dramas, and cartoons to novels.
>
> (Chung, A. Y., 2014)

Snack culture was first coined by *Wired* in 2007 to explain a modern tendency to look for convenient culture that is indulged within a short duration of time, similar to how people eat snacks like cookies within a few minutes. Snack culture mostly depicts the changing habit of cultural consumption: consuming popular culture, such as music, television programs, games, and movies, within such a short time period, even less than ten minutes at a time, instead of watching films for two hours due to the emergence of digital technologies, in particular smartphones (Miller, 2007).

Snack culture has become a new trend in the global cultural industries, and Korea especially develops this new culture, including webtoon,[1] web-dramas,[2] and web-entertainment, due to the convergence of a newly emerging cultural genre—webtoon—and smartphones. As one of the most wired countries in the world, Korea has advanced several cutting-edge technologies, including broadband and smartphones—the highest in terms of penetration—and these digital technologies have greatly changed not only people's daily lives but their habits in consuming popular culture.

Many Koreans started to enjoy webtoons on the two largest web portals—Naver and Daum—with their notebook computers at home and work in the early 2000s. Now, on a subway, one witnesses people, regardless of their ages, looking at their smartphones and scrolling down the screen quickly with their thumbs. If a smile can be spotted on the smartphone user's face, it would not be far-fetched to say they could be reading their favorite webtoon (Jin, E. S., 2014). The Internet and the smartphone have become drive engines for the growth of snack culture, and many new creators in the realm of popular culture, including webtoon, film, and drama, quickly started to utilize media convergence between digital technologies and cultural content to consequently develop a new type of culture. In other words, with the rise of the smartphones, people's lifestyles and consumption patterns have substantially shifted, and in this new media environment, webtoons flourish in the early 21st century. What is interesting is that this small culture has become a new resource for big screen culture as webtoons have continued to be turned into films, dramas, and digital games. Seemingly tiny, trivial, and conveniently packaged culture has become one of the most significant sources for digital media storytelling.

Three major concepts—webtoon, smartphone, and snack culture—arrived in Korean society only a decade or so ago, and therefore, there has been little research about the socio-cultural reasons for the growth of webtoons as snack culture and its influences on big screen culture. In order to fill the gap, by employing media convergence supported by transmedia storytelling as a major theoretical framework alongside historical and textual analyses, this chapter first historicizes the emergence of snack culture. It divides the evolution of snack culture—in particular webtoon culture, —followed by becoming big screen culture, into three major periods according to the surrounding new media ecology. Then, it examines the ways in which webtoons have become one of the major resources for transmedia storytelling. Finally, it addresses the reasons why seemingly small snack culture becomes big screen culture in the 2010s with the case of *Along with the Gods: The Two Worlds*, which has transformed from a popular webtoon to a successful big screen movie.

The evolution of webtoons and transmedia storytelling in the digital media era

The webtoon-based transmedia storytelling age can be divided into three historical stages. The first generation could be represented by drawing characters on personal homepages between the late 1990s and the early 2000s, which also became the initial stage of digital transmedia storytelling. The second generation was the time when webtoonists started to post webtoons on Internet portals between 2003 and 2008, when selected few webtoons turned into big screen culture, but commercially were not successful. The third generation began with the introduction and growth of smartphones starting in 2009, which symbolizes the boom of digital transmedia storytelling, both commercially and aesthetically.

The first generation of Korean webtoons and early transmedia storytelling

The history of webtoons dates back to the late 1990s when personal webpages were launched. The expenses of production on the web were not as high as they were with magazines, and independent *manhwa* creators could also create new works based on their own ideas (K-Studio, 2013; Jin, D. Y., 2015). Back in the 1990s, before the coinage of the term webtoon, again, Korean comic artists began publishing on the Web (Marshall, 2016). Park Kwang-su's *Kwang-su Thinking* starting in April 1997 became the first digital cartoon, and it was transformed into a play with the same title in November 2006 (*Yonhap News*, 2009).

Regardless, Chollian, an old form of the Internet service engine, established Chollian Webtoon to provide webtoons to the readers on August 8, 2000. The webtoon was defined as manhwa which was created to post on the web with web-focused attributes, such as vertical layout, color drawing, speedy production and consumption (Seo, C. H., 2017). Chollian, therefore used the term webtoon for the first time in history and *Invincible Hong Assistant Manager* (*Daeri*) created by Hong Yun-pyo became the first webtoon on this particular service (Lee, K. W., 2000). In other words, in 2000, a Korean web portal managed by Chollian created a new site for Internet comics termed webtoon. Most of the comics appearing on this site followed conventional print formats (Cho, H. K., 2016).

While there are several differences between print formats and webtoons, the most important dissimilarity is the webtoon's vertical layout. Before the emergence of vertical-layout webtoons, comics writers who published their works on Internet portal sites such as N4 and Comics Today in 1999–2000 created horizontal pages that were designed to fit the landscape layout of a computer screen. Once the vertical layout came out, however, it was quickly adopted by artists and now dominates the webtoon format (Cho, H. K., 2016).

More importantly, Kwon Yoon-joo—a comic artist of the new generation—created *Snow Cat* in 2001, an endearing comic about the diary of a white cat. In the first stage, she used Cool Cat as a pen name in her homepage in February 1998, but changed it to *Snow Cat* in August 2000. Soon after, *Marine Blues* became one of the most famous webcomics. *Marine Blues* is about the everyday life of Sea Urchin boy, composed of many stories not connected with each other. The webcomic started in 2001 with great popularity, becoming one of the most successful webcomics of all time in the 2000s. There have been several transmedia releases, including online gaming in 2006 and an Android game released in 2012 (Lee, D. W., 2012).

In the late 1990s until the very early 2000s, several cartoonists opened their own webpages to showcase their works instead of trying to debut through magazines. *Papepopo Memories* by Shim Sung-hyun, *Snow Cat* by Kwon Yoon-ju, and *Marine Blues* by Jeong Chul-yeon were big hits (The Age of Webtoons, n.d.; Bae, S. M., 2017). As Hancox (2017) points out, the early form of webtoon can be categorized in digital storytelling, because the creators developed cartoons for a two-to-four-minute multimedia story in which drawings were used to convey a personal story on the webpages. More importantly, although there were some limitations, these early forms of webtoon-like comics as snack culture already became a new source to diverse cultural production. As they opened a door toward a transmedia storytelling format, Korean webtoons have continued as new resources for many cultural forms, including digital gaming, broadcasting, film, and stage performance.

The second generation of Korean webtoons and transmedia storytelling

In the early 2000s, socio-economic milieu surrounding the Korean manhwa industry substantially changed, resulting in the beginning of the boom of webtoons. Most of all, the creation of webtoon portals by the largest Internet portals—Naver and Daum—became a turning point. Daum created a webtoon portal in 2003, followed by Naver in June 2004.[3] During this era, many webtoonists published their works on Internet portals such as Naver and Daum, and some webtoonists also started to receive a writer's fee, although it was small (Park, S. K., 2013; Seo, C. H., 2017).

While there were several famous webtoons that appeared back then, Kang Full's *Sunjeong Manhwa* reached a milestone as it attracted two million viewers per day on average (Lee, M., 2008). Since it was published on Daum by developing a vertical display, it was considered as the first webtoon in the contemporary manhwa industry (Korea Creative Content Agency, 2016). Kang Full combined epics with a vertical scroll method unlike previous digital comics consisting of only a few episodes. He also started to develop a webtoon-serial to be published on the portal site (Korea Creative Content Agency, 2015). These portals, including Naver and Daum, have continued to be the leaders in the webtoon market; however, with the introduction of a fee-based subscription system by another webtoon portal Lezhin, it has become the largest platform to publish webtoons since 2013. For example, during 2017, Lezhin published 157 webtoons, ahead of Naver (87) and Daum (54) (Figure 4.1).

Most of all, webtoons have started to play a central role within transmedia cultural production while being distributed through multiple platforms and re-created since the mid-2000s. Webtoons also become sources for transmedia tie-ins in which several media features converge to produce novel aesthetic effects and new cultural genres (Cho, H. K., 2016). Since debuting in 2003, a sweet and wistful online comic *Sunjeong Manhwa* had become a pop culture phenomenon, generating countless Internet hits. This webtoon was adapted into a film titled *Hello, Schoolgirl* in 2008. The film deviated a lot from its original webtoon; however, it kept the webtoon's main themes intact as the director of the film Ryu Jang-ha preserved the original's essence—the gradual growth and buildup of love regardless of age difference (Soh, J., 2008).

During the second-generation era, Korean webtoons developed different features as webtoons were published as a long vertical strip. They are often

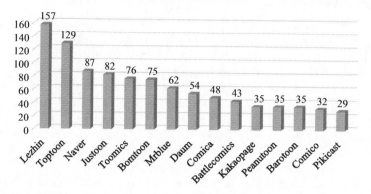

Figure 4.1 Top 15 platforms for the production of webtoons in 2017.
Source: Korea Manhwa Contents Agency (2018).

in color, because, unlike previous *manhwa*, which was mainly printed in black ink due to the cost and time of coloring the *manhwa*, webtoons were posted online; therefore, there was no extra cost to coloring (Jin, D. Y., 2015). This period certainly developed webtoons not only as new youth culture but also as the new source of transmedia storytelling.

The adaptation of webtoon into film and drama fully started with several webtoons developed in this particular period: Kang Full's *Apt* (2006) and B Class Dal-gung's *Dasepo Naughty Girls* (2006) were filmed and released at the same time. Another of Kang Full's webtoons *Ba:Bo*, which was started in 2004, was also adapted into a film in 2008. However, these films based on webtoons were not box office successes (Ha, 2016). *Dasepo Naughty Girls* was originally started in 2004, and Super Action, a cable channel, made it as a drama between 2006 and 2007.

One of the major attributes of transmedia is spreadability—spreading a narrative across platforms—and the Korean webtoon industry started to play a role as a source of transmedia storytelling (Jenkins et al., 2013). As Stavroula (2014, p. 34) points out, "transmedia is especially contextualized from a film perspective because films are key components of transmedia productions," and therefore, many film producers especially pay attention to webtoons. Unlike novels, webtoons consist of visual images supported by text, which are good sources for filmmakers. The adaption of Korean webtoons, however, was limited to a few famous webtoons, and these movies did not achieve commercial successes as a reflection of the difficulty in transmedia storytelling. For example, webtoons are sometimes too simple and at other times too complicated, which demand film directors and television producers to expand or constrict the original stories. During the process, webtoon-based films and television programs lose the originality of webtoons, which bring about controversies among webtoon and/or webtoon-based movies fans.

The third generation of Korean webtoons and storytelling

The third generation starting in the late 2000s has characterized the close convergence between webtoons and smartphones, which further drive the popularity of webtoons and webtoons-based transmedia storytelling. Korea developed its own smartphones in 2009, and webtoonists started to target this new form of digital technology, which has resulted in the growth of webtoons in the 2010s. For example, as a reflection of smartphones, many people were able to read the webtoon *Misaeng* on their smartphone application supported by the Korea Creative Content Agency two weeks in advance by paying fees, while people could read a free-version of *Misaeng* on Daum two weeks later (Daum Webtoon, 2012).

During this period, Yoon Tae Ho has become one of the most influential webtoonists who creates several famous webtoons, including *Moss* (2008–2009), *Inside Men* (2010), and *Misaeng* (2012–2013). The webtoon industry has continued to grow, from 529 million won in 2010 to 5,097 million won in 2018 (estimation), a 9.6 times increase during the same period (KT Economic Management Institute, 2013, 2015).

This period of time marks the boom era of webtoons and webtoon-based transmedia storytelling. For example, *Misaeng* (Incomplete Life) turned into cable tvN's drama in 2014. *Misaeng* was an eponymous webtoon about the office life of a fictional trading company, portraying a hopeless intern's office life, and the television series had been sensational, which has been turned into very successful movies and/or television dramas.

To respond to the needs of busy digital users on the go, in the 2010s media content providers released more webtoons, web-dramas, and web-entertainment materials short enough to be enjoyed in under ten minutes on smartphone devices. Snack culture is a result of digital users' desire to enjoy cultural content shortly on the go rather than make time for cultural consumption activities (Baek, B. Y., 2014). Webtoons have become optimized for smartphones, from a prototypical webtoon with pictures and quotes on a vertical display to carrying special effects such as sound, background music, and vibration (Lee, S. Y., 2016). Consequently, webtoons have witnessed a surge in the cultural market.

Webtoons as snack culture become the norm for transmedia storytelling

Several elements explain the growth and development of webtoons as snack culture, including free content, diversity in genre, speedy publication, full color, and optimization for mobile devices. These socio-cultural factors along with the rapid growth of smartphone technologies have greatly contributed to the recent surge of webtoons (Jin, D. Y., 2015; Kim, Y. S., 2016). In other words, with the soaring use of smartphones, cultural content is at people's fingertips. Snack cultural content guarantees convenience and entertainment in a short period of time. Prior to the emergence of snack culture, most cultural content could only be indulged through time-consuming activities, such as going to movie theaters, reading a book for several hours, and watching television dramas at home (Kim, Y. S., 2016).

To begin with, one of the major reasons for the high popularity of webtoons is easy accessibility (Sohn, J. Y., 2014; Jin, D. Y., 2015). Previously, the readers bought comic books or borrowed them from comic book rental stores; however, the growth of new platforms including smartphones has made it more convenient for people to access webtoons anywhere and anytime. In this sense, media convergence is about the process in which digital technology adopts content, not only through production but also through consumption. Digital technologies drive easy accessibility, resulting in the boom of webtoons in the most networked Korean society.

Second, diverse genres and themes that webtoons represent appeal to readers with varying tastes (Sohn, J. Y., 2014; Hwang, 2018). Unlike its first stage focusing on romance, webtoons develop diverse genres, including thriller, fantasy, Sci-Fi, and mystery. From political dramas to murder thrillers, webtoon genres have rapidly involved several socio-cultural issues deeply embedded in Korean society, which make webtoons the most reliable source for big screens.

Third, stories are not only diverse but also subtle compared to previous manhwas. When the webtoonists publish each episode, it looks like snack people digest quickly. However, the story itself is not short, nor compact because the entire story is like an epic, which needs diverse structures, conflicts, harmonies, and distinctive themes. They seem to be like a snack because people have no choice but to enjoy them partially as webtoonists publish them day by day unlike novels that people read after publication.

These webtoons' visual images are also intriguing, and many cultural producers are able to imagine the transformation of webtoons into movies and television dramas. As Zur (2017, p. 203) points out, webtoon actualizes its potential as the source for other cultural production due to its distinctive story structure:

> it is a storytelling mechanism that can capture complex reality and the psychological state of its characters without having to commit to one particular narrative voice. Even with minimal text, webtoons give us access to the inner state of a wide variety of characters through suggestive images.

Many webtoonists keep this transmedia storytelling in mind during their creation and publication. A movie critic (Song, C. R., 2014) indeed states that one of the major reasons for the transformation of webtoons into other cultural forms is their subjects and themes that are dauntless and interesting. When movie directors and television producers cannot find good scenarios, they turn their attention to webtoons.

Fourth, people's changing consumption habits have promoted the growth of webtoons. In the 21st century, many people like casual mobile gaming over online gaming, in which the players finish each game within 3–5 minutes, and therefore, again, many Koreans like to consume popular culture within such a short time period, even less than 10 minutes at a time on their own smartphones (Miller, 2007).

Last, but not least, the boom of the so-called "loser" syndrome among Korean youth has increased the popularity of webtoons (Ha and Lim, 2012; Jin, D. Y., 2015). In particular, millennials have suffered from all kinds of socio-economic barriers, in particular employment, housing, and promotion in companies, which make their lives miserable. Therefore, many of them feel like they are losers. These young people, even those in their 30s, show sympathy with some webtoons portraying loser-like characters. For example, *Misaeng* revolves around a precarious intern worker at a trading firm. Instead of portraying a salaryman's myth of being CEOs, it depicts a hopeless salaryman's office activities. Many people who work at various companies, in particular people in their 20s who do not have regular jobs, but part-time positions, sympathize with the protagonists and other office members. As both the webtoon and the webtoon-based drama similarly show people who are very nervous about their futures, they greatly appeal to audiences who are themselves either office workers or job seekers.

The loser-like syndrome is also connected to "moron-taste." For example, the webtoon written by Lee Mal-nyeon titled *Lee Mal-nyeon Series* is unrivaled in terms of being moron-like. To be specific, well-organized plots always have steps like introduction, development, turn, and conclusion in composition. In Lee's webtoon's case, it has introduction, development, turn, and moron taste. The final step could result in either disaster of a whole story or display some unique charm (Sora's Webtoon World, 2012). His improvisation is likely to count on trends on the Internet or funny things captured in society. As many Koreans have no jobs after college graduation, they feel like they are losers who pursue snack-like light humor and fun. Some webtoonists reflect this kind of social milieu in their webtoons, which make the contemporary webtoons popular.

Webtoons symbolizing snack culture have become the major part of big screen culture due to their own unique characteristics, which ironically fit into movies and dramas. As snack culture itself gains popularity, it acts as a source of contents for other cultural contents, which means that webtoons and web novels have been turned into several big screen cultural contents, like films, television dramas, and games. Seemingly trivial, light snack culture has delivered profoundly significant and timely socio-cultural issues, making itself a great source for big screen culture. As *Misaeng*'s producer Lee Jae Moon said, "webtoons are great resources for content producers because the original messages and episodes are already strong, and it is easy for us to add dramatics" (Lee, J. Y., 2015).

Of course, film adaptations of popular webtoons have not guaranteed financial success of films as many webtoons-turned into films recorded poor results, contrary to the expectations at the beginning. According to the box office data provided by Korean Film Council, when *APT* was screened in 2006, the number of attendees was only 540,539, and it ranked 42nd in the box office that year. It was not until *Moss* that movie adaptations of webtoons started to achieve success (Park, C. I., 2016, p. 246). *Moss* (2010) was based on Yoon Tae Ho's webtoon of the same name, and the movie was directed by Kang Woo-suk.[4] The movie organized the scenes in a visual format that maximized the images of the original cartoon based on the vertical scroll-based presentation method unlike the previous movie adaptions (Park, C. I., 2016). Since the successful release of *Moss*, the film adaptions of webtoons have been booming by emphasizing the characteristics of webtoons and expanding on the attractions of webtoons (Jin, D. Y., 2019).

Several movies and television dramas show off diverse genres and styles based on webtoons. *Secretly, Greatly*—about a North Korean spy in a neighborhood, disguised as a mentally deficient young man—was very successful at the box office in 2013 as it successfully transferred its story to the big screen. *Steel Rain* (2017)—another action thriller film portraying a secret mission between North and South Korean intelligent agencies to prevent the breakout of a nuclear war on the Korean peninsula—was based on Yang Woo-suk's 2011 webtoon of the same name, which was moderately successful. Meanwhile, *Inside Men* (2015) as a new noir action film based on Yoon Tae Ho's webtoon became a national sensation due to its focus on the corruption within Korean society.

As these webtoon-based films did well at the box office, many movie directors in the 2010s started to pay attention to well-made popular webtoons. According to Daum Webtoon (2018), for example, from the start of its webtoon service in 2003, it has transformed about 280 webtoons of the 500 published in total into diverse cultural forms, including film, drama, musicals, and novels until May 2018. Webtoons become transmedia platforms that create a virtuous cycle in which cartoon characters and stories can move into other cultural forms, such as television, film, and musicals (Park, H. K., 2014). In other words, film directors and television producers are increasingly keen about the possibility of commercialization and commodification of webtoons by transforming them into big screen culture.

Bringing webtoons to the big screen offers more opportunities to filmmakers and drama producers by taking advantage of the original ideas along with their solid fanbase and familiar storylines. As You and Kang (2016) point out, this trend will continue because webtoons are a treasure trove of original stories. The increasing number of webtoon fans has also been an encouraging element. Unlike manhwa whose major audiences are between their mid-teens and early 20s, webtoons' audiences vary between early teens and late 30s, which overlap with the major audiences of movies. Also, webtoons are distributed through online portals, so the movie producers and corporations can get the original stories cheaper than they would from other resources (Song, Y. S., 2012). In the late 2010s, webtoons have substantially fulfilled their dream of big screen culture equipped with diverse subjects, visual and colorful images, well-made plots, and huge fanbase, which could not be seen in other original stories in novels and manhwa.

Snack culture's dream comes true: *Along with the Gods: the Two Worlds*

While there are several successful examples of transmedia storytelling based on webtoons, *Along with the Gods: the Two Worlds* (2017), which was developed from Joo Ho-min's webtoon, is one of the most successful webtoon-based movies. *Along with the Gods* was released in December 2017 and became a huge hit at the box office. Directed by Kim Yong-hwa, the movie was a blockbuster movie with a production cost of $40 million as he produced two films at the same time. The second film was screened in August 2018. The story is the blend of melodrama, humor, action, and fantasy, and it is about a dead man who is guided by reapers to be judged in seven hells for 49 days after his death. The webtoon provides a modern twist to Korean folklore about the afterlife, depicting deceased souls who receive judgment for their actions by various gods and their courts. The text was "pretty satirical and provided some sharp commentary on the state of contemporary society, while also acting as a fascinating mini-course on traditional Korean mythology" (Tipsymocha, 2017, para. 2).

The movie made some tweaks to the original webtoon story and attracted as many as 14.4 million movie goers by the end of May 2018 (Korean Film Council, 2018). This is the second highest, only behind *The Admiral: Roaring Currents* (2014), and the highest among webtoon-turned-movies. This certainly proves webtoons are the most successful transmedia storytelling sources and, furthermore, drives this form of transmedia cultural production (Jin, M. J., 2017).

The movie depicts an earnest and heroic firefighter (Cha Tae-hyun) who, when he is killed in the line of duty, becomes a candidate for reincarnation. But first he must face seven judges in the afterlife who review key moments in his existence. Fortunately, he is represented by three guardians who defend his eligibility. En route to these celestial magistrates, the four pass through perilous realms with names like the Volcano of the Damned, Murder Hell, and the Blade Forest, battling the computer-animated likes of toothy fish with humanoid heads and so-called hell ghouls, with glowing red weapons vaguely resembling light sabers (Webster, 2017).

Since the movie is an adaptation of the webtoon, there are several significant similarities and differences between these two different cultural forms. Most of all, there are some variances between the webtoon and the movie, while the basic premise remains the same. The director Kim Yong-hwa stressed that,

> The film version has the same storyline and characters of the original work. The only difference, if I should tell, is that the dramatic impact from the original was maximized because movies have to immerse viewers only in a limited time. I had to satisfy both of those who love the original and who haven't seen it yet.
>
> (Shim, S. A., 2017, para. 9)

Despite his assertion, there are several major differentiations, which make the film unique on the big screen more than the webtoon itself.

To begin with, the nature of the major character and relevant plots have changed. While Cha Tae-hyun's charter in the webtoon was an average salaryman who died of work-related alcohol abuse, his pre-death occupation in the film version is a firefighter. In the webtoon, the dead are all assigned defense attorneys for their various trials in front of the underworld's gods, but the film is conflating the reaper and lawyer roles together.

The film in fact took out a key character—lawyer Jin Gi-han—of the webtoon and changed the occupation of the main character, Ja-hong, who plays a key role in determining how the protagonist's journey unfolds in the story that deals with his afterlife. Jin Gi-han as a new lawyer worked for Ja-hong to safely pass the seven trials. Upon entering the afterlife, Ja-hong is guided by three grim reapers, Kangrim, Haewonmaek, and Deok-choon.

Big screen culture could not be the same as snack culture, of course. As Franco (2015, pp. 44–45) points out, "the transmedia practice contains both continuities and contrasts with the source text, with producers' perceptions of intended viewers' preferences" factoring into the webtoon's transformation into a film text. Hills (2015) also points out that it is inevitable to modify the original text in another platform due to narrative complexity. As webtoons like *Along with the Gods* provide some very complicated epics, cultural producers adjust the story to meet different audiences, regardless of some criticisms by popular magazines and critics who are concerned about the interference of the original meaning.

Another significant transformation is that the movie connects an unrelated subplot from the original story to the main plot of the movie by transforming a relationship among characters. A soldier who turns into an anger-filled lemur after dying as a result of an accident, for example, turns into Ja-hong's younger brother Su-hong (Kim Dong-wook), who unintentionally distracts Ja-hong's trials in the underworld (Jin, M. J., 2017). As Giovagnoli (2011) claims, transmedia means that it creates the original project's contents available on different platforms without damaging or interfering with the stories. Through this form of transmedia storytelling, audiences who either do experience or do not experience the originality of stories feel similar themes and subjects; however, once the original stories

go into the transmedia storytelling process, it is inevitable to change originality in order to appeal to different audiences.

What is interesting is that these changes may appeal to the audiences.
From the point it was revealed that the average office worker Ja-hong from
the webtoon had been turned into a righteous firefighter, the direction in
which the filmmaker wanted to take the movie was quite clear: a maudlin
tear-jerker (Jin, M. J., 2017). Ja-hong at the age of 39 on webtoon died
because of cirrhosis after drinking alcohol everyday as part of his work-
related daily routine in the webtoon; however, Ja-hong as a firefighter in the
movie plays a very brave man that saves and helps many people as a hero,
becoming a very noble man in the hell. The film stresses the importance
of fulfilling one's duties to their parents and highlights the significance of
forgiveness (Jin, M. J., 2017). As KayRosa (2017)'s movie review indicates;

> the film touches upon the sensitive values that strongly evoke Korea's
> traditional values of brotherly love and filial piety. It wouldn't be an
> exaggeration to say that at least 80% of the audiences around me wept
> throughout the film; this one is a strange mix of an up-to-date super-
> hero action thriller and a tear-jerker drama endorsing historically con-
> servative values.
>
> (para. 4)

Merely showing the sins committed by Ja-hong to his speech-impaired
mother, who is portrayed as nothing more than an angel who has done
nothing but unconditionally love her son, is an element powerful enough
to force tears out of the audience. And Ja-hong's continuous cries for his
mother throughout the journey, begging grim reapers for the safety of his
mother, is another controversial aspect that could raise eyebrows of some
audiences who are not into sentimentality (Jin, M. J., 2017).

For example, during a flashback to 15 years ago in the final scene of the
movie, Ja-hong planned to kill his mother following his brother's suicide because there was no hope. However, the younger brother Su-hong restrained
him from killing their mother. Ja-hong beat Su-hong hard and left home
because he felt guilty and never returned to his mother. When Ja-hong is
confronted at the final trial in front of the king of the underworld, he almost lost his opportunity to return to the human world because of this
secret misbehavior. This incident reveals the reason why Ja-hong wanted
to see his mother so desperately just once as he wanted to apologize for
his wrongdoing. However, his mother was then actually awoken and for-
gave Ja-hong's wrongdoing, which was seen through computer-generated
imagery. The king of the underworld let him go back to the world by saying
that "the people who were forgiven truly could not be asked the same sin
in the underworld. Therefore, I order your immediate return to the human
world." Starting as a form of snack culture, *Along with the Gods* has become a great part of big screen culture, and it has also turned into other
cultural forms, including musical.

What we have to understand is that *Along with the Gods*, and in general some webtoons cannot be considered as snack culture due to several significant dimensions. Most of all, the subjects that webtoons touch on are not trivial. As the genres of webtoons vary, the themes are diverse and good enough to be turned into big screen culture. *Along with the Gods* as a webtoon focused on justice so that the author might give a message to the readers, and the movie is not much different as it shows that in the afterlife they must pass seven trials, focusing on murder and deception, which are some of the major crimes that we witness in the current life. Although the movie version has shifted its focus from justice to family values, these ideas are good enough for the big screen.

Webtoon-based cultural products, including movies and dramas are popular in the 2010s, because webtoons reflect various real lives that many people are able to easily sympathize with. As Scolari (2009, p. 589) argues, transmedia storytelling "not only affects the text but also includes transformations in the production and consumption processes," as producers "visualize new business opportunities for the media market as new generations of consumers develop the skills to deal with the flow of stories and become hunters of information from multiple sources."

Second, some webtoons, including *Along with the Gods* eventually turn into a long novel-length literature. This particular webtoon has been transformed into eight books, and it includes several conflicts, betrayals, and harmonies, which can be seen in many good movies and novels. This means that some webtoons are not trivial although the webtoonists publish only a few pages at a time. Based on the epics of the webtoon version, the movie clearly connects the human world's story and the underworld's story that are seemingly separated to make the movie more enjoyable and easier to understand.

Third, the computer-generated imagery (CGI)-filled movie set new ground in the local film industry by demonstrating that a film with such a high reliance on CGI can also be created in Korea (Jin, M. J., 2017). As discussed, webtoons are mostly printed with color so that they immediately provide vivid images to big screen creators. Unlike novels or manhwas, which cannot provide this kind of visual image, webtoons have their own big advantages because they do not have any limitations in expressing the subjects and styles. When film and drama producers read webtoons, they are able to create their plan to use CGI based on this colorful and vivid webtoon drawing. The film has as many as 2,300 shots with visual effects (VFX), which represents 88% of the entire movie (Kim, S. H., 2017). Kim Youn-hwa easily got the ideas on VFX because the webtoon with visual images in color provides enough ideas for the movie.

Last, but not least, the film's focus on family values and filial piety is timely and desirable. As briefly discussed, the webtoon version focused on justice by portraying several social issues surrounding Korean society.[5] By judging the dead people seven times, the webtoon clearly emphasized the importance of social responsibilities to the readers. However, these kinds of webtoon-turned-into-movies, like *Inside Men,* were too numerous before the impeachment of the former president Park Geun-hye. In the much liberalized and democratized social milieu, the director aptly turned his focus to family, and therefore, audiences of all ages, in particular those with families, enjoy this heartbreaking tear-jerker movie. In this regard, *Along with the Gods* deftly connects two actors' main roles—Cha Tae-hyun in the underworld and Ha Jung-woo in the human world—so that it coordinates the inimitable ensemble of the two characters in developing a seemingly similar, but different story.

In sum, snack culture is not snack culture anymore for both the readers and cultural producers. As Stavroula (2014) argues, webtoons as the convergence of digital technologies and digital content have created new forms of stories in the Korean context. Webtoons have diverse tastes because they represent various genres and subjects. More importantly, due to their vivid visual and epic images, cultural creators have to transform the original webtoons into several cultural forms through modifying webtoons' subjects, genres, and styles. Transmedia storytelling in the era of digital media has become a norm in the cultural industries as it shifts the major resources of cultural products while providing creative and convergent ideas.

Conclusion

This chapter has analyzed the socio-cultural milieu surrounding the rapid growth of webtoons representing Korea's snack culture. By developing media convergence between digital technologies, in particular smartphones and content, it discussed the possibility of webtoons as sources of transmedia storytelling in the Korean cultural industries. In the smartphone era, Korea has rapidly developed webtoons as a new form of popular culture, known as snack culture. Although Korea created and advanced webtoons before the smartphone era based on the growth of Internet portals, the country has rapidly advanced webtoons right after the introduction of smartphones. As the smartphones have become the most significant digital technology for Koreans, webtoons as snack culture continue to grow and turn into big screen culture. Based on the popularity of webtoons, the Korean *manhwa* industry and portals have developed their strategies in utilizing webtoons as a primary source for several cultural forms, including film, games, and dramas.

Many cultural producers, such as film directors, television producers, and game developers, are keen to adapt and transform webtoons into films, dramas, and games. Korea's webtoons can be regarded as a transmedia phenomenon in terms of the convergence of old and new media, as well as technology and content. As Jenkins (2011) claims, "transmedia storytelling represents a process where integral elements of a fiction get dispersed systematically across multiple delivery channels for the purpose of creating a unified and coordinated entertainment experience," and the webtoon sector has utilized transmedia storytelling strategies through media convergence. Digital technology has also transformed the rules of engagement and currency for other storytelling formats (Iezzi, 2006).

As the story of webtoons is amusing and fresh with visual images, now even with sound, which provides the possibility of a transformation into the big screen, the remediation of webtoons has been increasingly popular in the Korean cultural industries. Regardless of some concerns, such as commodification of webtoons and webtoonists, losing webtoons' originality during the modification process, and market dominance by a few portal giants, webtoons' dream of big screen culture will be further increased. This new form of transmedia storytelling will also be the norm in the global cultural industry as well as the domestic cultural industry in the 21st century.

Notes

1 Webtoon is the neologism combining Web and cartoon—meaning comic strips distributed via the Internet originally, but now via the smartphone. The webtoon is a *manhwa* style webcomic that is typically published in chapters and published online (Kwon, 2014).
2 As Kang (2017, p. 762) explains, "web-dramas, which are original serialized dramas that are released primarily on online platforms, are a recent development of digital content in South Korea." Some exemplary web-dramas are *Aftermath, Love for Ten,* and *Twenty Years Old* that are less than 20 minutes per episode.
3 In 2004, Naver Webton began as an in-house startup at Naver. It established itself as its own company from Naver in May 2017. According to its own history, "Naver Webtoon dedicated to innovative storytelling that changes with the world by developing a platform where creators can truly meet their audience" (Naver Webtoon, 2018)
4 *Moss* as a mystery thriller film portrays the cruelty of human nature, set in a small village in the countryside. It was ranked fourth at the Korean box office with 3.3 million viewers, which was commercially successful.
5 Some of the movies released around 2017 focused on the relationship between Korean movies and the corrupt society. Films like *A Taxi Driver, The Battleship Island, I Can Speak,* and *1987: When the Day Comes* mainly touched on the conflict of social justice between the corrupt who are in power and the general people who stand up for what is right (Jeong, M. A., 2017).

References

The Age of Webtoons (n.d.). Retrieved from http://phonetimes.co.kr/php/phone/news_print.asp?uid=274&code=knowledge
Bae, S. M. (2017). Korea starts webtoons: We should export the system and webtoons. *Money Today.* 21 August.
Baek, B. Y. (2014, July 9). Rise of snack culture. *The Korea Times.* Retrieved from http://www.koreatimes.co.kr/www/common/printpreview.asp?categoryCode=688&newsIdx=160731
Cho, H. K. (2016, July 18). The webtoon: A new form for graphic narrative. *The Comics Journal.* Retrieved from http://www.tcj.com/the-webtoon-a-new-form-for-graphic-narrative/

Chung, A. Y. (2014, February 2). Snack culture. *The Korea Times*. Retrieved from http://www.koreatimes.co.kr/www/common/printpreview.asp?categoryCode=688&newsIdx=150813

Daum Webtoon (2012, January 17). Yoon Tae-ho's Misaeng started. Retrieved from http://bbs.cartoon.media.daum.net/gaia/do/announce/read?articleId=763&&bbsId=notice&pageIndex=1

Daum Webtoon (2018). About U.S. Retrieved from http://biz.webtoon.daum.net/about

Franco, C. P. (2015). The muddle earth journey: Brand consistency and cross-media intertextuality in game adaptation. In R. Pearson & A. Smith (eds.). *Storytelling in the media convergence age: Exploring screen narratives* (pp. 40–53). Berlin: Springer.

Giovagnoli, M. (2011). *Transmedia storytelling: Imagery, shapes and techniques*. Pittsburgh: ETC Press.

Ha, J. M. (2016, May 20). [Cine feature] New platforms and new sources for new Korean cinema ③: webtoons. *Hankyoreh*. Retrieved from http://www.hani.co.kr/arti/english_edition/e_entertainment/735818.html

Ha, S. J., & Lim, S. M. (2012, April 9). Webtoon, why so popular? Webtoons are now a syndrome among the young generations, but how has they become so popular? *The Dongguk Post*. Retrieved from https://www.dgupost.com/news/articleView.html?idxno=1247

Hancox, D. (2017). From subject to collaborator *Transmedia storytelling and social research*. *Convergence: The International Journal of Research into New Media Technologies* 23(1): 49–60.

Hills, M. (2015). Storytelling and Storykilling: Affirmational/transformational discourses of television narrative. In R. Pearson & A. Smith (eds.). *Storytelling in the media convergence age: Exploring screen narratives* (pp. 151–173). Berlin: Springer.

Hwang, S. T. (2018). *Crowdsourcing webtoon storytelling*. Seoul: Communication Books.

Iezzi, T. (2006, November 6). Web weaves new opportunities for comic-book artists and readers. *Advertising Age* 77(45): 14.

Jenkins, H. (2011) *Transmedia 202: further reflections*. Retrieved from http://henryjenkins.org/2011/08/defining_transmedia_further_re.html

Jenkins, H., Ford, S., & Green, J. (2013). *Spreadable media: Creating value and meaning in a networked culture*. New York: New York University Press.

Jin, D. Y. (2015). Digital convergence of Korea's webtoons: Transmedia storytelling. *Communication Research and Practice* 1(3): 193–209.

Jin, D. Y. (2019). *Transnational Korean cinema*. New York: Columbia University Press.

Jin, E. S. (2014, June 11). Smartphones set off webtoon boom. *JoongAng Daily*. Retrieved from http://koreajoongangdaily.joins.com/news/article/article.aspx?aid=2990396

Jin, M. J. (2017, December 14). Epic undertaking fails to impress: Fans of the 'Along with the Gods: The two worlds' webtoon may find the film to be overly sentimental. *Korea JoongAng Daily*. Retrieved from http://koreajoongangdaily.joins.com/news/article/article.aspx?aid=3042069

Jeong, M. A. (2017). The relationship between Korean movies and society: Social issues succeed as the people desire justice. *Korean Cinema Today* 30: 60–63.

Kang, J. (2017). Just another platform for television? The emerging web dramas as digital culture in South Korea. *Media, Culture and Society* 39(5): 762–772.

KayRosa (2017, December 23). Along with the Gods: The two worlds'. Allkpop. Retrieved from https://www.allkpop.com/article/2017/12/movie-review-along-with-the-gods-the-two-worlds

Kim, S. H. (2017). Korea VFX today. *Korean Cinema Today* 30: 48–55.

Kim, Y. S (2016, March 6). Snacks emerging as the new entrée: How snack culture permeates the contemporary era. *The Yonsei Annals*. Retrieved from http://annals.yonsei.ac.kr/news/articleView.html?idxno=1607

Korea Creative Content Agency (2015). *Webtoon industry status analysis*. Naju: KOCCA.

Korea Creative Content Agency (2016). *2015 Manhwa content white paper*. Naju: KOCCA.

Korea Manhwa Contents Agency (2018, March 5). *2017 Manhwa statistics card news*. Press Release.

Korean Film Council (2018). Box Office. Retrieved from https://www.kofic.or.kr/kofic/business/infm/introBoxOffice.do

K-Studio (2013). History of digital Manhwa in Korea. Retrieved from http://comics.plus21kr.com/digital-manhwa-in-korea/history-of-digital-manhwa-in-korea/

KT Economic Management Institute (2013, September 22). *The evolution of webtoon platforms and future of Korean webtoon*. Seoul: KT Economic Management Institute.

KT Economic Management Institute (2015, January 7). *Webtoon market dreams of 1 billion market*. Seoul: KT Economic Management Institute.

Kwon, O. S. (2014, March 6). Korean webtoons go global with LINE. Medium. Retrieved from https://medium.com/the-headline/korean-webtoons-go-global-with-line-b82f3920580e

Lee, D. W. (2012, June 12). Marine blues turned into a go-stop game. *ZDNet*. Retrieved from http://www.zdnet.co.kr/news/news_view.asp?artice_id=20120612182001

Lee, J. Y. (2015, January 5). Webtoon-based drama and films will be boom in the New Year. *Dong-A Ilbo*. Retrieved from http://news.donga.com/List/3/all/20150105/68905908/4

Lee, K. W. (2000, August 9). Chollian, Manhwa Special Site Webtoon. *etnews*. Retrieved from https://www.etnews.com/200008090020

Lee, M. (2008, November 11). Does love break iced theaters: Kang full's love story opens. *Cine 21*. Retrieved from http://www.cine21.com/news/view/?mag_id=54086

Lee S. Y. (2016, October 6). Snacking on the online snack culture. Retrieved from http://www.theargus.org/gisa_print.asp?no=1064

Marshall, C. (2016). Korean webtoons entertain the world. *Korea Magazine*. March. Retrieved from http://www.korea.net/NewsFocus/Culture/view?articleId=133278

Miller, N. (2007, March 1). Minifesto for a New Age. *Wired*. Retrieved from https://www.wired.com/2007/03/snackminifesto/

Naver Webtoon (2018). Naver webtoon corp. Retrieved from https://webtoonscorp.com/en/

Park, C. I. (2016). Study the phenomenon of cross-media between video media and webtoon. *International Journal of Multimedia and Ubiquitous Engineering* 11(5): 245–252.

Park, H. K. (2014, December 17). Daum webtoon goes global. *The Korea Herald*. Retrieved from http://www.koreaherald.com/view.php?ud=20141217000431

Park, S. K. (2013, March 20). The golden days of webtoon. *Postech Times*.

Scolari, C. (2009). Transmedia storytelling: Implicit consumers, narrative worlds, and branding in contemporary media production. *International Journal of Communication* 3: 586–606.

Scolari, C. (2013). Lostology: Transmedia storytelling and expansion/compression strategies. *Semiotica* 195: 45–68.

Seo, C. H. (2017, December 20). Chosun webtoon history that can be read within 10 minutes. *Hangyereh Shinmun*. Retrieved from http://www.hani.co.kr/arti/special-section/esc_section/824448.html#csidx387ee681d94001eb764f9f92ed99646

Shim, S. A. (2017, November 14). Movie 'Gods' maximizes dramatic impact of original story: Director. *Yonhap News*. Retrieved from http://english.yonhap-news.co.kr/news/2017/11/14/0200000000AEN20171114011700315.html

Soh, J. (2008, December 4). Soonjeong stays true to its heart. *The Korea Times*. Retrieved from http://www.koreatimes.co.kr/www/news/art/2008/12/135_35552.html

Sohn, J. Y. (2014, May 25). Korean webtoons going global. *The Korean Herald*. Retrieved from http://www.koreaherald.com/view.php?ud=20140525000452

Song, C. R. (2014, January 10). From a movie director to a composer. *Maeil Business Newspaper*. Retrieved from http://news.mk.co.kr/v7/newsPrint.php?year=2014&no=49947

Song, Y. S. (2012, August 23). Webtoons' current status and features and webtoons-based OSMU strategies. *Kocca Focus* 57: 3–27.

Sora's Webtoon World (2012, December 18). Here comes moron-taste webtoon. Retrieved from https://podosora.wordpress.com

Stavroula, K. (2014). *Transmedia storytelling and the new era of media convergence in higher education*. London: Palgrave.

Tipsymocha (2017, October 7). Welcome to the afterlife in with the Gods. Retrieved from http://www.dramabeans.com/2017/10/welcome-to-the-afterlife-in-with-the-gods/

Webster, A. (2017, December 21). Review: 'Along with the Gods' is a fantasy journey with C.G.I. at Every Turn. *The New York Times*. Retrieved from https://www.nytimes.com/2017/12/21/movies/along-with-the-gods-review.html

Yonhap News (2009, March 3). Play Kwang-su thinking got the seventh encore stage. Retrieved from http://news.nate.com/view/20090303n12996

You, E., & Kang, C. (2016, January 18). Webtoons as the new trend for Korean dramas and films. Korea.com. Retrieved from http://www1.korea.com/bbs/board.php?bo_table=SHOW&wr_id=1501

Zur, D. (2017). Modern Korean literature and cultural identity in a pre-and post-colonial digital age. In Kim, Y. N. (ed.). *Routledge handbook of Korean culture and society* (pp. 193–205). London: Routledge.

5 Sword art everywhere

Narrative, characters, and setting in the transmedia extension of the *Sword Art Online* franchise

Andrew Hillan

Online digital media has transformed how people experience and pursue their preferred forms of entertainment, and we are amidst what many have referred to as the "transmedia" era in which stories are often told across different platforms (Jenkins, 2006). Entertainment franchises thrive in this era by making use of the technological, industrial, and cultural patterns of the time to extend their texts through as many avenues as possible for audiences and potential fans. Japan has proven very influential in this era due to its own transmedia growth over the last couple of decades, as well as the radiating impact of its growth on the global state of transmedia industries and fan cultures (Napier, 2001; Steinberg, 2012). This paper will discuss how the extension of a franchise's texts to different media platforms serves to transform the textual content of each adaptation, as well as consider the industrial and cultural contexts surrounding these transformations. It will specifically examine the popular Japanese novel, anime, and video game series entitled *Sword Art Online* (*SAO*) for how its unique extension across media contributes to our understanding of the state of Japanese and global transmedia.

The discussion will start by briefly outlining the specific story, characters, and setting of *SAO*. Then, it will review the existing academic literature on transmedia's industrial and cultural contexts to frame the discussion of how *SAO* fits into these contexts both within Japan and globally. The next three sections will discuss how the transformations of *SAO*'s three most pertinent textual elements—story, characters, and setting—are connected to, and can reveal insights into, corresponding industrial and cultural contexts during processes of transmedia extension. It will be seen that *SAO* is unique compared to a lot of other Japanese and transnational media franchises, as its setting, and not its story or characters, is the only element that remains consistent across its novel, anime, and video game adaptations. This is significant because *SAO*'s specific prioritization of textual elements shows that a Japanese media franchise about Massively Multiplayer Online (MMO) video games can focus primarily on its MMO environment at the expense of story and characters – with implications for new ways of both producing and consuming the transmedia texts surrounding this franchise.

Overview of *Sword Art Online*

SAO takes place in Japan in 2022, where 10,000 players log in to "Sword Art Online," the highly anticipated "virtual reality massively multiplayer online role-playing game" – or "VR MMORPG" (Kawahara, 2014a, p. 12). The players' five senses are fully immersed in the virtual world through their VR headset, called the "NerveGear," so that their virtual surroundings are experienced and navigated as though they were physically there (Kawahara, 2014a, p. 10). The players soon realize that the logout button has been removed from their in-game menus, and it is revealed that they are being held captive inside the game by its genius programmer until they reach the 100th floor of the game's world and defeat the final boss (Kawahara, 2014a, p. 30). Characters who die in the game die in real life, and any in-game pain is experienced as real physical pain, so that characters must continue to "level up" their abilities and combat skills in order to survive and escape back to the real world (Kawahara, 2014a, p. 43). The main protagonist, "Kirito," is a lifelong gamer who embodies a familiar gaming stereotype of the socially awkward loner, preferring to be a "solo player" instead of interacting with other players or joining one of the game's many guilds (Kawahara, 2014a, p. 44).

The novels are narrated from the first-person perspective of Kirito, who frequently references the game's omnipresent user interface to remind the reader that he is constantly inhabiting this virtual reality game. For example, when describing the sensation of getting hit by an enemy in *SAO*, he says, "I felt a chilly hand squeeze deep within my chest as the thin line fixed to the corner of my vision shrank slightly. That blue horizontal line – my HP [health points] – was a visualization of my remaining life force" (Kawahara, 2014a, p. 3). The story takes place entirely within this VR game world of *SAO*, so that the characters must deal with and take strategic advantage of the unique quirks associated with living inside of an MMO – which produces much of the material for plot points and memorable moments in the series (Kawahara, 2014a, p. 43).

SAO started as an online serial written by Japanese author Reki Kawahara on his personal webpage from 2002 to 2008, and it was later printed in paperback by the publishing firm Dengeki Bunko beginning in 2009 as an ongoing series of "light novels" aimed at young Japanese readers (2014a, p. 247). The series quickly gained popularity in mainstream media, and in 2012 the novel was made into a successful television anime series, followed by manga adaptations written by Kawahara and illustrated by various artists, as well as several widely released video games (Kawahara & Ito, 2013; Bandai Namco, 2016; GREE, 2017). The entire body of *SAO* novels, anime, and video games is not only popular in Japan, as these texts have been translated and localized for many other regions to generate attention, engagement, fan works, and fan communities amongst media consumers worldwide.

Literature review of transmedia studies

This section outlines the existing literature on transmedia studies, and where this chapter fits in and contributes to these ongoing discussions. Henry Jenkins first conceptualized our present state of media as one of "convergence culture," which entails coordinated production and consumption across media platforms, and franchises deploying strategies of "transmedia storytelling" (2006, p. 20). Jenkins sees this approach to transmedia production as necessary to facilitate more synergistic relationships of "co-creation" in which the whole is greater than the sum of its parts, and producers of various media products benefit from sharing labor and resources amongst each other (2006, p. 105). Since the introduction of convergence culture, scholars have used and interrogated the concept to help study distinctive textual traits of various media franchises, and if—or how—they are related to economic and cultural contexts underlying them (Lamarre, 2009; Hays & Couldry, 2011; Steinberg, 2012; Clarke, 2013).

An often-identified insufficiency of the concept is that there needs to be a more explicit connection made between examining textual elements and the various subcultures that emerge around them (Hays & Couldry, 2011; Johnson, 2013). Textual elements can be analyzed for insights on wider contexts surrounding them, because these observable texts are ultimately the products of cultural and industrial factors that underlie and condition our experiences of consuming these media products. So, studying what occurs on the surface texts and consumer-level experiences of these media products can yield useful connections to the industrial and cultural processes involved in their production (Allison, 2006; Havens, Lotz, & Tinic, 2009).

For example, several scholars have remarked on the Japanese governmental and industrial policies in the late 1990s and early 2000s aimed at making a "Cool Japan," which facilitated the rise of the Japanese "media mix" such as manga and anime in popular culture and global markets (Condry, 2009; Yano, 2009, p. 687; Steinberg, 2012; Steinberg & Zahlten, 2017, p. 81). This governmental intervention helped to shape many Japanese consumers' identities and largely characterize contemporary Japanese society throughout this era, affording it more cultural "soft power" but also unintentionally facilitating the emergence or re-emergence of certain subcultures that are tied to media consumption (Shiraishi, 1997, p. 235; Yano, 2009, p. 683). These include "otaku," "hikikomori," and other overlapping subcultures in Japanese contemporary society, which comprise a generation of youth who obsessively depend on media consumption in their daily lives at the expense of social interaction and real-life responsibilities (Napier, 2006, p. 33; Zielenziger, 2007, p. 14; Azuma, 2009, p. 98; Rosenthal & Zimmerman, 2012, p. 83; Wada-Marciano, 2012, p. 26). The now-widespread Otaku subculture has a longer history than recent government protocols for a Cool Japan, but it has grown exponentially since around 2000 when these policies converged with newly available digital technology to allow these subcultural traits and practices to proliferate among Japanese youth (Azuma, 2009).

Scholars have also shifted the focus of transmedia studies to integrate more organizational considerations of how various interrelated producers do the creative labor necessary to make transmedia products (Caldwell, 2008; Johnson, 2013; Hartzheim, 2015). These kinds of studies view trans-media franchises through the lens of co-creative networks, where agents from different media backgrounds, such as authors, artists, animators, directors, actors, and editors, collaborate and negotiate to jointly create, manage, and cross-promote media products (Condry, 2013). Other studies attribute more important roles to fans in production, trying to remove the binary analyses of production versus consumption, and replace it with a more open-ended perspective in which creative works can emerge across different categories of amateur and professional producers (Allison, 2006; Steinberg, 2013).

The literature on transmedia has largely congregated around the textual elements of story, characters, and setting, because they are seen to have the most focus put into them throughout the creative aspects of the production process, as well as the most fan works and cultural impact surrounding them (Boni, 2013). So, the industrial and cultural contexts behind these texts can more easily come to the forefront when viewed through the lens of these textual components (Clarke, 2013). The next three sections will cover the major textual elements present in each of *SAO*'s adaptations, and observe how they change as the franchise extends across these various media. This discussion will contribute to the previously outlined literature on transmedia studies by asking how and which textual elements of the *SAO* franchise are connected to specific industrial and cultural factors dur-ing its transmedia extension—such as co-creation, otaku subculture, and fan works.

Compared to *SAO*'s specific prioritization of textual elements, other Japanese transmedia franchises about MMOs that span anime, video games, novels, and manga include: the *.hack* (2002) series, which focuses on coordinating multiple concurrent interweaving plotlines; *Digimon Adven-ture* (1999), which focuses on expanding and promoting a collectible array of virtual pet characters; *No Game No Life* (2012), whose more thoroughly developed characters are deliberately designed as "hikikomori"—shut-ins who prefer social isolation over coping with societal pressures—to appeal to specific demographics of fans who can strongly relate; and *Btooom!* (2009), which has a darker plot, grittier style, and more distinctive characters that are meant for a smaller and more mature audience, as opposed to the looser assemblages of plot and characters in *SAO* that help market it to a wider audience (Martin, 2012). It will be seen that, for *SAO*, setting matters the most across different media, and what makes it unique and successful as a Japanese transmedia franchise is its emphasis on world-building as the highest priority. Other textual elements such as narrative and characters still serve important supplemental roles across various adaptations—but most of the franchise's co-creative production efficiencies, distinctive identity for specific subcultures to relate to, and works generated by its fanbase, are based not on its plot or characters but its video game setting, and, the accompanying potential for further exploration of the premise of what it is like to live, eat, and sleep inside of an MMORPG.

Story in *Sword Art Online*

Many scholars in the field of transmedia studies focus primarily on how a franchise maintains narrative cohesion amongst its various media adaptations, and these studies tend to analyze the narrative modes used within each media product to better understand its surrounding historical, industrial, or cultural conditions (Napier, 2001; Steinberg, 2013). They observe that many Western transmedia franchises, such as *The Matrix* (Jenkins, 2006), *Doctor Who* (Evans, 2011), *LOST* (Bertetti, 2014), and *Battlestar Galactica* (Bourdaa, 2018), continue the overarching narrative after their original runs by loosening the other textual elements, such as characters and setting, to open up multiple points of access and attract as wide a cross-platform audience as possible into their meticulously detailed and interconnected stories, which serve as the main attraction for fans interested in that specific kind of mediated entertainment experience (Jenkins, 2006).

SAO's plot, however, is not necessarily a focal point for producers of the series, as the story is derivative of several classic stories from older media, such as the 1924 short story *The Most Dangerous Game*, as well as the live-action films *The Running Man* (1987), *Battle Royale* (2000), and the novel and film series *The Hunger Games* (2008), which all feature plots wherein characters are forced to participate in games with their lives at stake. In *SAO* and a lot of other Japanese media, there is an impermanence in how its general template of a story is told, so that each new adaptation can benefit the most by telling the story in a way that best suits their respective formats (Napier, 2001; Clarke, 2013). For example, the second volume of the *SAO* novels restarts the story at the beginning of the first volume's events from a different perspective, and the anime reorders the novels' sequence of events to flow more linearly, while the video games aim to tell a condensed story through intermittent narration and dialogue between gameplay (Kawahara & Ito, 2013; Kawahara, 2014b; GREE, 2017). *SAO*'s de-emphasized story is not necessarily a consistent feature of the franchise, and this has allowed the franchise to adapt to the changing media landscapes and usage patterns of each new platform it extends to, without being restricted by a painstakingly intricate plot that hinders any producer other than the original from taking the source material in their own direction for new adaptations.

A major reason why the *SAO* franchise does not follow a single coherent narrative, carefully constructed and dispersed over multiple media, is that each adaptation has involved some degree of co-creation between different parties in the production process, so that its overarching cross-media narrative is not controlled by any single visionary but is instead repurposed and given different meanings and modes of fan engagement by diverse groups of producers (Hartzheim, 2015; Saito, 2015). For example, one of *SAO*'s most heavily featured story arcs, from volume eight of the novels, features a player circumventing the game's programmed rules to murder other players in game-designated "safe zones," and it was retroactively inserted into the story of the anime's first season when it was produced—with the added benefit of hindsight and having ten volumes worth of accumulated novels from which to draw story elements and insert as early as the first season (Kawahara & Ito, 2013). This rearranging of story is due to the original publishers, Dengeko Bunko, giving up a significant degree of control to the veteran animation studio, A-1 Pictures, to rearrange the plot points of the anime so that they best fit this new medium (Saito, 2015).

The video game adaptations of *SAO*, however, involve little to no collaboration between the original publisher and game designers, but its narrative content is de-emphasized anyways—whereas battles, character customization, and levelling up are its primary modes of conveying the story and engaging fans on this specific medium (GREE, 2017). *SAO*'s media adaptations vary in their capacity to communicate the narrative thread to readers, viewers, and players respectively. The novel and anime installments are better equipped to weave a complex narrative, while more recent adaptations excel at capturing other elements of the series besides narrative, ensuring that this franchise does not rely on complex or brilliant story construction for success in both maximizing the potential of their production resources and resonating with their targeted demographics across different platforms.

Co-creation can be used with narrative as the primary focus, but it is a more involved and intensive process that requires close coordination between a relatively small group of producers who have a long-term vision of how and on which platforms they want to tell the story, and it can go wrong much more easily than simply transporting characters or settings across media (Bourdaa, 2018). This idealized type of synergetic narrative-based transmedia content can be very rewarding for consumers who are looking for an in-depth and detailed media experience, but it often does not retain the attention of people who are more suited to devoting only partial time and attention to consuming their media in short bursts (Jenkins, Ford, & Green, 2013; Hjorth & Richardson, 2014). The varying degrees of narrative detail and intensity in each of *SAO*'s adaptations, with the novels and video games occupying opposite ends of the narrative depth spectrum, represents the larger shift in Japanese and global transmedia franchises offering different-sized portions of their story across media to accommodate the increasingly diverse and fluctuating usage patterns of consumers (Saito, 2015).

Characters in *Sword Art Online*

Several scholars, particularly in and of Japan, do not view the state of transmedia as a result of storytelling strategies, but instead as more of a "transmedia character-telling" in which fictional characters are used as the basis for new stories as well as merchandising and cross-promotion opportunities (Condry, 2013, p. 57; Steinberg, 2013; Saito, 2015). Unlike Hollywood's focus on cohesive and tightly coordinated storylines across platforms, Japan's media mix is more character-oriented, prioritizing the need for a franchise to have a database of recognizable—and often collectible—characters who endure in the public imagination and become ubiquitously associated with their respective franchise on whatever medium they appear on, such as "Pikachu" or "Goku" from the *Pokémon* and *Dragon Ball* series (Allison, 2006; Azuma, 2009; Scott, 2009; Condry, 2013; Clements & McCarthy, 2015).

The character-centered transmedia strategy is successful for many Japanese media producers because it better suits the cultural context of Japan, whose practices of consumption are heavily populated with character images at the expense of narrative depth, due to the media mix era's proliferation of image and animation-based media (Condry, 2013). It is easier for fans to form a strong emotional bond with an identifiable character as opposed to a complex storyline that audiences cannot identify with at that same primary level (Bourdaa, 2018). Consumers also engage in and create character-related works in order to live out certain culturally-informed fantasies, such as otakus pairing up their favorite media characters or inserting themselves into fan art or fan fiction to live out romantic fantasies that go unfulfilled in their everyday lives (Azuma, 2009).

For example, many Japanese transmedia franchises, such as the roleplaying game series *Fire Emblem*, acknowledge and cater to these fantasies by allowing players to pair up almost any male and female character to produce different combat boosts, dialogue lines, and even offspring characters whose appearance and stats depend on each specific pairing (Intelligent Systems, 2015). The mobile game *Fire Emblem Heroes* (Intelligent Systems, 2017) expands the database of possible interactions for players to explore, as its developers regularly update and add to the roster of characters by retrieving and inserting any number of characters from the large reservoir of all previous installments in the series. The kinds of textual practices that obviously cater to the desires of a significant portion of a media franchise's fanbase are referred to as "fan service" (Beaty, 2016). Reki Kawahara, the author of the *SAO* novels, even acknowledged and apologized for the fact that there is a different heroine in each of the four stories in volume two, but the male lead that they are accompanying in all four stories is always Kirito (2014b, p. 248). Fan service also exists in Western transmedia, but they more commonly take the form of hidden details or "Easter eggs" (Beaty, 2016, p. 322) in the narrative that reward the most observant and dedicated fans—which once again denotes an existing difference between the Japanese and Western focuses on character and narrative elements, respectively.

Consumers, through their own increasingly common experiences of belonging to specific subcultures, like youth culture, computer culture, gaming culture, or otaku culture, can identify with relatable archetypal characters and more easily form a bond with them (Azuma, 2009). This increased cultural focus on media characters is representative of the Japanese media mixes' shift away from linear narratives and towards nonlinear databases of combinable elements, including characters' appearance, personality traits, and other characteristics that can be easily arranged, combined, and transferred across media producers to generate new characters as well as alternative versions of existing characters (Azuma, 2009). By consuming these character-centered franchises, members of otaku and other subcultures are engaging in what Hiroki Azuma (2009) calls "database consumption" (p. 53), because they are not just consuming a text, but instead the smaller extratextual elements, chunks of data, and digital processes that underlie and give motion to our experience of the text.

SAO's database of characters includes an array of major and minor characters from various installments of the series, and the mobile game adaptations make use of this database to have an endless supply of different versions of characters that are collectible in the game and give fans a reason to stay engaged and spend money, such as pirate, Santa Claus, or groom versions of Kirito (Clarke, 2013; GREE, 2017). As the database grows, it becomes exponentially easier for *SAO* to maintain momentum in production because it has more resources to draw from, as the video game adaptations can reuse assets from previous media, such as visual illustrations from the anime as well as dialogue from the novels, to construct new iterations of existing characters (GREE, 2017).

Most Japanese character designers avoid average archetypes and aim for designs that are odd in extreme or distinctly memorable ways, but instead of creating iconic characters that stand out, *SAO* inversely pursues generic archetypes for its ambassadors of the series (Condry, 2013). Kirito, being a Japanese youth obsessed with computer and gaming culture to the detriment of his social skills, is a stereotype that serves as a somewhat empty vessel for otaku and gamers in the audience, who can step into his perspective and live out the fantasy of escaping into a world that is reminiscent of the video games they are familiar with and nostalgic for (Azuma, 2009; Kawahara, 2014a).

The novels and anime are structured with a lack of in-depth character construction, so that fans cannot get overly attached to any official character identity, and these characters can be more easily interchanged amongst others or have modified physical and personality traits in later volumes, seasons, game adaptations, and other various installments of the series. For example, the character "Asuna," who becomes Kirito's constant companion and love interest for the first volume's series of events, is given little to no backstory and has only a very loosely bounded identity that is largely an assembly of various tropes related to female action heroes in media. She is made to resemble well-known stereotypes such as *Wonder Woman*, *Charlie's Angels*, and *Laura Croft: Tomb Raider*, in the sense that Asuna is featured as a very capable fighter but is still physically depicted as a sexual object that exists for the male character in the plot as well as the male readers (Ormrod, 2018). *SAO*'s later mobile game adaptations reap the benefits of Asuna's general template character design from the original novels, as it is used as the basis to continually create alternative versions of her in various costumes to maximize her sexual appeal and prompt players to spend additional money trying to collect them.

From a co-creation perspective, the looser collaborative networks that produce *SAO*'s various adaptations are better suited for more generic, blank-slate characters who have few defining traits, as each new producer can exert in some agency in constructing these characters' personalities and actions so that they are more accessible to producers when transported over to their respective media platforms (Hartzheim, 2015). Creators can work with the characters created by others, allowing each one to not be limited to telling one particular story, and instead flexibly recombine character traits to form alternative characters with whom to tell new and divergent stories (Condry, 2013; Steinberg, 2013; Bertetti, 2014). The original author's open-ended writing of these characters in the novels also reflects the kind of limited character design found in customization menus for MMO video games, so that the character design at the very outset of the series is influenced by—and already lends itself to be adapted into—video games.

In the *SAO* anime, there is co-creation between the original author and various scriptwriters and animators, as they insert characters that were not present in the events of the original novels to generate interest in future spin-offs and sequels. For example, a character from a future *SAO* spin-off called *Alfheim Online*, who was not present in volume one of the novels, "Yui," is inserted into the first season of the anime through a time travel plotline in which she befriends Kirito and gets involved in the events of the first volume (Kawahara & Ito, 2013). Inserting characters that were not present in the events of the original novels facilitates fans' eventual transition to subsequent installments of the series that no longer involve its original characters or the same game-world, ensuring the franchise's transmedia extension is sustainable even after the original narrative material is fully expended on all available media.

In the mobile game adaptations, *SAO*'s characters are easily converted to combinations of images, dialogue lines, and combat statistics – and characters can be exchanged amongst a wide assortment of others for fans to play as while completing the games' quests and storylines (GREE, 2017). Many of the *SAO* console game adaptations even allow for complete customization of the player's character (Bandai Namco, 2016). So, even though *SAO* does not emphasize the need for iconic and enduring characters like in other Japanese transmedia franchises, its specific construction of weak characters is a useful approach to transmedia because it acknowledges what relevant subcultures want out of the characters in this franchise, and makes use of various co-creation production efficiencies that come with having an open and flexible character design.

Setting in *Sword Art Online*

Setting is the final textual element to be discussed, and there are roughly three ways that transmedia scholars have interpreted setting in texts: world, feeling, and premise. Some scholars emphasize the shared fictional world or universe in which the franchise exists, where different characters can live and stories can continuously emerge (Jenkins, 2006; Evans, 2011; Boni, 2017). Another way of conceiving setting is as the general atmosphere or "feeling" induced in fans through a franchise's distinct visual style (Gray, 2010). A third element of setting is the dramatic premise or setup, which is the governing logic that defines and mediates character-world relationships (Condry, 2013; Saito, 2015). It is necessary to distinguish between the three aspects of setting—world, feeling, and premise—because *SAO* emphasizes each to varying degrees throughout its extension across media, opting to arrange these elements in altogether unique ways compared to the rest of the Japanese or global media mixes.

World-focused scholars study certain franchises that use online media and fan engagement to build their fictional universe, which functions as the backdrop in which characters and stories unfold (Condry, 2013; Bertetti, 2014; Boni, 2017; Bourdaa, 2018). The emphasis is not so much on placing characters in different stories as it is on placing them within a consistent and appealing world that can continue to be developed by professional and fan producers within the franchise's ongoing shared universe—even after the original series of events have ended (Scolari, Bertetti, & Freeman, 2014; Boni, 2017; Bourdaa, 2018).

In the case of *SAO*, the reason why fans form a strong emotional bond and identify with its rather generic characters is because they can understand and empathize with the typical video game obstacles that characters encounter and must overcome in its fictional game-based world, as they know from experience how it feels to deal with these familiar aspects of playing video games (Condry, 2013; Bourdaa, 2018). Therefore, the video game adaptations of *SAO* are especially popular, because players can better experience how they would personally fare in *SAO*'s game world instead of having to experience it passively through Kirito's storyline (GREE, 2017). In this case, world is more important for fan participation than characters or story, since fans of *SAO* cannot insert themselves as readily into character roles or plot points compared to its video game world (Gray, 2010; Steinberg, 2013; Bourdaa, 2018). *SAO* is similar to many franchises in how it caters to a demographic of fans who in turn sustain it economically and ensure its place in popular culture—but what makes it unique is how *SAO* structures its textual elements to fit the specific consumption patterns of subcultures who identify more with an overarching fictional world than any single character.

Whereas interpreting setting as world is most effective at the conceptual level and better described through a literary medium like novels, the aspect of setting that gives fans a distinctive and consistent "feeling" or atmosphere of a franchise is more suitably expressed through audiovisual texts such as manga illustrations or televised animations (Condry, 2013; Saito, 2015). Feeling allows fans to relate to the setting on a more primary level, as a franchise's world can be conceptually strong and detailed, but it needs a certain visual style and symbolic references to make it a living environment (Napier; 2001; Lamarre, 2009; Gray, 2010). In terms of *SAO*'s feeling, its specific visual style is the virtual reality videogame interface—with its menus, inventories, dialogue boxes, etc.—through which characters navigate and interact with the fictional world (Kawahara, 2014a).

SAO generates a certain feeling through its interfacial visual style, but it also maintains a strong dramatic premise with regards to the video game rules and game mechanics that characters must adhere to while they are trapped in its virtual reality world. *SAO*'s premise is the only consistent element of the franchise, as later novel, anime, and video game installments in the franchise take place in different video game worlds, each with a completely different feeling, set of characters, and story – such as the spin-offs *Alfheim Online* and *Gun Gale Online* (Kawahara & Ito, 2013, 2014). These spin-offs are different than *SAO* in term of aesthetic, as their characters, stories, and world are modelled in fantasy style and warzone styles, respectively, as opposed to the futuristic style of *SAO*. However, these spin-offs are similar where it matters: the videogame premise and rules that govern how characters can interact with their setting to progress the story. The foundational premise of human characters trapped inside a VR MMO game remains as the defining consistent linkage that is parlayed across various media platforms, as this is the part that appeals most to the gamer contingent of its audience (Saito, 2015).

SAO's emphasis on transporting its videogame premise across media has allowed its video game adaptations to feel consistent within the larger backdrop of the franchise—even if they do not have as much narrative or character depth as previously used media. For example, the *SAO* mobile games have a less intact world that is segmented into short levels meant to be played in quick spurts throughout the day, and it is played from a third person perspective so that the feeling invoked by its interface is not as strong (Hjorth & Richardson, 2014; GREE, 2017). These particular adaptations may not satisfy fans' expectations on the level of being immersed in their lesser interpretations of *SAO*'s world, but they surpass the novels and anime in regard to premise, because in those previous media the passive audience could not experience the actions-consequences feedback of the premise firsthand – whereas playing a game adaptation allows them to directly grasp the game mechanics and rules that governed *SAO*'s fictional world and characters (Hutcheon, 2006; Gray, 2010; GREE, 2017). The medium of video games is better equipped in its interactive properties to simulate the distinctive experience of *SAO* by directly integrating the fictional world's user interface and game rules—which were previously only used as narrative devices—and making them functional parts of the game that impact players' experiences and actions to get as close as possible to simulating characters' experiences of story events (Werning, 2014).

In terms of *SAO*'s different setting-related elements, world is best expressed conceptually through novels, feeling is best expressed sensorially through anime, and premise is best expressed interactively through games. *SAO* is unique in how it starts its franchise on the traditional medium of the novel but with a fictional setting of a new medium video game, and then as the franchise has extended to newer media, it has rendered functional the textual characteristics of its setting to let fans play within the same world and under the same game rules that the earlier texts could only describe, abstractly conceptualize, and display through image and animation.

Conclusion

It is the setting of a fictional videogame world and its rules of play which appeal most to fans of *SAO*, and keeps this series relevant and successful on various adaptations by keeping its world, overall feeling, and—most importantly—premise as the distinctive experience of *SAO*, with not as much priority placed on maintaining consistent stories or characters across various platform adaptations (Evans, 2011; Hartzheim, 2015; Freeman, 2016; Bourdaa, 2018). *SAO* is unique in that most Western transmedia franchises focus on their narrative, and Japanese franchises focus on their characters, whereas *SAO* and a select few others prioritize setting as the element on which their financial and cultural success hinges. This reflects the industrial and organizational expediency with which professionals and fans alike can produce and co-create *SAO*-related media products through the textual element of setting, as well as the local and increasingly transnational subcultures that consume—and thus sustain—*SAO* for this specific element above all others. For *SAO*, the unique qualities of the VR MMO setting and its game mechanics are carried across media more consistently than the other comparatively interchangeable textual elements. *SAO*'s plot is often rearranged and its characters are mostly archetypes belonging to and generated from a database, but its world, feeling, and premise of living inside a videogame is what gives this franchise its distinctive identity across different media adaptations.

SAO is similar to transmedia franchises for how it structures its textual elements to appeal to, and even engender, the emergence of subcultures whose values and practices of consumption match the specifically ordered elements of certain franchises. However, *SAO* is unique amongst the

Japanese media franchises who cater to localized otaku subcultures by focusing on character identification for fantasy fulfillment, as it caters instead more to a slightly different but overlapping Japanese and global audience of people who enjoy video games to the point where they share the fantasy of living inside a video game world.

This chapter showed how the relevant subcultural contexts in which each transmedia franchise's adaptations are consumed and produced help to reciprocally shape their textual characteristics. It also emphasized the industrial and organizational implications behind the deployment of textual elements in transmedia franchises, and how the latter can reveal a lot about the former, such as the shifting collaborative networks of professionals and amateurs in interconnected processes of co-creation that operate before and after consumers experience the text on a screen. Even though *SAO's* category of setting-centered transmedia franchise is currently the least populated, it may be a vanguard of future cultural, industrial, and textual practices in the transmedia era. Transmedia franchises want to leave nothing unturned as they explore opportunities for expansion, and as the already brimful media mixes of character and narrative-centered franchises reach a point of oversaturation, creators will increasingly seek other textual characteristics through which to capitalize on currently untapped subcultural demographics and production efficiencies.

References

Allison, A. (2006). *Millennial monsters: Japanese toys and the global imagination*. Berkeley: University of California Press.

Azuma, H. (2009). *Otaku: Japan's database animals*. Minneapolis: University of Minnesota Press.

Bandai Namco. (2016). *Sword art online: Hollow realization* [PlayStation 4 game]. Tokyo, Japan: Bandai Namco Entertainment Inc.

Beaty, B. (2016). Superhero fan service: Audience strategies in the contemporary interlinked Hollywood blockbuster. *The Information Society*, 32(5), 318–325.

Bertetti, P. (2014). Toward a typology of transmedia characters. *International Journal of Communication*, 8, 20.

Boni, M. (2013). *Romanzo criminale: Transmedia and beyond*. Venezia, IT: Edizioni Ca'Foscari.

Boni, M. (Ed.). (2017). *World building: Transmedia, fans, industries*. Amsterdam, The Netherlands: Amsterdam University Press.

Bourdaa, M. (2018). *Character, time, and world – The case of Battlestar Galactica*. In *The Routledge companion to transmedia studies*. M. Freeman, & R. R. Gambarato (Eds.), 133–140. New York, NY: Routledge.

Caldwell, J. T. (2008). *Production culture: Industrial reflexivity and critical practice in film and television*. Durham, NC: Duke University Press.

Clarke, M. J. (2013). *Transmedia television: New trends in network serial production*. New York, NY: Bloomsbury Publishing USA.

Clements, J., & McCarthy, H. (2015). *The anime encyclopedia: A century of Japanese animation*. Berkeley, CA: Stone Bridge Press.

Condry, I. (2009). Anime creativity: Characters and premises in the quest for Cool Japan. *Theory, Culture & Society*, 26(2–3), 139–163.

Condry, I. (2013). *The soul of anime: Collaborative creativity and Japan's media success story.* Durham, NC: Duke University Press.

Evans, E. (2011). *Transmedia television: Audiences, new media, and daily life.* London, UK: Routledge.

Freeman, M. (2016). *Historicising transmedia storytelling: Early twentieth-century transmedia story worlds.* New York: Routledge.

Gray, J. (2010). *Show sold separately: Promos, spoilers, and other media paratexts.* New York, NY: New York University Press.

GREE, Inc. (2017). *Sword art online: Memory defrag* [Mobile game]. Tokyo, Japan: Bandai Namco Entertainment Inc.

Hartzheim, B. H. (2015). *Inside the media mix: Collective creation in contemporary manga and anime* (Doctoral dissertation, UCLA).

Havens, T., Lotz, A., & Tinic, S. (2009). Critical media industry studies: A research approach. *Communication, Culture, and Critique*, 2(2), 234–253.

Hay, J., & Couldry, N. (2011). Rethinking convergence/culture: An introduction. *Cultural Studies*, 25(4–5), 473–486.

Hjorth, L., & Richardson, I. (2014). *Gaming in social, locative, & mobile media.* New York, NY: Palgrave MacMillan.

Hutcheon, L. (2006). *A theory of adaptation.* New York, NY: Routledge.

Intelligent Systems. (2015). *Fire emblem: Fates* [Nintendo 3DS game]. Kyoto, Japan: Intelligent Systems Co., Ltd.

Intelligent Systems. (2017). *Fire emblem heroes* [Mobile game]. Kyoto, Japan: Intelligent Systems Co., Ltd.

Jenkins, H. (2006). *Convergence culture: Where old and new media collide.* New York, NY: New York University Press.

Jenkins, H., Ford, S., & Green, J. (2013). *Spreadable media: Creating value and meaning in a networked culture.* New York, NY: New York University Press.

Johnson, D. (2013). *Media franchising: Creative license and collaboration in the culture industries.* New York: New York University Press.

Kawahara, R. (2014a). *Sword art online, volume one: Aincrad* (S. Paul, Trans.). New York, NY: Yen Press.

Kawahara, R. (2014b). *Sword art online, volume two: Aincrad* (S. Paul, Trans.). New York, NY: Yen Press.

Kawahara, R. (Writer), & Ito, T. (Director). (2013). *Sword art online* [Television series]. Aniplex of America (Producer), North America: Netflix.com.

Kawahara, R. (Writer), & Ito, T. (Director). (2014). *Sword art online II* [Television series]. Aniplex of America (Producer), North America: Netflix.com.

Lamarre, T. (2009). *The anime machine: A media theory of animation.* Minneapolis: University of Minnesota Press.

Martin, T. (2012, December 19). Btooom! episodes 1–7 review. *Anime News Network.* Retrieved from https://www.animenewsnetwork.com/review/btooom/episodes-1.

Napier, S. J. (2001). *Anime from Akira to Howl's moving castle: Experiencing contemporary Japanese animation.* London, UK: St. Martin's Griffin.

Napier, S. (2006). "Excuse me, who are you?": Performance, the gaze, and the female in the works of Kon Satoshi. In *Cinema anime.* Brown, S. T. (Ed.), 23–42. New York, NY: Palgrave Macmillan.

Ormrod, J. (2018). Wonder woman 1987–1990: The Goddess, the Iron Maiden and the sacralisation of consumerism. *Journal of Graphic Novels and Comics*, 9(6), 1–15.

Rosenthal, B., & Zimmerman, D. L. (2012). Hikikomori: The Japanese phenomenon, policy, and culture. *International Journal of Mental Health*, 41(4), 82–95.

Saito, S. (2015). Beyond the horizon of the possible worlds: A historical overview of Japanese media franchises. *Mechademia*, 10, 143–161.

Scolari, C., Bertetti, P., & Freeman, M. (2014). *Transmedia archaeology: Storytelling in the borderlines of science fiction, comics and pulp magazines*. New York, NY: Springer.

Scott, J. (2009). The character-oriented franchise: Promotion and exploitation of pre-sold characters in American film, 1913–1950. In *Cultural borrowings: Appropriation, reworking, transformation*. Smith, I. R. (Ed.), 34–55. Nottingham, UK: Scope.

Shiraishi, S. (1997) Japan's soft power: Doraemon goes overseas. In *Network power: Japan and Asia*. Katzenstein, P. J., & Shiraishi, T. (Eds.), 234–272. Ithaca, NY: Cornell University Press.

Steinberg, M. (2012). *Anime's media mix: Franchising toys and characters in Japan*. Minneapolis: University of Minnesota Press.

Steinberg, M. (2013). Copying Atomu. *Mechademia*, 8, 127–136.

Steinberg, M., & Zahlten, A. (Eds.). (2017). *Media theory in Japan*. Durham, NC: Duke University Press.

Wada-Marciano, M. (2012). *Japanese cinema in the digital age*. Honolulu: University of Hawaii Press.

Werning, S. (2014). Manga, anime and video games: Between adaptation, transmedia extension and reverse remediation. *Mediascape*. Fall. Retrieved February 5, 2018, from: http://www.tft.ucla.edu/mediascape/Fall2014_MangaGames.html.

Yano, C. R. (2009). Wink on pink: Interpreting Japanese cute as it grabs the global headlines. *The Journal of Asian Studies*, 68(3), 681–688.

Zielenziger, M. (2007). *Shutting out the sun: How Japan created its own lost generation*. London, UK: Vintage.

Part II
Digital media and storytelling

6 Dynamics between agents in the new webtoon ecosystem in Korea

Responses to waves of transmedia and transnationalism

Jane Yeahin Pyo, Minji Jang, and Tae-Jin Yoon

What is "webtoon"? Dissecting the terminology, webtoon is a combination of two words, "web" and "cartoon." These terms are quite familiar words as we easily come across in our everyday lives. Taken together, they denote a series of cartoons or comics that are published on the Internet sphere (KOCCA, 2016a). Then, why is this simple combination of two mundane words seem so unique, or even unfamiliar? Moreover, how does it differ from other cartoons?

First, webtoon is different from "digital comics." Whereas the latter is simply a scanned and digitally web uploaded version of paper printed, webtoon is digitally produced from its very origin and intended to be uploaded, circulated, and consumed online. It follows traits of television dramas or newspaper comic strips in that it is uploaded regularly on a weekly basis mostly, but interactions between the authors and readers become much more spontaneous and direct in the online environment. Moreover, webtoon is also distinguishable from "webcomic" in terms of its contents. Although webcomics similarly aim to be published on the web, webtoon is essentially different in that the targeted period of serial publication is usually longer, and thus requires a longer narrative. Tailored to the size of digital screen, each episode takes advantage of readers' vertical scroll down activity. The industry's focus is increasingly centered around the mobile mediascape as Internet access via smartphones is becoming ever more prominent and prevalent.

Webtoon is also a uniquely Korean phenomenon: it is a cultural product that stemmed from Korea's Internet culture, along with native Korean platforms. Indeed, the unique service model of providing and circulating webtoon originated from Korea. When encountering the word "webtoon," one may simply think of Korean comics that are uploaded on Korean Internet platforms. Even in Wikipedia, webtoon is defined as Internet cartoons that are uploaded on the Internet in Korea (Chung, 2016). Witnessing webtoon's market potential and the profitability of the service model, Korea's Internet platform companies and newly arising webtoon service providers are turning their eyes to the global markets of Southeast Asia, Japan, and U.S.A. (KOCCA, 2016b). Korean webtoon also achieved successful settlement in foreign markets: the annual revenue is expected to be about 92 million dollars (KOCCA, 2016a). Also, in an attempt to break away from cultural boundaries, webtoon providers are incorporating glocalization strategies, such as fostering local cartoonists who can reflect their own cultural connotations rather than merely translating Korean into local languages. Hence, apart from exporting Korean contents themselves, the webtoon industry is exploring ways to export webtoon service platforms, comic artist management systems, and cinematized versions of preexisting webtoon.

Transmedia and transnational waves of webtoon

Webtoon has become an outstanding example of hybrid and convergence culture in this digital and global era, in the sense that it is a cultural form embodying transmedia phenomenon and transnational media environment. The term transmedia, introduced by Jenkins (2006) for the first time, is widely applicable to various phenomena: from a media production standpoint specifically, a transmedia production delivers similar story across different media. Transmedia is a safe tool to build an entertainment brand that attracts global audiences for television and film producers (Bernardo, 2014). Yet, transmedia does not merely refer to something like a screen adaptation. In transmedia, there is one narrative world, where variations of stories and forms spin out of. For instance, the mega-hit movie made in Korea, *Along with The Gods: The Two Worlds (2017)*, was based on a popular webtoon, but was initially criticized for digressing too much from the original webtoon. Meanwhile, webtoons are in the midst of the transnational phenomenon as appropriated versions of webtoons are exported to various countries. For example, Lezhin Comics, a Korean webtoon platform, was reported to be ranked in best grossing mobile applications on U.S. Google Play in the first quarter of 2018, outpacing Marvel and DC Comics (Venture Square World, 2018). Webtoon today is at the center of the crossroad between transmedia and transnationalism.

It is the intersection of webtoon's transmedia and transnational traits within the new mediascape that this chapter aims to investigate. New ways of production, circulation, and consumption create a new ecosystem, with new agents and power dynamics. Hence, our objective is to introduce the field of Korean webtoon and its significance in today's culture industry, and then analyze the dynamic between agents in the webtoon production field. We aim to explore how various agents are responding to and being influenced by the two most important factors impacting the ecosystem: transmedia and transnationalism. While there are numerous agents in the field, such as advertising companies or management agencies, we focus on three core agents: Webtoon creators, producers (from hereafter, we would indicate as PD), and platform companies. Webtoon creators are the artists[1] who debuted and signed contracts through a new process that is different from the traditional apprentice system, while PDs are essentially the employees of platform companies who recruit and manage creators and plan new projects. Various platform companies have newly emerged, either from the mergers between companies or business expansions from preexisting web service companies.

The structure and agents in the webtoon ecosystem

In illustrating the power relations in the new media ecosystem, the term agent helps to depict how agents are influenced by the structures and vice versa. Such a phenomenon is what Giddens (1984) acknowledged as the duality of structure. In advancing the idea of duality, Giddens stressed that structural properties of social systems exist only insofar as social practices are reproduced by social actors through routinization of processes. Hence, structure and agents are co-constitutive: structure constrains and enables agents' everyday practices, and agents reproduce and change structures. Giddens' theorization of co-constitutive relationship between individual agency and organizational structure has been an important framework to understand cultural production process, especially in settings in which routinized rituals are essential, like the newsroom (Ryfe, 2009; Usher, 2013).

Following Giddens' duality of structures, this article does neither attempt to create a dichotomy between structures and agents nor to assess how one overpowers the other. Rather, we meticulously portray the interplay between the structures and agents, focusing on how they influence each other in the context of transmedia and transnationalism. Moreover, according to Giddens, agents have knowledgeability of their practices that allows them to tacitly act in contexts of social life, as well as reflexivity. As will be further explained, since agents have knowledge and reflexivity, they set the rules to govern and monitor themselves and expect others to do the same. This allows us to capture the power dynamics among the agents as they understand, enforce, and restrain the rules to each other.

Moreover, webtoon industry is a cultural industry where the role of creative workers is foundational. Hesmondhalgh (2012) points out that creativity has become the main mechanism of cultural industries. When creativity becomes an important source of value in capitalist society, economization of creativity is inevitable: securing aesthetic autonomy and professional autonomy becomes an essential source of profit. Because individual cultural producers become part of the collective production process, they are assigned as knowledge workers in the social division of labor.

This means that we need to undergo a complex process of debate in order to properly grasp and understand the relative power, privilege, status, and interests of the cultural producers (Hesmondhalgh & Baker, 2013). Creative laborers are struggling to secure aesthetic autonomy and professional autonomy in labor process, and this creates tension within the cultural production process. As a result, the creative industry is the field where the workers' desire to demonstrate their creativity, fulfill industrial goals, and meet socio-cultural needs are combined (Hesmondhalgh & Baker, 2013). Webtoon artists, as creative laborers, know fully well that they are a part of the economic system of cultural industry and that their products are commercial goods. Yet, they do not discard the identity of artists.

This chapter is divided into two parts. First part will delineate the status quo of webtoon ecosystem, from briefly reiterating the history of Korean webtoon to showing how the webtoon industry has expanded, and how its production structure has developed along with the birth of web portal platforms. This section will focus on describing the overall webtoon ecosystem. The latter part focuses on the agents, in terms of their identity and role, and their power relations. Important factors that affect agent's identity and power dynamics are transmedia and transnationalism, which will be discussed in the final part. To deeply explore each agent, nine in-depth interviews were conducted. Capturing their liveliness in the field, this chapter hopes to contribute to a more comprehensive understanding of the webtoon ecosystem and its changes in responding to the waves of transmedia and transnationalism.

The historical context of Korean webtoon: industry, culture, and new media environment

The advent of webtoon and its embryonic phase: from the late 1990s to early 2000s

The history of webtoon can be traced back to the 1990s. As of other Korean popular culture, in the vestiges of webtoon's history lies neoliberal ideologies that prevailed in Korea during 1990s and the nation-state's intervention in creating a "global" popular culture that can be exported (Jin, 2014). Similar to government-driven business of Hallyu (the Korean Wave), webtoon was originally introduced as the Korean government's plan to further modernize Korean economy: to the stage of "digitalization" and "informatization" (Park, 2015). While the traditional, paper-based comic industry faced severe struggle due to the IMF Crisis in 1997 and increase in import of Japanese anime during 1998, Internet-based comics enjoyed a new possibility with open and easy access, and high speed (Yoon, Jung, Choi, & Choi, 2015). In other words, technological developments, economic crisis, the government's policies, and (inter-)cultural factors led to the decline of the paper-based comic industry while contributing to the birth of the webtoon ecosystem.

For creators, open space of the Internet allowed amateur artists' public debut, without going through years of traditional master-apprentice learnings (Yoon et al., 2015). Additionally, digitalization of the comics also indicated that the comic industry would have to embrace a new profit structure that does not rely on subscription fee or book sales, as online comics could be copied multiple times and distributed widely.

The prosperity of webtoon and portal sites: from 2003 to mid-2000s

After its embryonic stage, webtoon industry faced another important shift in 2003. In 2003, with Daum as the forerunner, major portal sites started to provide webtoon services. In the case of Daum, published an already popular work series of a famous comic artist, KangPool, on its web. In 2005, Naver, Korea's current number one portal site in terms of market share, officially launched webtoon division as a part of its business.

Indeed, the early 2000s marks the turn in the great success of webtoon: bringing the essential changes in its narrative, its ways of access, and showing definite possibility of webtoon's marketization and commercialization (Chung, 2016; KOCCA, 2016b; Park, 2015). Moreover, with powerful portal sites such as Daum and Naver regularly providing and updating webtoons in their platforms, webtoon's publication changed from a personal space to a public space. As mentioned before, whereas early webtoons were mostly uploaded on personal webpage of each creator, major portal sites allowed more convenient access to the general Internet users who were not avid fans of specific creators.

New technology and new platform in the smartphone era: from 2010 to present

Early 2000s was a period that showed numerous possibilities that webtoon could provide as one of the entertainment industries. However, webtoon became the leading industry with new digital technology: the advent of smartphones was a significant game changer in the circulation and consumption of webtoon. As users turned away from accessing webtoon via computer to smartphones, consumption of webtoon experienced an exponential increase. The number of new webtoon release increased drastically after 2010, showing about 62.2% increase compared to the previous year, which is the estimated year that smartphones became widespread in Korea (Yoon et al., 2015). In 2014, webtoon field also showed dramatic hype, as the number of users (Daum and Naver) was estimated to be six million (KOCCA, 2015). The shift in predominant way of webtoon access from personal computers to smartphones fostered a change in revenue structure. As users consumed webtoon via their smartphones, platforms could no longer solely rely on revenues from selling ad-space, commercial model as such would not fit with smartphone interface where there is no separate space for advertisement.

Recognizing marketability of webtoons, new platforms started to jump into the webtoon industry around 2012. Internet platforms that focused solely on providing webtoon were launched, such as Lezhin Comics and KakaoPage. Lezhin positioned itself as the first platform to provide "adult webtoons": R-rated webtoons that deal with sexual and/or violent topics. KakaoPage is a smartphone application that is based on the messenger application, KakaoTalk. With the help of KakaoTalk's market power, Kakao-Page successfully became one of the leading webtoon service providers and stretched its boundaries to other areas such as web drama and web novel, expanding its market to transmedia contents.

Now, webtoon ecosystem involves intricate web of relations between webtoon creators, users, and economic and cultural intermediaries. Particularly, the new media environment, in which content is spreading rapidly over territorial and cultural boundaries, has created a more participatory and complex mixed-model of content creation from different cultures and different genres (Jenkins, Ford, & Green, 2013). Yet, there is no concrete formula to which media contents become "spreadable." While Jenkins suggested the term spreadable media, Lotz (2015) described that the entertainment-based media industry is different from most other business sectors, often in frustrating ways for practitioners because of the audience's fickleness that prevents effective prediction: "I suspect the 'nobody knows' maxim is likely to be true of the circulation of spreadable media" (Lotz, 2015, para. 3.). This structure of "nobody knows" becomes a crucial factor for the webtoon industry, creating both anxiety and hope among agents in the webtoon field.

The Korean webtoon ecosystem's transnational and transmedia flow and expansion

Webtoon-specialized platforms, or so-called the second wave webtoon platform, have recently begun their own services in overseas. Comico (Comico. jp) opened in Japan in 2013, and Line Webtoons (webtoons.com) launched its Japanese, English, and Chinese services in 2014. Since then, Line Webtoon has launched its services in Indonesian and Thai. Lezhin Comics is also expanding its global services steadily since 2013, and as of September 2017, it has 120 Korean webtoons on the Japanese platform and 150 on the U.S. platform. Professional and global webtoon platforms, including Top-Toon (toptoon.com) and the KakaoPage (picoma.co/web), take advantage of the mobile and digital media environment to publish the webtoons or to find local creators.

The global expansion of the Korean webtoon platforms propels certain changes in comics and cartoon industries worldwide. Typical forms of publication—for example, one episode a week, 70 cuts an episode, and 30 episodes per title—are very new to most markets. Some say the general forms of webtoon publication cannot succeed in certain countries due to the sociocultural differences, while some find it very interesting and compelling. Meanwhile, transmedia conversions help readers to more actively participate in the field, as respondents or potential creators. Transmedia conversion is a way to expand and adapt the original story to reach various media and platforms (Seo, 2015). For example, *Incomplete Life* (*Misaeng, 2014*) and *Cheese in the Trap (2016)* are television dramas that are based on famous Korean webtoons, reaching wider television audience. Such appropriation works at the global level as well. In the film field, the Marvel series urge audiences to "study" each hero and their relations to grasp the whole picture of the Marvel Cinematic Universe (Richter, 2016). It makes people stay loyal, but loyalty happens only when they become active participants in transmedia process.

Agents in the production field: identity and power relations

Total of nine formal interviews were conducted, with four webtoon creators, four PDs from different companies, and one CEO of Korea's major webtoon service provider. All PDs, coined as A through D in the article, are employees of webtoon platform companies. Among the creators, two (Interviewees E and F) were currently publishing works on a weekly basis, one (G) had previous experience but was currently on rest, and the other one (H) had not officially debuted yet but was currently working as an assistant to the established creators. All the names of the platform companies are anonymized (A through H and Z; the CEO referred as Z). The interviews were semi-structured and ranged from one hour to less than two hours. All were recorded and later transcribed to be interpreted.

Who are they and what do they do?

Amid the emergent agents, PD is a relatively new and composite position that emerged with the changing webtoon ecosystem. The term webtoon PD was adopted from the field of television production, but the webtoon PD's role differs. First is to plan and direct future works, suggesting new topics and themes to publish, and recruiting new creators. PDs individually judge works submitted by the creators and select publishable ones. They also actively search for the new creators to recruit and contact them to suggest contracts.

The second role of PD is to manage creators and their work. As webtoons are mostly uploaded weekly, PDs are responsible for constantly keeping in touch with creators so that they meet the deadline. B even defined PD's job as "a service job" where they provide "mental care service." Another is to manage the quality of webtoons, which A described as the most important job as a PD. Mostly, this means giving feedbacks to creators. Moreover, PDs act as mediators between creators and audience. PDs would sometimes read user comments and deliver general reactions. Some creators replied they make PDs read comments instead because they do not wish to read for themselves.[2]

The vast ranges of the PD's role suggest their mobile identity. Because it is a relatively new job, each PD's task is not clearly defined, and the wide spectrum of their backgrounds add up to the confusion. Still, many had experiences as editors or relevant educational backgrounds. Interviewees mostly compared their job to editors; yet, they constantly pointed out the differences. C mentioned: "Yes, webtoon PDs work in a similar logic to that of the publishing house editors, but it is different." Differences included how PDs should be responsive to the cultural trends, have a larger number of creators to manage, and work to expand intellectual property.

Mobility in PD's identity and their differing backgrounds influenced creators when giving feedback; some feedback was from the editor's point of view, so mostly on narrative, while others were from comic artists' point of view and were on sketching style. Due to their fluid identity, PDs struggle in accumulating knowledge about the webtoon field. All PDs stated that despite their experience working as a PD, they still cannot tell which webtoon will succeed in the market or understand the rules of success. Experiences with book publishing or marketing did not mitigate confusion. D mentioned that it is neither quality of narrative nor drawing that brings the popularity of webtoon but could only vaguely answer that "fun" is the determining factor. As the webtoon industry expands, readers' responses become even more unpredictable, making it harder for PDs to corroborate their identity with their previous knowledge. This is precisely what Lotz (2015) means by the spreadable media's "nobody knows" maxim. It is almost impossible to create "a formula for producing creative content likely to catch the cultural fancy of any particular audience" (Lotz, 2015, para. 3). She suggests intentional overproduction and the production of sequels as the primary strategies for dealing with the uncertainty. Most webtoon platforms know this, and these strategies sometime make PDs' work harder because they need to keep managing creators' works to deal with uncertainties of creative cultural products.

Unlike PDs, webtoon creators appear to have a stable identity. When asked to identify oneself, E clearly expressed that she is an "artist who draws and tells stories," and that she would have become a paper-based comic artist had she been born in that era. Others identify themselves either as a cartoonist or a storyteller, who pursue creativity and originality. Their strong sense of identity was reflected in their works, particularly in the topics they chose. Based on her previous experience working as a nurse, E's work is about working in a hospital, whereas G reflects her love toward video games and shares episodes about gameplay. Moreover, their educational background suggested artist identity, as the creators mostly received professional trainings in animation or digital imaging. In fact, having a strong and solid identity was regarded as the essence of creators. All pointed out that creators should have strong characteristic and thematic focus. As those creators are more desired by the industry, some creators try to individually establish their reputation by uploading works on their social media.

Simultaneously, webtoon creators show great adaptability to the new webtoon ecosystem, which shows how they assert agency within the industrial structure. Even though they have a strong sense of identity as artistic creators, they acknowledged that they were ultimately laborers trying to make a living. E still works as a part-time nurse due to flexible work hours as a webtoon creator. Creators also show different coping mechanism, when their identities clash. H, who had not officially debuted yet, commented: "I try to separate myself when working as an outsourced worker who meets every demand from my employer. That is another me, not when I put my pen name up front and draw my work. That's more comfortable."

New digital media technology was also essential in agents' purposive agency. Creators understood the importance of mastering digital technology. They signed up for extracurricular education and bought state-of-the-art devices when necessary. They also actively sought tactics and advices from senior creators regarding how to well build relationships with PDs after debut, how to deal with physical and psychological stress, and successfully writing contracts. Their actions were shaped by unpredictable webtoon structure, but at the same time changing the structure through their own ways of coping.

Platform companies naturally emerged as a powerful agent as webtoon ecosystem experienced a "digital turn." Renowned CEO, interviewee Z, acknowledges that the webtoon industry fortuitously expanded with the Internet boom. Platforms play the role of displaying and curating webtoons as if readers are subscribing to a weekly magazine. Their unique political economic structure particularly posed limitations to agents like the creators. Like the word platform connotes, they provide open, neutral, egalitarian and non-elitist space, where creators can compete fairly to win their debut (Gillespie, 2010), particularly within the amateur leagues. Yet, creator E responded that a certain logic exists behind weekly curation of webtoons, so having the opportunity to debut may not necessarily depend on quality. Additionally, platforms work to perform audience research (Andrejevic, 2002), which provides lucrative grounds for attempting transmedia and transnationalism. For instance, Z had an exact understanding through audience data because webtoons first need to verify marketability in Korea in order to be exported. The platforms' role is to channel the audience's interests into transmedia production or global export.

Dynamics among agents: power relations between agents

In reality, power relations are not visible or consistent. Yet, dynamic interplay was evident among agents. All acknowledged that the webtoon creator is crucial in the production field: they are not only an important source of value, but also a force that can bring tremendous changes in webtoon eco-system. Z notices that the webtoon industry was able to take the current form because the star creators were born:

> It is more of a Big Bang in the webtoon industry through the birth of one genius creator, such as KangPool, than gradual industrial expansion. KangPool was so powerful. Whenever he updated his series the whole Internet server went unstable.

Even as the industry solidified today, F said "There is a mascot to every platform. If one famous creator migrates to a new platform, it becomes huge news because it brings in a lot of new users."

Creators sit at the center of the dynamic, but their relationship between the platform companies is not always amicable. H defines the relationship as a tug-of-war. She says "(Creators and Platforms) move forward together, constantly. But it is not together peacefully but with constant clash." This "clash" is interesting as it reveals their ambient relationship. However, creators expressed that they clearly benefited from platforms. G even expressed that she is "grateful" because the platform "tries to pay me at least $50 a month. That did not exist before." Although her series ended few years ago, she was still receiving royalty fee. Platform companies provide opportunities and benefits to creators, and creators realized that it was a good opportunity. Z also acknowledged that the webtoon industry turned to the paid readership to protect creators and provide an environment where they could freely create innovative works.

Nonetheless, creators expressed their discontent with the system. Problems were about unfair income, excessive workload, strict policies on late submission, and required modifications of their contents in order to meet platform's demand. Usually, the creators would compromise by sacrificing quality. G explicitly mentioned how she "gave up on quality." F states:

> It is important during work that I maintain my humanity, and that requires compromise. I use this program that allows me to copy and paste background drawings. I cannot afford an assistant and the platform will not pay me, so I just use ready-made sources ... Before debuting, my artistic universe was all that mattered but now, let's say I gained how to do tug-of-war between myself and reality.

Platforms would require around 80 cuts per week, which creators thought as a very demanding workload. Furthermore, making the deadline was more important than quality, because tardiness would directly impact their income. H mentioned that she is deliberately delaying debut because she feels a "sense of shame" in meddling between platform's demands and her artistic pursuit. She notes "even if my work is more suitable for black-and-white, I have to color it if the platform requires colored work. I feel shame or disheartened."

As they struggle to make dispiriting compromises, creators still try to claim agency. Although they may compromise, creators hold the authority to make the final decision on their work. Since they have rights to their intellectual property, all business must go through them, especially when the platform company is trying to expand intellectual property. By asserting a solid identity as the creator and owner of their work, creators attempt to claim their power in this tug-of-war. In their attempt to claim power, creators demonstrate a great amount of knowledgeability and adaptability. Over the past years, creators have gained a great depth of knowledge regarding the webtoon ecosystem. Born during the hype of webtoons and having witnessed new debut process such as amateur league, creators are the "webtoon generation." Moreover, creators learned about the irrationality of platform companies from their seniors and sharing with their co-workers. Then, they attempted to break the routine by passing on their knowledge: "I tell my school's freshmen about what companies to avoid. I got help so I try to give help," says F. In their day-to-day enactment of social life, while they reproduce structure, they also attempt to make structural changes and produce new rules.

Having been avid readers of webtoon before debuting, they also show great adaptability to the traits of each platform. All platforms had different preferences. Creators who debuted acknowledged that their platforms suited their work in terms of the company's target markets. E stressed the importance of tactical positioning and said

> You cannot just draw, but from the planning, you need to choose a platform and plan your work. (...) Actually, you carve out yourself to fit into one platform. Either you fit yourself into the platform, or make it want you.

This shows that E had an exact understanding of each platform's characteristics, whereas H similarly understood that the genre of his work was not favored on any of the platforms. C, who is a PD, compared that whereas the former creators were those who simply loved drawing, the young creators nowadays know much more about the industry and intentionally aim for the target platform that is already in their mind. Creators show a great deal of knowledgeability and struggle to adapt to the new webtoon ecosystem made by dominant digital intermediaries in order to assert their power.

PDs mediate between the conflict between creators and platform companies. As they directly interact with the creators, they understand creator's discontent. At the same time, being a part of platform companies, they stand by the commercial side. They are the mediators, yet assert their own authority within the power relations. PDs know that the creators' stability, satisfaction, and amiable environment are of utmost importance when it comes to publishing successful webtoons. Thus, they try to respect creators in their work and remain cautious when giving feedback. D stated that "Creators are human. They are not factories so I cannot force them to listen to me. Creators are the first. When they do not have fun with their work, then their work shows that." Similarly, B said

> Basically, I try to respect creator's opinion. If creator really does not want to accommodate my feedback, it does not make sense to push it, because it is the creator who makes the story. If the creator is not enjoying the creative process, the result is not good either.

According to A, creator's autonomy is directly related to the contents' consistency and liveliness, so PDs try to refrain from aggressively giving feedback. D commented that PDs should trust the creators. This underlines that as original creators of their works, PDs show leniency toward creators so that they can produce a masterpiece.

Nonetheless, PDs described their relationship with creators as "strictly business" and attempted to keep a certain distance for that reason. B compared the relationship to moneylending: "it is a relationship where one provides work and the other pays." It rather created discomfort when they were too close. Mostly, the distance between them could naturally be maintained as PDs and creators do not have to communicate face-to-face. Most of the feedback process was through email, texts, or phone calls. Platform companies sometimes had rules to prevent close contact. Professional distance allowed PDs to assert their power over creators when necessary. B replied that

> Sometimes, when you get too close, you expect what you should not. For example, deadline exists, but creators may ask for late-submission without any penalty because they think we are close. If I do it, they will think that rules can be bent and repeat it. That cannot happen. I have to enforce rules.

This reveals that although PDs respect creators' privilege, they still have their duties to enforce rules and prevent creators' power overcoming theirs. Hence, they cannot yield too much latitude or allow creators stepping over "business" boundaries because PDs are a part of the company. PDs' primary role was to represent their companies, from which they received authority. B admitted that "I cannot simply stand for creators because in the end, I am affiliated with the company." He defined his position as a "mediator," working out conflicts between the company and the creators. Such conflicts occurred the most when creators were demanding a wage increase, as in the case of creator E with her PD. In the end, she did not achieve her goal as the PD drew a strict line.

To claim superiority in this power relationship, such as when creators refuse to accommodate their feedback, PDs assert their authority in various ways. Sometimes it was PDs' long experience in the related fields such as publishing as in the case of A and B, or exterior power relations such as gender or age, as E exemplified. Mostly, it was the power transferred to the PDs from the company's technological affordance. B commented, "Creators trust me. Because when I say 'it would be better this way' and they accept it, most of the times it receives a better response from readers than when they don't take my advice." Having access to the data about the readers' response puts them in a superior position and grants authority to their feedback. D further elaborated that if creators do not take his feedback, he presents statistical numbers such as daily click rates, number of user-views, number of revisits, and paid view rate. If the numbers are declining, he would strongly urge the creator to make necessary changes again. In C's case, because PDs have access to the demographic data of the audience, he tries to ease out gender-sensitive issues and provide advice based on audience data. As employees of the platform companies, PDs have access to the bigger structure where data is centralized, and this creates new forms of accountability and control (Goulden, Tolmie, Mortier, Pietilanien, & Teixeira, 2018).

Creators also understand the ambivalent position of PDs. Although they saw PDs as good people trying their best to respect the author's freedom and creativity, they realized that they essentially follow the platform company's commercial logic. In their own ways, creators tried to win back their power. They realized that if they follow PDs' feedback too much, their work would lose its identity and become tainted. In these cases, creators would simply disagree and refuse to make changes to their work: "I say I'm sorry but I will just trust my decision," says E. They would again make compromises, mostly enduring until they gain enough authority and power. As renowned creators mostly have absolute freedom in planning and carrying out their work, F said she was persevering until she accumulates enough social capital. In the case of E, she said she would only heed to PDs until she fully seals the contract. Nonetheless, creators' struggle for autonomy becomes harder especially when platform companies or PDs have pre-planned projects. In those cases, PDs "make sure their requirements are made," and such attempts occur more frequently as platform companies prepare to meet the oncoming wave of transmedia and transnationalism.

New challenges to respond to transmedia and transnationalism

Transmedia and transnationalism have become inevitable forces that bring change to the structure. Transmedia and transnationalism goes side by side: producing multiple texts through multiple media adds values to the franchise, and fostering transmedia production is a response to globalization so that global audience are encouraged to collaborate on decoding multiple texts (Pamment, 2016). Although interviewees replied that two factors are immensely restructuring webtoon ecosystem, their opinion greatly varied in terms of the future. In the struggle for power, Z's blueprint suggests how the platform company envisions future webtoon industry. Ultimately, he envisions a structure where companies have "absolute control of works":

> We are beginning on this project to work more efficiently for us to expand the business. It is like hiring creators to make webtoons and give them some royalty on original works while we have all copyrights... We need works that we have absolute control of, which we have the decision-making power.

Z notes that transmedia is currently the best solution to maximize the value of webtoon. He explains that webtoon as a sole content cannot become "super IP," which is intellectual property that has a business value of five billion dollars. It must cooperate with moving pictures industry. As his company is big enough, he nowadays brings webtoon creator, his platform company, and film production company to one roundtable to build webtoon product from scratch. Because he constantly takes transmedia into consideration, he prefers genres with strong characters and story world because they are more feasible to apply into various fields. Characters are essential glues that allow successful transition between media (Sánchez-Mesa, Aarseth, Pratten, & Scolari, 2016).

PDs also agreed that when they select works, they consistently keep the transmedia possibility in mind. For instance, when B encountered webtoons with a universal theme or which would not require much special effects such as romantic comedy, he immediately thought of cinematization. Similarly, creators were also responding to the transmedia demand as they worked on new projects, reminding themselves that successful cinematization would bring them great fortune. Potential transmedia conversion put pressure on both PDs and creators, and the dynamics of webtoon ecosystem may be changing because of this extrinsic variable: PDs have to constantly persuade creators to adapt to the change while creators have to either accept or confront it.

Nonetheless, creators stated that there are risks in prioritizing transmedia possibilities. There were definite "webtoon traits" that cannot be translated into moving pictures. Moreover, focusing only on transmedia would critically harm the diversity of webtoon genres. To creators, identities as a webtoon creator and as a visual arts producer were entirely different, F noted. H declared that she would not justify changes or alter her priorities just because it would better suit cinematization. A evaluated that although there are numerous attempts in cinematization, not many remain successful, which suggests the difficulty of producing a quality transmedia. Transmedia matters for sure, but it needs to be seen how strong this variable will be in transforming the whole webtoon ecosystem.

When it comes to transnationality in a more general sense, interviewees displayed greater difficulty in having unified opinions. PDs generally expressed that transnationality is an ongoing process: their companies were mostly exporting webtoons to China, Japan, and Thailand. All acknowledged that the Korean market was limited and that foreign markets provided greater opportunities for expanding the industry. Creators expressed great expectations toward exportation, as E mentioned she always considers and hopes for her work to be exported. Thus, she would be cautious not to criticize certain countries, but to talk about universal subjects. F's work was already in the process of overseas expansion to China, so she had to extend the story because China prefers seasonal series. Yet, concerns and doubts still lingered. Successful localizing was the key to success but had multiple barriers. Problems of the cultural gap and language barrier were the greatest. F worried that her work, which is a horror webtoon, has strong Korean connotation because the setting is in a Korean school. The overseas expansion would also require modifying drawings to fit the local style or rearranging speech bubbles to fit differing language configurations. Lack of interaction with the audience was also problematic, as G stated "Webtoon creators are in a symbiotic relation with the audience through constant interaction. But I don't know for foreign audience." Creating webtoon just to target foreign markets was also dangerous, as in the end foreign markets also preferred works that have been successful in Korea. A and B noted that ultimately, the Korean market comes first.

Although transnationalism is fraught with difficulties and risks, foreign markets are crucial targets that the current Korean webtoon industry must tackle in order to accelerate its growth. Z acknowledges that Korean market has clear limits on the amount of webtoons that platforms can sell. Even to expand intellectual property, such as producing action figures, having a bigger market is efficient due to the economy of scale. Yet, because the webtoon industry is encountering numerous obstacles in its attempt of achieving transmedia and transnationalism, one could easily question whether this is a naturally occurring phenomenon. While platforms would clearly run the risk of pushing the industry toward new flow, it seemed that some creators would not willingly accept such a demand, if not unwittingly. They expressed concerns regarding mistranslation, over-modification, and possible failures. There were also possibilities that in order to meet the company's demands for transnationalism and transmedia, webtoons' diversity and creators' freedom may be limited. This suggests that the two waves are not necessarily the natural forces that restructure the webtoon ecosystem; yet, in order to maximize the profit, the industry would make carefully calculated attempts to successfully attain transnationalism and transmedia.

Moreover, a discussion on technological change, geospatial boundaries, social and cultural tension, inequality, and social penetration naturally follows when discussing transnational attempts (Christensen, 2013). However, for the webtoon industry, transnationalism is rather an industry-enforced and export-oriented wave to increase the influx of capital. This explains Z's comment on creators' stance regarding the changing structure: "I think it will be difficult for this system, like weekly updates, to change greatly...It would be better for the creators to change their environment to fit with the system."

Discussion

The webtoon industry's structure is constantly evolving as webtoons gain great popularity in and out of Korea and the number of different agents entering the production field is growing. The field is becoming ever more complex and dynamic, as agents are interacting and struggling based on their power relations. This article is an attempt to capture the dynamics and power relations that exist in the webtoon production field, based on live and vivid experiences to which each agent attests. Moreover, webtoon ecosystem is experiencing another big transition with the flow of trans-media and transnationalism. These factors greatly impact the structure of webtoon production field, wherein agents are constituted and constituting at the same time. The idea of duality of structure, wherein agents reproduce structural properties and also alter the structure based on their knowledgeability and reflexivity, enables us to shed light on how agents are responding to changes in the webtoon ecosystem. The results also have a strong implication for the history of theoretical discussions on the cultural industry, including Hesmondhalgh's emphasis on the aesthetic autonomy in the cultural industries and Jenkins' insight into spreadable media.

Responses to structural changes varied. Some are actively seeking to accommodate these factors by redirecting capital flows, as in the case of platform companies. Others, such as webtoon creators, are trying to react to these changes but essentially trying to maintain their identities as creators of Korean webtoon. Some are meddling; as the mediator between platform companies and creators, PDs understand the increasing importance of transmedia and transnational flow and are pressured to meet capital's demand; thus, they are also aware of the difficulties that creators face and essential obstacles such as genuine webtoon traits, language barriers, and cultural differences. Other than what is happening within the webtoon ecosystem, other external variables such as political relations, social change, and cultural preference were also making an impact on the way to adapt to transmedia and transnationalism. By providing online space where creators can present and share their work, platform companies open unprecedented methods for creators to debut, make a living, and interact with their audience. They also created the new job of PDs, who may or may not have the related experience, to conceive new ideas and projects.

To truly help soak the webtoon industry with the flow of transmedia and transnationalism, creators seem to be a genuine source of values. As the interviewees demonstrate, creators' unique and original works are what attracts the global audience regardless of the cultural or linguistic barriers. However, their reluctance to adapt to the changes could block the industry's efforts to cross the barriers of media and nation. At the same time, based on the interviews, we can see the possible collisions between the creators and companies/PDs because the former wants to claim their rights to intellectual property no matter how transmedia and transnationalism change the structure, while the latter seeks to have more control over creators' work to expedite transmedia and transnationalism. Nonetheless, the power of the agent, particularly creative power of creators is tantamount to capital forces as it is the creators' yearning to create art pieces and share their works that helped establish the webtoon industry in the first place.

The multiple interviews indicated that the future of webtoon ecosystem is too opaque to predict. Many new forces are ripe with possibilities of their utterly changing the structure. We cannot offer a clear blueprint of the webtoon industry's future based on the interviews but can at least grasp a vague idea about how to improve the industry, as understood from H's comments. She said, "I feel powerless and overwhelmed, more like suffocated from this structure, and how this structure still continues to exist in this way. Why doesn't it, so unfair and so consuming, change?" Perhaps a true change in the structure toward prosperity could begin with allowing agents to break away from the oppressive structure through constant reflexivity.

Notes

1 It may be controversial to call the webtoon creators "artists." However, most creators interviewed for this research consider themselves having double identities: artists and laborer. They produce webtoons for money, but at the same time they emphasize creativity and autonomy like film directors. Hence, we use the term "artist," borrowing from their own definition of their role. We use the terms "creators" and "artists" interchangeably depending on the context.
2 Most webtoon providers have comments section for complaints, praises, and debates. Sometimes audiences leave harsh criticisms that some creators do not want to read.

References

Andrejevic, M. (2002). The work of being watched: Interactive media and the exploitation of self-disclosure. *Critical Studies in Media Communication, 19*(2), 230–248. doi:10.1080/07393180216561

Bernardo, N. (2014). *Transmedia 2.0: How to create an entertainment brand using a transmedia approach to storytelling.* London, UK: beActive Books.

Christensen, M. (2013). TransNational media flows: Some key questions and debates. *International Journal of Communication, 7*, 2400–2418.

Chung, I. H. (2016). A study on remediation of digital contents in N-Screen environments: Focused on <Misaeng>. *Social Science Research Review, 32*(3), 155–183. doi:10.18859/ssrr.2016.08.32.3.155

Giddens, A. (1984). *The constitution of society.* Berkeley: University of California Press.

Gillespie, T. (2010). The politics of 'platforms.' *New Media & Society, 12*(3), 347–364. doi:10.1177/1461444809342738

Goulden, M., Tolmie, P., Mortier, R., Pietilanien, A., & Teixeira, R. (2018). Living with interpersonal data: Observability and accountability in the age of ICT. *New Media & Society*, *20*(4), 1580–1599. doi:10.1177/1461444817700154

Hesmondhalgh, D. (2012). *The cultural industries*. New York, NY: SAGE Publications.

Hesmondhalgh, D., & Baker, S. (2011). *Creative labour: Media work in three cultural industries*. London and New York, NY: Routledge.

Jenkins, H. (2006). *Convergence culture: Where old and new media collide*. New York, NY: The New York University Press.

Jenkins, H., Ford, S., & Green, J. (2013). *Spreadable media: Creating value and meaning in networked culture*. New York, NY: The New York University Press.

Jin, D. Y. (2014). The power of the nation-state amid neo-liberal reform: Shifting cultural politics in the new Korean Wave. *Pacific Affairs*, *87*(1), 71–92. doi:10.5509/201487171

KOCCA (Korea Creative Contents Agency). (2015). *Webtoon industry's structural problems and improvement plans*. Retrieved from http://www.kocca.kr/cop/bbs/view/B0000147/1825421.do?menuNo=201825

KOCCA (Korea Creative Contents Agency). (2016a). *Report on the improvement of cartoon distribution environment: Focusing on the webtoon business*. Retrieved March 10, 2019, from http://bitly.kr/Exj9m

KOCCA (Korea Creative Contents Agency). (2016b). *Strategy of Korean webtoon business toward East Asian market: The case of Indonesia and Thailand* (9th ed.). Retrieved March 10, 2019, from http://bitly.kr/0cjFc

"Lezhin Comics beats Marvel and DC on U.S. Google Play." (2018). *Venture Square World*. Retrieved from http://www.venturesquare.net/world/lezhin-comics-beats-marvel-dc-u-s-google-play.

Lotz, A. (2015). What old media can teach new media. *Spreadable Media Blog*. Retrieved from http://spreadablemedia.org/essays/lotz/#.XEFwR1z7Q2x

Pamment, J. (2016). Digital diplomacy as transmedia engagement: Aligning theories of participation with international advocacy campaigns. *New Media & Society*, *18*(9), 2046–2062. doi:10.1177/1461444815577792

Park, S. H. (2015). Policy recommendation for promoting Korean webtoon ecosystem. *The Korean Journal of Animation*, *11*(3), 65–81.

Richter, Á. (2016). The marvel cinematic universe as a transmedia narrative. *Americana: E-Journal of American Studies in Hungary*, *12*(1), 1. Retrieved from http://americanaejournal.hu/vol12no1/richter

Ryfe, D. M. (2009). Structure, agency, and change in an American newsroom. *Journalism*, *10*(5), 665–683. doi:10.1177/1464884909106538

Sánchez-Mesa, D., Aarseth, E., Pratten, R., & Scolari, C. (2016). Transmedia (storytelling?): A polyphonic critical review. *Artnodes*, *18*, 8–19. doi:10.7238/a.v0i18.3064/

Seo, S. E. (2015). *The study on media conversion storytelling* (Doctoral dissertation). Retrieved from Ewha Womans University, Seoul. http://www.riss.kr/link?id=T13668789

Usher, N. (2013). Marketplace public radio and news routines reconsidered: Between structures and agents. *Journalism*, *14*(6), 807–822. doi:10.1177/1464884912455903

Yoon, K. H, Jung, K. H., Choi, I. S., & Choi, H. (2015). Features of Korean webtoons through the statistical analysis. *Cartoon & Animation Studies*, *1*, 177–194.

7 Do webtoon-based TV dramas represent transmedia storytelling?

Industrial factors leading to webtoon-based TV dramas

Ji Hoon Park, Jeehyun Lee, and Yongsuk Lee

With the proliferation of mobile devices and snack culture, the webtoon (a type of online comic) has become one of the leading forms of popular culture in Korea. In 2017, a total of 1,759 webtoons were published on various online platforms, such as Naver, Daum, Lezhin Comics, and Toptoon (Korea Manhwa Contents Agency, 2018). In response to their increasing popularity, TV production companies, broadcasting stations, and webtoon platforms are actively seeking for opportunities to transform webtoons into TV dramas. The huge successes of *Misaeng* (tvN, 2014) and *Cheese in the Trap* (tvN, 2016), the drama series based on the webtoons of the same titles, are known to have accelerated the trend of turning webtoons into TV dramas (Baek, 2016).

Critics and scholars have discussed the reasons underlying the popularity of webtoons in Korea (Doo, 2017; Jin, 2014). However, few studies have been conducted to identify the industrial context and production practices that motivate the TV industry to utilize webtoons as a source of TV drama storytelling. On the basis of in-depth interviews with individuals closely involved in the production of webtoon-based TV dramas, we investigate the industrial context of the collaboration among webtoon platforms, broadcasting stations, and production companies. This study is driven by our particular interest in the transmedia potential of webtoon-based TV dramas in the age of convergence culture (Jenkins, 2006). Is the use of the webtoon narrative across different media platforms indicative of the larger phenomenon of transmedia storytelling? Or is webtoon-based TV drama production a part of an industrial practice of cross-media adaptation or one source multi-use (OSMU)? An examination of the production practices specific to the Korean TV industry will enable a closer look into the factors that are currently encouraging or precluding the transmedia potential of webtoons.

Transmedia potential of webtoon

The optimistic prospect of the Korean webtoon arises from the markedly growing diversification of webtoon content to dramas, movies, animation, games, and musicals. Han (2014) has also reported on the webtoons' potential as transmedia storytelling sites revealing that there are webtoons planned from the onset to develop as easily adaptable transmedia texts. According to Han, Lezhin Entertainment is taking steps to move beyond OSMU strategies, as it plans to collaborate with CJ ENM to create webtoons suited for transmedia stories, which will later be expanded into films. Another notable transmedia project is the collaboration between Neowiz Games and Naver, which has transformed the webtoon *Sound of Heart* into a game of the same name (Y. Lee, 2016). Also, popular webtoon *Along with the Gods* has been adapted into a musical in 2015 before its transition to the big screen in 2017. When *Along with the Gods* was released as a blockbuster film in 2017, it was an epic success. Attracting more than 14.4 million viewers, it ranked second in Korea's all-time box office records (Na, 2018). Most recently, the film's sequel *Along with the Gods 2* (2018), released on August 1, has dominated Korea's box office, selling 3.85 million tickets within the first week (Jin, 2018). Other than *Along with the Gods*, webtoon-based movies have fared extremely well, examples including but not limited to *Moss* (2010), *Secretly, Greatly* (2013), and *Steel Rain* (2017), all proving the great potential of webtoons as a primary source for Korean films (Na, 2018).

Following movies, there have been many successful cases of TV remakes of webtoons in recent years, making webtoons also a popular primary source for Korean dramas. Since 2013, there have been approximately 40 webtoon-based dramas (Table 7.1).

Misaeng (2014) and *Cheese in the Trap* (2016), which have been adapted into TV drama series aired on tvN, a cable network, each enjoyed viewer ratings over 7%, which is rare for shows on cable TV. In 2018 alone, more than five webtoon-based dramas have been planned, with the most recent *What is Wrong with Secretary Kim* ending with a viewer rating over 8%, outperforming many popular webtoon-based dramas. Alongside the commercial success of webtoon-based dramas and movies in recent years, S. Lee (2018) also describes 2017 as a year of "pilot content" for the Korean webtoon market, as numerous webtoons have participated in OSMU and transmedia projects by expanding the webtoon story to secondary media contents. One notable example is the "Super String" project, the content collaboration among Naver Webtoon, content corporation Y-lab, and film company Young Film. The project, which is still in its developmental stages, will integrate popular webtoon characters from *Blade of the Phantom Master*, *Reawaken man*, and *Terror man* into a single narrative space (S. Lee, 2018). This grand transmedia project plans to expand the webtoon narrative into films and games, creating a universe similar to the cinematic universes of Marvel and DC Comics.

Aside from the collaboration, Naver has also reported on its plan to establish a corporate body called Naver N that will be in charge of adapting webtoons into TV dramas and films, which Park (2018) observes as an

Table 7.1 Webtoon-Based TV Drama Series

Drama Title	Webtoonist	Aired from – to	Channel
Flower Boys Next Door (이웃집 꽃미남)	Yoo Hyun-Sook	2013.01.07–02.26	tvN
Misaeng: Incomplete Life (미생)	Yoon Tae-Ho	2014.10.17–12.20	tvN
Dr. Frost (닥터 프로스)	Lee Jong-Beom	2014.11.23–2015.02.01	OCN
Hyde, Jekyll, Me (하이드 지킬 나)	Lee Choong-Ho	2015.01.21–03.26	SBS
Hogu's love (호구의 사랑)	Yoo Hyun-Sook	2015.02.09–03.31	tvN
A Girl Who Sees Smells (냄새를 보는 소녀)	Seo Soo-Kyung (Man Chwi)	2015.04.01–05.21	SBS
Orange Marmalade (오렌미 마말레이드)	Seok-Woo	2015.05.15–07.24	KBS2
The Scholar Who Walks the Night (밤을 걷는 선비)	Jo Joo-Hee	2015.07.08–09.10	MBC
Last (라스트)	Kang Hyung-Kyu	2015.07.24–09.12	JTBC
The Awl (송곳)	Choi Kyu-Sok	2015.10.24–11.29	JTBC
Cheese in the Trap (치즈인더트랩)	Soonkki	2016.01.04–03.01	tvN
My Lawyer, Mr. Jo 1 (동네변호사 조들호 1)	Kim Yang-soo (Hatzling)	2016.03.28–05.31	KBS2
Lucky Romance (운빨 로맨스)	Kim Dal-Nim	2016.05.2–07.14	MBC
Hey Ghost, Let's Fight (싸우자 귀신아)	Im In-Su	2016.07.11–08.30	tvN
The Gentlemen of Wolgyesu Tailor Shop (월계수 양복점 신사들)	Lee Jong-Kyu	2016.08.27–2017.02.26	KBS2
Sweet Stranger and Me (우리 집에 사는 남자)	Yoo Hyun-Sook	2016.10.24–12.13	KBS2
Save Me (구해줘)	Jo Geum-San	2017.08.05–09.24	OCN
Avengers Social Club (부암동 복수자들)	Sajatokki	2017.10.11–11.16	tvN
Confession Couple (고백부부)	Hong Seung-Pyo, Kim Hye-Yeon	2017.10.13–11.18	KBS2
My First Love (애간장)	Kim Byoung-Gwan, Kim Hee-Ran	2018.01.08–02.06	OCN
What is Wrong with Secretary Kim (김비서가 왜 그럴까?)	Kim Myung-Mi	2018.06.06–07.26	tvN
Your House Helper (당신의 하우스헬퍼)	Seong Jeong-Yeon	2018.07.04–08.29	KBS2
My ID is Gangnam Beauty (내 아이디는 강남미인)	Gi Maeng-Gi	2018.07.27–09.15	JTBC
Clean with Passion for Now (일단 뜨겁게 청소하라)	Aengo	2018.11.29–2019.02.04	JTBC

attempt by Naver to become a Korean style Marvel. Kwon Mi-Kyung, the former head of the Korean Film Business department of CJ ENM and an illustrious figure behind Korea's biggest box office hits that include *Ode to My Father* and the *Roaring Currents*, was hired as the new head of Naver N (Na, 2018). By acquiring the intellectual property (IP) rights of webtoons, Naver is attempting to capitalize on its transmedia potential.

Similar attempts have been made by CJ ENM whose TV Network, Orion Cinema Network (OCN), has recently brought together major heroes and villains from six of its popular dramas to the webtoon series *Original Sin* (Cho, 2018). *Original Sin* is an unprecedented case of universe building in Korea, with the superhero multi-universe extending the stories of major characters beyond the narrative of their respective dramas. As CJ ENM is the mother company of OCN, with its own game, music, entertainment and movie industry, future transmedia franchises are expected to arise from its current endeavors.

Transmedia storytelling vs. cross-media adaptation

Transmedia storytelling is a concept most comprehensively theorized by media scholar Jenkins, who describes highly integrated works with narratives expanding across films, games, and novels in the age of media convergence. In his web blog "Confessions of an ACA Fan," Jenkins (2007) defines transmedia storytelling as "a process where integral elements of a fiction get dispersed systematically across multiple delivery channels for the purpose of creating a unified and coordinated entertainment experience" (para. 2), with each new medium making distinctive contributions to the overall story. Therefore, there is no single text in which viewers can acquire all the information they need to understand the whole story. For example, Jenkins (2006) explains how in the world of *Matrix*, numerous texts are integrated to create a narrative so expansive that it cannot be enclosed within a single medium.

The theorization of transmedia storytelling developed in tandem with the exclusion of cross-media adaptation to distinguish the transmedia phenomenon from other similar, long dated practices of employing multiple media platform in the unfolding of the same story world (Dena, 2018). Jenkins (2009) differentiates the two practices; adaptation "reproduces the original narrative with minimum changes into a new medium and is essentially redundant to the original work" and transmedia is an "extension which expands our understanding of the original by introducing new elements into the fiction" (para. 11). Therefore, transmedia practice has firmly established itself as an extension process rather than an adaptation practice, where the latter was regarded as simple retellings of the same story (Bourdaa, 2013; Evans, 2011; Phillips, 2012). However, many adaptation theorists have challenged such distinctions, maintaining that adaptations are neither redundant nor mere retellings. Instead, adaptations "always involves (re)interpretion and (re)creation" (Hutcheon, 2006, p. 8) and constantly engage in balancing out the elements of familiarly and novelty (Wells-Lassagne, 2017). Dena (2009) regards adaptation as part of the transmedia phenomena as it can have "many roles in the meaning making process" (p. 149), resonating "with the spirit of transmedia, in which each medium is seen as an equally viable expression of a fictional world" (p. 158).

Recently, transmedia theorists have softened their stance on the "no adaptation rule," acknowledging that adaptations are rarely simple retellings of the story (Harvey, 2015; Jenkins, 2011). Jenkins (2017) has recently noted,

> those of us who study transmedia (and fan fiction) and those who study adaptation are asking a related set of questions, though as of now we are often talking past each other, because our terminological and methodological assumptions lead us to underestimate the materials the other is studying.
>
> (para. 10)

The no-adaptation rule no longer seems to sufficiently characterize transmedia storytelling, as transmedia extensions do a bit of both, grounding itself in the original text while engaging in the extensions of the story world in adherence to transmedia sensibility (Dena, 2018; Jenkins, 2017).

In Korea, the theorization of transmedia storytelling is still in its early development stage with a significant number of studies focused on differentiating the practice with the more prevalent OSMU projects. Korean media scholars have employed the similar rhetoric of the "no adaptation" rule by excluding OSMU projects from the transmedia phenomenon by defining the former as a replica of the original source across different mediums and transmedia texts as novel additions to the original story world dispersed across multiple mediums (Han & Nam, 2009; M. Lee, 2014; Shin & Kim, 2010).

Importance of capital and IP rights in transmedia storytelling: the case of Marvel

The launch of the Marvel Cinematic Universe (MCU) by Marvel Studios in 2008 is a prime example of fictional world building through transmedia storytelling. In 2008, Marvel Studios commenced its universe with its feature film *Iron Man* (2008), followed by a combination of films exclusively centered on Marvel Studio's characters (Ritcher, 2016), including *The Incredible Hulk* (2008), *Thor* (2011), *Captain America: The First Avenger* (2011), and films which have assembled the superheroes together, such as the *Marvel Avengers Assemble* (2012), *Avengers: Age of Ultron* (2015), and most recently the *Avengers: Infinity War* (2018).

Marvel's world building illustrates the importance of capital in transmedia storytelling. The acquisition of Marvel Studios by Walt Disney Corporation in 2009 greatly galvanized Marvel's Cinematic Universe building, as it released many commercially successful films and created games based on the universe. More importantly, Walt Disney Corporation's recent reclamation of Marvel's previously relinquished film rights of some of its major characters is expected to further enrich and enhance the universe. When Marvel was at the brink of bankruptcy in the 1990s, it responded by selling off the film rights of some of its most popular superheroes—*Spider-Man* to Sony, and *X-Men* and the *Fantastic Four* to Fox. Fragmented film rights also meant a splintered universe, as many of the Marvel comic stories could not be told on the big screen. For example, Marvel's crossover comic story *Avengers vs X-Men* could not transition to the big screen (Abad-Santos, 2017). Also, the crossover comic book event *Captain America: Civil War* has been told without X-Men and the Fantastic Four, integral characters who all exist in the comic world (Abad-Santos, 2017).

In 2016, Disney proposed to acquire 21st Century Fox, a deal which will bring *X-Men, Fantastic Four,* and the other previously Fox-owned Marvel characters back to Marvel Studios (Abad-Santos, 2017). Also, the cinematic universe has recently incorporated *Spider-Man* who had belonged exclusively to Sony Picture's Entertainment until 2015 (Ritcher, 2016). This incorporation makes *Spider-Man: Homecoming* (2017) the first *Spider-Man* movie in the Marvel Cinematic Universe (Ritcher, 2016). Although it is unclear as to when we will be able to see these newly incorporated characters in Marvel's Cinematic Universe due to Fox's previously set schedule for its film projects, Disney's acquisition of Fox marks the first time in Marvel's history to have all the major superheroes and villains within the same cinematic universe (Abad-Santos, 2017). Now with all its major superheroes under the same roof, Marvel Cinematic Universe illustrates the indispensable role of IP rights in transmedia storytelling.

Transmedia audiences

Audience behavior in this changing media terrain has also been of increasing interest to media scholars (Atkinson, 2014; Evans, 2011; Simons, 2014). In her research of *The Inside*, a social film project led by Intel and Toshiba, Atkinson (2014) introduces a concept called "dramatic community," which she defines as audience members "who take on a range of different performative identities within the social media spaces of an online fictional arena" (p. 2002). *The Inside* enhanced the performativity of audiences, as it invited them to participate in the protagonist Christina's quest in escaping from an unknown location through a combination of puzzles, games, and role-playing opportunities.

Jenkins (2007) has indicated an increased performativity on the part of audience members in transmedia environments, as transmedia texts "provide a set of roles and goals which readers can assume as they enact aspects of the story through their everyday life" (para. 10). Würfel (2014) also makes parallel observations in her study of transmedia appropriation by German adolescents as they partake in transmedia storytelling in the construction of their identity. By transmedia appropriation, Würfel refers to the ways in which people engage and consume popular media contents born out of technological and content convergence. She notes how a substantial number of German adolescents actively engage in transmedia appropriation by consuming their favorite media content across a wide range of media forms alongside the primary source. For example, they would participate creatively in web blogs and other online forums related to their favorite media contents.

However, unlike the optimistic discourse surrounding the increased interactivity and performance of transmedia audiences, some research has revealed otherwise. Evans (2011) investigates the telling difference between audience response and industrial expectations. In her case study of two transmedia projects—the Flash games of *Spooks*, a British TV series, and mobisodes of U.S. counterterrorism serial *24*—Evans found that audiences felt their enjoyment was being compromised by discrepancies between the original content and their secondary extensions. For example, some reported to feeling uncomfortable experiencing the discrepancy between the spectator role given to viewers in the series *Spooks* and the active participant role required of them as game characters in the flashgames. In the case of *24*, some of the lukewarm responses came from the fact that mobisodes did not adapt the split screen structure of *24*. The observed mixed responses by audiences indicate that the audience expects a certain level of well-blended consistency between secondary forms of the original content.

Method

The purpose of this study is to identify the industrial factors that promote webtoon-based drama production practices. What are the industrial contexts in which webtoons have become a critical source for TV drama productions? What are the main issues that arise when webtoons are turned into TV dramas? Are webtoon-based dramas indicative of transmedia storytelling? Or, are they a part of the continuing tradition of cross-media adaptation?

We conducted nine in-depth interviews with ten individuals who work at webtoon platforms, cable TV stations, and production companies. All respondents have been closely involved in the production of webtoon-based TV dramas as producers, directors, and webtoon producers (Table 7.2). Their experience helped us map out the industrial practices and the contexts in which many webtoons have recently been made into TV dramas. While the respondents offered a variety of information, such as the procedure of acquiring webtoon's TV rights, we particularly probed into the industrial implications of the recent expansion of webtoon businesses by asking questions that included: "Why are drama producers/directors interested

Table 7.2 Interviewee Information

Interview Number	Name	Company Type	Position
1	A	Webtoon platform	Producer
2	B	Cable TV station	Drama director/producer
3	C	Drama production company	Producer
4	D	Drama production company	Producer
	E	Drama production company	Producer
5	F	Drama production company	President
6	G	Drama production company	Producer
7	H	Cable TV station	Drama director/producer
8	I	Webtoon platform	Vice president
9	J	Webtoon platform	Webtoon producer

Notes: A director is widely referred to as a producer in the Korean TV industry because (s)he also oversees all the aspects of the TV production. For the readers, we made a distinction between director/producer and producer. A producer in this study refers to a person whose main task is to search for novels, foreign shows, webnovels, or webtoons to be made into TV dramas.

in webtoons?", "What benefits do the webtoon platforms and production companies gain when they sell and obtain webtoons' TV rights?", and "What are the advantages and challenges of turning webtoons into TV dramas?". The interviews were conducted at the respondents' office or at a coffee shop, with each lasting approximately (60–80) minutes.

Webtoon as a basis of TV dramas

In recent years, webtoons have emerged as a reservoir of creative stories. In Korea, the proliferation of mobile devices fostered the so-called "snack culture," where web-based cultural content that can be consumed in minutes (Chung, 2014). The weakening of the comics publishing market has also galvanized the migration of traditional cartoonists to the webtoon industry. Since the webtoon industry is not only a lucrative market, but also has relatively low entry barriers, many young creative storytellers have found their career as webtoonists. Moreover, compared to comics and TV dramas, the webtoon is a medium that can convey innovative stories and unconventional characters with more freedom from editorial intervention and production budget constraints (e.g., webtoonitsts can draw whatever they imagine, and upload to an online platform). Interviewee J stated that the audiences are attracted to the unique ways of webtoon storytelling that depart from conventional narrative structures. For example, the protagonist in webtoons often dies, and the villain turns into a hero. There is no clear boundary between good and bad. All interviewees commented that they were most impressed by the webtoon's imaginative ideas and narratives that go beyond their expectations.

It has been a common practice for the Korean TV industry to use various forms of popular culture as a basis of drama series, such as novels, comic books, and Japanese and American TV dramas. Given that the webtoon is "a warehouse that contain numerous story ideas" (Interviewee C), it comes as no surprise to learn that most TV production companies have several employees and internees who specialize in reviewing almost all webtoons published on major webtoon platforms to find ideal candidates waiting to be transformed into TV dramas. Many webtoon platforms have a division that recommends promising webtoons as sources for TV dramas to production companies and broadcasting stations.

The Korean drama industry has relied on the live shoot system that involves hectic schedule changes and last-minute script changes (Kil, 2017). While notorious, the system has advantages because it allows the directors and writers to integrate audience feedback and alter the development of the drama, just as Brazilian telenovelas are heavily influenced by audience feedback (Rosas-Moreno, 2014). For example, they can change the plotlines to satisfy the audience's requests and increase the screen time for popular characters. They may shorten or lengthen the entire series based on the popularity of the drama. The fact that the webtoon actively reflects audience feedback also makes it an ideal source for TV dramas. Each episode comes with a message board where viewers can leave their comments that webtoonists can incorporate into subsequent episodes. Since the webtoon platforms have immediate access to audience demographics (e.g., age, gender, viewing patterns), they can develop recommendation systems for the viewers, and effectively decide when to upload particular webtoons that cater to audiences' tastes (Interviewee J). According to Interviewee F, both webtoon and TV dramas take the audience feedback seriously, but the former is much more responsive because webtoonists can read the comments immediately. He considers popular webtoons as exemplary sources for TV dramas because their popularity implies that they contain many story components that a large audience finds attractive.

The cost-effectiveness of webtoon-based drama production

The most important factor underlying the increasing number of webtoon-based TV dramas has a great deal to do with the limited pool of top TV scriptwriters, widely referred to in Korea as "level A writers." TV drama is regarded as a writer's medium, due to its heavy reliance on the writer's competence. The production context of the TV industry in Korea also contributes to the importance of scriptwriters. Under the circumstances in which approximately 80% of drama series are outsourced to independent production companies (Jang, 2018), a large number of production companies must compete for available broadcasting time slots for TV drama series. Typically, production companies start their drama production only after a TV station agrees to broadcast the TV drama series, and provides them with sizeable budgets. Therefore, production companies must succeed in selling their program ideas to TV stations.

In the process of pitching a drama to a TV station, the scriptwriter's reputation is critical. Along with casting, the scriptwriter is also a determining factor when TV stations make a purchasing decision. Traditionally, three terrestrial TV stations in Korea—SBS, MBC, and KBS—have been the major outlets for TV dramas. In the past decade, cable channels have also started to broadcast drama series. For example, OCN began to present original drama series from 2006. JTBC started to showcase quality drama series from 2011. Most importantly, tvN, a channel owned and operated by the media giant CJ ENM, began to broadcast drama series. While these cable channels appear to give more opportunities to production companies (and thus less competition), the competition among production companies has become fiercer for two reasons. First, there has been an increase in the number of production companies. There are over 100 production companies who have produced at least one TV drama series in the past three years (Interviewee D). Recently, top entertainment talent agencies, such as SM, YG JYP, and FNC, also joined the drama production business because they can take advantage of their own actors and actresses whom they can cast easily. Second, top scriptwriters have become difficult to hire because they are limited in number. As most interviewees mentioned, a TV station would buy a drama idea immediately if it is written by first-rate writers, such as Kim Eun-Sook, Park Ji-Eun, Noh Hee-Kyung, Kim Eun-Hee, and Kim Soo-Hyun, all of whom have written many hit dramas.

In the circumstances where only a few production companies can manage to hire top scriptwriters, most production companies prefer to base their dramas on popular webtoons, instead of working with what they call a "mediocre writer." Since webtoon is one of the most popular forms of culture in Korea, production companies can strategically utilize the success of celebrated webtoons as a way to sell drama ideas to TV stations. Almost all webtoon-based drama productions are retroactive. New production companies also use the TV rights of a webtoon as an opportunity to enter the TV industry (Interviewee D). TV stations have also recognized the value of the webtoon as a source of TV drama series after the huge success of webtoon-based dramas such as *Misaeng* (tvN, 2014) and *Cheese in the Trap* (tvN 2016). TV stations consider webtoon-based drama ideas seriously, since successful webtoons are deemed to have a solid narrative structure and attractive characters.

> Interviewee F: My company doesn't have renowned scriptwriters to work with. This is a big weakness. Since TV stations do not trust unknown writers, I use the reputation of the webtoon, instead of persuading TV stations to buy my drama idea. Webtoon indeed serves as a powerful weapon for production companies.

Webtoon reduces the risks of relying solely on a mediocre writer's original drama script. The drama production in Korea begins (2–3) months before the series airs on TV. Typically, production companies complete the production of (2–4) episodes before the airdate, and the rest of the episodes are written, filmed, and edited as the drama series airs. While the live shoot system has many advantages as discussed earlier, it also creates a high chance that the scriptwriter fails to meet expectations, because (s)he must work on several episodes of the drama within limited time constraints. When there is a lack of trust for the lesser-known writers, the webtoon as the basis of a drama series reduces the risk of the story going off track, since a popular webtoon already has an established narrative that has been proven successful. In other words, the webtoon serves as a safety net for both production companies and TV stations when they work with mediocre scriptwriters.

> Interview H: For an original drama script, only the scriptwriter knows how the story will unfold in the later episodes. A story can head in the wrong direction, or end unexpectedly on a shock twist. But, if a drama is based on a webtoon, we don't have to worry about this uncertainty because we already know the overall story of the webtoon. A webtoon is like an 'insurance.'

Webtoon-based drama production has many strengths in terms of cost-effectiveness. In comparison to hiring top scriptwriters for an original drama series, a production company can save its production budget by purchasing the TV rights of a webtoon and hiring a writer who adapts the webtoon into a TV drama script. According to interviewees, the price of TV rights for a webtoon to be turned into a drama series of (16–24) episodes normally ranges between USD (20,000 and 100,000). Then, an "adaptation" writer is paid about USD (5,000–10,000) per episode. Given that a production company normally pays well-known writers USD 20,000–30,000 per episode for an original drama script, the cost of creating webtoon-based drama scripts is half the cost of creating original drama scripts.

Drama production based on webtoons is also cost-effective because it can substantially shorten the length of time to develop TV scripts. For an original drama series that starts from scratch, it typically takes a year to create an overall story structure and complete scripts for two episodes. The time required for this pre-production can be reduced to half for a webtoon-based drama because the content of a story and the main characters are already available (Interviewee G). Long-running webtoons with over 100 episodes are ideal ones for TV remakes. For example, webtoon *Cheese in the Trap* has been running for seven years with over 200 episodes, and thus has a vast amount of raw materials to choose from for the 16-episode series (Interviewee E). Interviewee B regards the webtoon as a "treasure" because it offers numerous story elements—setting, characters, events, and dialogues—with which to construct attractive TV drama series. Relatively flexible as regards to its subject and content, the genre of romantic comedy is preferred for TV remakes because cost-effectiveness is a major driving force for webtoon-based drama production. Not only is the genre of romantic comedy most popular among mainstream TV audiences, but it also requires a smaller production budget to remake compared to other genres, such as science fiction, action, or fantasy. Interviewee H stated that popular martial arts webtoons are unlikely to be turned into TV dramas because of the consideration of production budgets.

> Interviewee C: There are webtoons not suited for TV remakes. If the main character is an animal, an alien, a flying fairy, a senior fighter, or a man with supernatural power, the webtoon has little chance to be made into a TV drama, because the story is difficult and costly to portray on TV.

Webtoon-based dramas also have advantages in marketing. Based on the reputation of a webtoon, TV stations can easily build up much hype leading up to the launch of the drama. Usually, when news on popular webtoons being adapted to dramas is released, the webtoon-based drama goes viral before its airdate. Webtoon fans often participate in the so-called "virtual cast," a practice of fans sharing comments online on the casting that they would like for the TV remake of a webtoon. Virtual casting by fans is helpful not only for the promotion of the drama series but also for producing a drama that satisfies the fans' desires. Interviewee H stated that he did in fact cast the main actress for a webtoon-based drama who has been ranked number one in virtual cast lists. Interviewee H discussed how the reputation of a webtoon facilitates the promotion of its TV remake.

> Interviewee H: A familiar title matters. Let's say you hear the TV drama title *The Birth of a Married Woman*. If it is a title no one has ever heard of before, you need to explain to everyone what the story is about, what role the married woman plays. But when the drama is based on a popular webtoon, I don't need to explain in detail. Moreover, the fans of the webtoon are expected to watch its TV remake.

Due to the economic values of webtoons, production companies rush to purchase the TV rights of webtoons. Famous webtoons are preferred because their reputation helps promote their TV remakes. Due to high competition to acquire TV rights of hit webtoons, production companies are quick to purchase the TV rights of webtoons after the publication of its third or fourth episode. Commonly, several production companies compete for TV rights. In the case of the webtoon *Hogu's Love*, over ten productions submitted bids for the webtoon's TV rights (Interviewee E).

Transmedia possibility of webtoon-based TV dramas

Central to transmedia storytelling is the expansion of the story world. Jenkins (2007) claims that "transmedia stories are based not on individual characters or specific plots but rather complex fictional worlds which can sustain multiple interrelated characters and their stories" (para. 4). In other words, each text from different platforms must contribute to the overall story. Our interviews suggest that the process of turning a webtoon into a TV series is adaptation that does not take full advantage of the potential of transmedia storytelling, in that they rarely expand the story world. The general perception in the TV industry is that the audience evaluates the quality of the webtoon-based TV drama on the basis of its fidelity to the original webtoon. The importance fans place on fidelity resonates with one of the core principles of transmedia storytelling, the effort to "construct a very strong sense of continuity" (Jenkins, 2009, para. 17), which generates coherence with the original source. Accordingly, dedicated fans look at how consistently the webtoon world is portrayed in the drama remake. However, the fidelity Korean fans sought out is not the plausible continuity of the narrative of the webtoon to its drama adaptation but the faithful reproduction of the webtoon world in the drama remake. It is the outward believability of the webtoon characters and their stories that is most concerning to fans rather than the continued extension of the webtoon story world in the drama narrative. Thus, it is a common practice for TV producers and directors to cast actors and actresses who physically resemble webtoon characters for the TV remake. In addition, production companies have recently begun to hire webtoonists as TV drama scriptwriters to improve the drama's fidelity to the original work.

> Interviewee F: For the TV remake of *My ID is Gangnam Beauty*, my company hired the webtoonist as one of the drama scriptwriters. My experience tells me that a big gap is created when TV scripts are adapted from a cartoon or a webtoon. So to reduce this gap, I thought it would be best to have the original story creator participate in the development of the drama scripts.

Fans' prioritization of fidelity to the original webtoon has been especially vocalized in their reaction to *Cheese in the Trap*, one of the webtoon-based dramas mentioned earlier. While successful, the drama version of *Cheese in the Trap* infuriated hardcore webtoon fans (widely labelled as "Chee mothers" because they are like nagging moms) who thought that the drama had completely deformed the original story. The plotline of the drama in the later episodes focused on Baek In-Ho instead of Yoo Jung, the lead character in the original webtoon. Alongside devoted fans, actor Park Hae-Jin, who took the role of Yoo Jung, also publicly expressed disgruntlement over his reduced screen time (Interviewees A, E). Rather than perceiving the drama's emphasis on the perspective of another character as what Jenkins (2007) would describe as a "unique contribution" to the webtoon story world, dedicated fans regarded the change as a distortion of the original story. Accordingly, *Cheese in the Trap* set a precedent precluding the TV industry from noticeably changing the plotlines or character roles. Unfortunately, due to the aftermath of *Cheese in the Trap*, production companies perceive a high risk of significantly modifying the original webtoon.

The difficulty in expanding the webtoon's story world in the TV drama has also a great deal to do with the webtoonists' objections to the drama departing significantly from the original webtoon. Famous webtoonists, such as Yoon Tae-Ho and Kang Full, do not want to see their webtoons altered greatly for TV audiences. For example, Yoon Tae-Ho rejected all the offers from production companies that wanted to create a drama based on *Misaeng* because they wanted to turn the webtoon's realistic portrayal about office workers' everyday life into office-themed TV drama peppered with romance. Instead, Yoon sold its TV rights to a production company that promised to stick close to the original webtoon with no romance (Interviewee H). Interviewees generally attributed the success of the TV remake of *Misaeng* to its quality of being true to the original. Although *Misaeng* is discussed as Korea's first transmedia franchise (Kim, 2016; Seo, 2015), our interview reveals the difficulty in balancing the two factors—fidelity and novelty—which contribute to the difficulty in making novel extensions to the webtoon story world.

There is one TV drama that has not been discussed in previous studies but is noteworthy in its attempt to realize the potential of transmedia storytelling through a webtoon. The producer of *The Village: Achiara's Secret* (SBS, 2015) collaborated with KToon (a webtoon platform) to create a prequel: a webtoon series with 16 episodes entitled *The Village: Achiara's Winter* that explains the back story that led to the events in the original drama narrative. While this was the first innovative attempt to expand the TV drama narrative onto a different platform, no other drama has followed suit. Since the webtoonist does not own TV rights in this type of project, (s)he is not incentivized, and does not wish to participate. For this reason, the producer of *The Village* had difficulty finding a webtoonist who was willing to create the prequel.

Inspired by Marvel and D.C. Comics, major webtoon platforms have grand plans to utilize their webtoons to expand their businesses. They have recruited TV and film producers to get involved in the production of webtoon-based TV dramas and films. Most notably, Naver (the largest portal website and the third largest webtoon platform) co-produced the TV remake of *Sound of Heart* (Interviewee J). In addition, major webtoon platforms seek the possibility of acquisition or joint ownership of intellectual property (IP) rights of webtoons (currently held exclusively by the webtoonists) so that they can expand their business to include licensing, TV/film production, publishing, game production, book publication and merchandizing (Interviewee I). For example, Lezhin Comics changed its title to Lezhin Entertainment to redefine its identity as a global entertainment corporation.

Currently, webtoon platforms benefit mostly from the synergistic effects of webtoon-based drama production. Despite their great ambition, their immediate goal is to increase the number of webtoon viewers by drawing TV audiences to webtoon platforms. The case of *Misaeng* illustrates the marketing power of webtoon-based dramas. Thanks to the success of its TV remake, Yoon Tae-Ho sold over two million copies of the nine-volume book version of *Misaeng* (Yonhap News Agency, 2014). Since many webtoon platforms require readers to pay to view webtoons, webtoon-based dramas can substantially increase revenues by attracting TV audiences who wish to watch the original webtoon (Interviewee, D).

Interviewee J: The webtoonist was about to end the story of *A Girl Who Sees Smells*. But the platform wanted to extend the publication while the TV remakes air to maximize the synergy effects.

Conclusion

Why have webtoons transitioned to the TV screen? Overall, interviewees working in broadcasting stations and production companies considered the production of webtoon-based TV drama as part of existing practices of cross-media adaptation of popular cultural forms, such as novels and comic books. According to the interviewees in our study, there are no intrinsic characteristics of the medium of the webtoon itself that makes it an ideal source for a TV remake. There has been an increase in the number of webtoon-based TV dramas in recent years simply because the webtoon has emerged as a leading form of popular culture that contains many innovative, unconventional stories.

If the proliferation of mobile phone and the migration of traditional cartoonists to mobile platform contribute to the emergence of the webtoon as a reservoir of creative stories, it is the industrial factors and considerations that promote the current practice of webtoon-based drama production. More specifically, the following industrial factors lead to webtoon-based TV drama production: the big success of earlier webtoon-based dramas (e.g., *Misaeng, Cheese in the Trap*), the limited pool of top drama scriptwriters, the use of webtoon as a cost-saving option (as opposed to hiring a top scriptwriter), the strategy of reducing the risks of hiring a mediocre scriptwriter, the use of the webtoon as a deal point when production companies set out to pitch a show, and the effectiveness of promoting TV dramas on the basis of the existing reputation of a webtoon.

Despite there being changes made during the process of turning a webtoon into a TV drama, the TV remake of a webtoon resembles cross-media adaptation more than transmedia storytelling, as their diversification is in the form of adaptation, and not that of expansion. We do not consider it as part of transmedia storytelling, in that the original webtoon narrative rarely expands the story world across different media, which is a critical requirement of transmedia storytelling. For TV producers, high fidelity to the original webtoon is a major criterion for evaluating the quality of webtoon-based TV dramas. Moreover, the attempt to modify the plotlines or to assign different character roles only results in strong resistance by original webtoon fans. As seen in the controversy surrounding the TV remake of *Cheese in the Trap*, a considerable number of audiences neither sought to engage in the narrative development of dramas nor exhibited desire to participate in the expansion of the fictional world. In other words, not all audiences partook in transmedia contents with equal enthusiasm and engagement as predicted by webtoon-based drama producers. Therefore, the practice of maximizing fidelity, such as hiring the webtoonist as a TV drama scriptwriter, precludes the possibility of expanding the original webtoon.

More recently, Marvel and D.C. comics have motivated Korean webtoon platforms to adopt transmedia strategies and business models. While the transmedia business is still at an early stage, a small number of webtoon platforms, such as Naver and Lezhin Entertainment, have long-term plans to capitalize on IP rights. While Korea has witnessed the expansion of webtoon businesses into TV drama and other areas, including video games and animated films, the potential for transmedia businesses is nevertheless limited in Korea because the majority of Korean webtoon platforms lack capital and do not possess the IP rights of webtoons. Therefore, the imminent goal of the webtoon platforms remains confined to increasing webtoon sales by encouraging TV drama fans to pay to watch the original webtoon.

Our study suggests that the availability of multimedia platforms and advanced digital technologies does not necessarily enable transmedia storytelling when the expansion of the story world is constrained by the fans' prioritization of fidelity, a variety of industrial factors, and the lack of ownership over IP rights, etc. In order to realize the transmedia potential of webtoons, it is imperative for TV producers to take advantage of the full potential that transmedia storytelling can offer to webtoons and TV dramas. Besides, webtoon platforms need to bring more capital investment and acquire or co-own the IP rights of webtoons that webtoonists currently own exclusively.

References

Abad-Santos, A. (2017, December 15). What Disney's acquisition of Fox means for Marvel's superhero movies. *Vox*. Retrieved from https://www.vox.com/culture/2017/12/14/16738852/disney-fox-marvel-acquisition-x-men-superhero

Atkinson, S. (2014). The performative functions of dramatic communities: Conceptualizing audience engagements in transmedia fiction. *International Journal of Communication*, 8, 2201–2219.

Baek, B. (2016, January 27). Webtoons emerge as source for dramas, films. *The Korea Times*. Retrieved from http://www.koreatimes.co.kr/www/news/culture/2016/01/201_196512.html

Bourdaa, M. (2013). 'Following the pattern': The creation of an encyclopaedic universe with transmedia storytelling. *Adaptation*, 6(2), 202–214. doi:10.1093/adaptation/apt009

Cho, H. (2018). 국내 영상콘텐츠에 적용된 트랜스미디어 스토리텔링 연구: 웹툰 활용을 중심으로 [Study on application patterns or transmedia storytelling with focus on media extension sing webtoons]. *Journal of the Korea Entertainment Industry Association*, 12(30), 309–322. doi:10.21184/jkeia.2018.4.12.3.309

Chung, A. (2014, Feb 2). 'Snack culture.' *The Korea Times*. Retrieved from http://www.koreatimes.co.kr/www/news/culture/2014/02/386_150813.html

Dena, C. (2009). Transmedia practice: *Theorising the practice of expressing a fictional world across distinct media and environments* (Doctoral thesis, University of Sydney). Retrieved from http://ciret-transdisciplinarity.org/biblio/biblio_pdf/Christy_DeanTransm.pdf

Dena, C. (2018). Transmedia adaptation. In M. Freeman & R. R. Gambarato (Eds.), *The Routledge companion to transmedia studies* (pp. 195–206). New York, NY: Routledge.

Doo, R. (2017, February 5). Korean webtoon readership growing, themes need diversifying: report. *The Korea Herald*. Retrieved from http://www.koreaherald.com/view.php?ud=20170205000176

Evans, E. (2011). *Transmedia television: Audiences, new media, and daily life*. New York, NY: Routledge.

Han, H., & Nam, S. (2009). 트랜스미디어 콘텐츠의 스토리텔링 구조 연구: <로스트> 대체현실게임을 중심으로 [A study on storytelling structure of trans-media contents: Focus on the *LOST* alternative reality game]. *Humanities Contents*, 15, 7–27.

Han, S. H. (2014, February 11). 웹툰이 해외 영상시장 공략 '선봉'... 트랜스미디어 빅뱅 온다 [Webtoon leads the global content market: Transmedia big bang arrives]. *Etnews*. Retrieved from http://www.etnews.com/201402110343

Harvey, C. (2015). *Fantastic transmedia: Narrative, play, and memory across science fiction and fantasy storyworlds*. New York, NY: Palgrave Macmillan.

Hutcheon, L. (2006). *A theory of adaptation*. New York, NY: Routledge.

Jang, S. (2018, July 14). Warning for terrestrial TV drama series. *Sports Korea*. Retrieved from http://sports.hankooki.com/lpage/entv/201807/sp20180714070029136670.htm

Jenkins, H. (2006). *Convergence culture: Where old and new media collide*. New York, NY: New York University Press.

Jenkins, H. (2007, March 21). Transmedia storytelling 101 [Web log post]. Retrieved from http://henryjenkins.org/blog/2007/03/transmedia_storytelling_101.html

Jenkins, H. (2009, December 12). The revenge of the origami unicorn: Seven principles of transmedia storytelling (Well two actually. Five more on Friday [Web log post]. Retrieved from http://henryjenkins.org/blog/2009/12/the_revenge_of_the_origami_uni.html

Jenkins, H. (2011, July 31). Transmedia: Further reflections [Web log post]. Retrieved from http://henryjenkins.org/blog/2011/08/defining_transmedia_further_re.html

Jenkins, H. (2017). Adaptation, extension, transmedia. *Literature/Film Quarterly, 45*(20). Retrieved from https://lfq.salisbury.edu/_issues/first/adaptation_extension_transmedia.html

Jin, E. (2014, June 14). Smartphones set off webtoon boom. *Korea Joongang Daily*. Retrieved from http://koreajoongangdaily.joins.com/news/article/article.aspx?aid=2990396

Jin, M. (2018, August 7). 'Along With the Gods' dominates in first weekend. *Korean Joongang Daily*. Retrieved from http://koreajoongangdaily.joins.com/news/article/article.aspx?aid=3051542

Kil, S. (2017, April 3). Korean dramas adopt pre-produced format to mixed result. *Variety*. Retrieved from https://variety.com/2017/tv/asia/korean-dramas-descendants-of-the-sun-pre-produced-format-1202019925

Kim, E. (2016). 웹툰 미생의 재매개 과정에서 나타난 디지털 서사의 변주 [A study on the transformation of digital narrative: A case study on remediation of webtoon *Misaeng*]. *Media, Gender & Culture, 31*(2), 45–80.

Korea Manhwa Contents Agency. (2018). 숫자로 보는 2017 한국만화 [2017 Korean comics in numbers]. Retrieved from http://www.komacon.kr/dmk/manhwazine/zine_view.asp?Seq=3533&nowPage=1

Lee, M. (2014). 국내 미디어 콘텐츠의 장르 간 스토리 이동에 관한 연구 [Transmedia storytelling: Reuse of content in different media]. *Broadcasting & Communication, 15*(1), 51–81.

Lee, S. (2018, January 2). 간단하게 짚어보는 2017 웹툰 산업 결산 [2017 Korean webtoon industry report: A brief look into Korean webtoon industry report]. *The Web Daily*. Retrieved from http://news.webdaily.co.kr/view.php?ud=201801021822429684614104cae764_7

Lee, Y. (2016, August 22). 무엇과 섞어도 '케미 폭발' … 웹툰의 무한확장 [Chemistry explosion of webtoons, webtoon's unlimited potential]. *The Hankyoreh*. Retrieved from http://www.hani.co.kr/arti/culture/movie/757726.html

Na, W. (2018, June 29). Movie biz gets bunch of new players: Korean groups start producing, and even Chinese are investing. *Korea Joongang Daily*. Retrieved from http://koreajoongangdaily.joins.com/news/article/article.aspx?aid=3049939

Park, S. (2018, August 9). 네이버, 웹툰 IP 영화 법인 '스튜디오N' 설립. 한국형 마블 꿈꾼다 [Naver, establishes corporate 'Studio N' to turn webtoon IP into films. Dreams of Korean style Marvel]. *Financial News*. Retrieved from http://www.fnnews.com/news/201808091124567309

Phillips, A. (2012). *A creator's guide to transmedia storytelling*. New York, NY: McGraw Hill.

Ritcher, A. (2016). The Marvel cinematic universe as a transmedia narrative. *Americana: E-Journal of American studies in Hungary, 12*(1), Retrieved from http://americanaejournal.hu/vol12no1/richter

Rosas-Moreno, T. C. (2014). *News and novela in Brazilian media: Fact, fiction, and national identity*. Lanham, MD: Lexington.

Seo, S. (2015). 트랜스미디어 스토리텔링으로서 <미생>의 가능성과 한계 [Potentials & limitations of <Misaeng> as transmedia storytelling]. *The Korean Language and Literature, 128*, 277–308.

Shin, D., & Kim, H. (2010). 트랜스미디어 콘텐츠 연구: 스토리텔링과 개념화 [A study of transmedia contents: Storytelling and conceptualization]. *The Journal of the Korea Contents Association, 10*(10), 180–189. doi:10.5392/JKCA.10.10.180

Simons, N. (2014). Audience reception of cross- and transmedia TV drama in the age of convergence. *International Journal of communication, 8*, 2220–2239.

Wells-Lassagne, S. (2017). *Television and serial adaptation.* New York, NY: Routledge.

Würfel, M. (2014). Transmedia appropriation and socialization processes among German adolescents. *International Journal of Communication, 8*, 2240–2258.

Yonhap News Agency. (2014, October 27). Comic book 'Misaeng' sells 1 mln copies. *Yonhap News Agency.* Retrieved from http://en.yna.co.kr/view/AEN 20141027003300315

8   The multimedia life of a Korean graphic novel

A case study of Yoon Taeho's *Ikki*

Bruce Fulton

Yoon Taeho's *Ikki* (*Moss*), like other of his graphic novels and those of his contemporaries, has been made accessible through a variety of media.[1] Originally serialized online (2008–2009) as a webtoon, *Ikki* was honored with a Puch'ŏn Graphic Novel Award (2008; the city of Puch'ŏn, Kyŏnggi Province South Korea, is home to the National Graphic Novel Museum), and the grand prize in the amateur graphic novel competition (2010). It was then published in five print volumes in 2010 by Korea Datahouse, made into a feature film by Kang Usŏk the same year, then reissued in four print volumes in 2015 by Woongjin. In 2015–2016 *Moss*, the English translation by Ju-Chan Fulton and myself, was serialized online in its entirety by *The Huffington Post*.[2]

Hudson Moura's (2011) notion of snack culture and snack media conceptualizes the practice of sampling small helpings of popular culture on the Internet. Might we then view the life of *Ikki/Moss* as a multimedia feast, with the initial webtoon version of the novel serving as an appetizer, the initial print edition and the film version as the entrees, and the English translation at *The Huffington Post* as a cosmopolitan dessert that may very well be offered in different linguistic flavors in the future?

The dissemination of this graphic novel, both the original Korean version and the English translation, has implications for the marketing of Korean graphic novels in the English-speaking world. Access by mobile devices is especially promising. In this essay I analyze *Ikki* as a work of Korean fiction involving trauma and abuse of power, discuss its viability in English translation, and consider whether its multimedia life might serve as a model by which Korean graphic novels could attain the international visibility presently enjoyed by other manifestations of Korean popular culture, such as television dramas and K-pop music.

Yoon Taeho, the author

Yoon Taeho was born in 1969 in Chŏlla Province, home to several of modern Korea's most distinctive literary voices, such as Ch'ae Manshik (1902–1950; whose home area of Kunsan is where Yoon went to elementary school, and who in much of his writing echoes the voice of the performer of the traditional Korean oral narrative *p'ansori*); Sŏ Chŏngju (1913–2000), arguably modern Korea's most accomplished poet; Ko Ŭn (b. 1933), perennial nominee for a Nobel Literature Prize; and Cho Chŏngnae (b. 1943), a writer of epic novels. He began drawing as a child, as an outlet from life with an abusive father, and moved to Seoul at the age of 19 years and became a disciple of Hŏ Yŏngman ("Yoon Tae-ho," 2018), the doyen of Korean graphic novelists at the time. He published his first graphic novel, *Pisang ch'angnyuk* (Emergency landing), in 1993. His early work also includes intertextual novels inspired by stories from the Korean oral tradition. But it was not until 2007, when his work was honored with a Republic of Korea Graphic Novel Prize, followed by the success of *Ikki* and *Misaeng* (An incomplete life) that Yoon became recognized as perhaps the most accomplished graphic novelist in Korea in the new millennium. In 2013, he founded the webzine *A-Comics* in the hope of revitalizing the Korean graphic fiction industry (Lee, 2013). Currently he teaches creative writing with a focus on graphic fiction. Such is his visibility in Korea and his stature in the traditionally conservative and patriarchal power structure of Korean literature that he was the sole non-poet/non-fiction writer among the handful of Korean writers represented at the London Book Fair in April 2014, at which Korea was the featured country.

Ikki and internet infrastructure in South Korea

Not only *Ikki* but subsequent graphic novels by Yoon Taeho have enjoyed a long multimedia life. *Misaeng*, for example, was simultaneously serialized online (by Daum), published in book form a volume at a time (currently available on Amazon), and made into a six-part mini-drama. A feature film version is also in the works. *Oebuin* (The insiders), dating from 2010, was also made into a film (2015). Research by Park Seok-hwan (2014), a professor at the Korea University of Media Arts, reveals that *Misaeng's* online version registered one *billion* views in 2013 alone, its print version sold more than half a million copies, and the six-part drama received three million hits from mobile devices (Park, 2016 see also Park, 2014)—the last statistic offering compelling evidence that digital dissemination is transcending desktop and laptop computer access and expanding rapidly to include access from smartphones and tablets; the webtoon is becoming the "smarttoon."

Research by Dal Yong Jin (2016) substantiates the crucial impact of the advent of the smartphone in 2008—and the surge of activity in social media occasioned thereby—in the dissemination not only of graphic novels but also of *Hallyu* ("Korean wave") in general. It is perhaps no coincidence that the initial serialization of *Ikki* gained popularity around the time that smartphones were hitting the market, a period that also coincides with what many consider the emergence of the second wave of K-pop music. Such is the impact of the arrival of the smartphone and the mushrooming of social media that Jin cites the year 2008 as the genesis of Hallyu 2.

In a discussion with Goran Topalovic, executive director of the New York Asian Film Festival, following a screening of the film adaptation of *Ikki*, Yoon emphasized that much of the appeal of webtoons lies in the ease of online browsing. Accessing webtoons on Korean Web portals is like visiting a department store, he said ("Yoon Taeho on the culture of webtoons and *Moss*," 2015). Consumers consider webtoon producers to be service providers, and not just a few users start their day by accessing the latest episodes. According to Yoon, some 30 Korean platforms provide webtoon service to consumers, and at any given time, some 200 webtoons are available ("Yoon Taeho's discussion about webtoon" 2014). Conservative estimates place the number of webtoon viewers in Korea at about six million (Lynn, 2016b). With Korean webtoons now appearing in Japanese and Chinese translation in addition to English versions, Korean graphic novels seem poised to join K-pop, Korean television dramas, Korean cuisine, and Korean film as integral elements of popular culture worldwide (Lynn, 2016a).

Ikki could not have become the multimedia success it is today without the South Korean Internet infrastructure to support it. South Korea is consistently ranked as one of the most wired nations in the world (see, e.g., Ismail Wu, 2003), and the ease of online access has resulted in a burgeoning of creativity in drawing and writing, two creative arts that have traditionally enjoyed an elite cachet and employed an elaborate and restrictive gatekeeping structure. But with access to the Internet has come an increasing variety of pictorial and literary content by writers and artists both amateur and professional, much of it reflecting the lives of the creators. We might say, then, that just as lifestyle has informed online creation, online creation in the form of webtoons has become part of the lifestyle of webtoon consumers.

Ikki the film

Ikki was one of the first Korean graphic novels to be adapted into a film following its webtoon incarnation, and is credited with enhancing the visibility of the source text (Han & Hong, 2011)—just as the film version of Gong Jiyoung (Kong Chiyŏng)'s novel *Togani* (2009) catapulted that publication to the domestic best-seller list. *Ikki* the film is generally faithful to *Ikki* the graphic novel, though the events at the crux of the novel—Ryu Mokhyŏng's Vietnam War trauma and the mass murder at the prayer retreat where he subsequently isolates himself—are variously absent or downplayed. Notable in the film version are the expanded roles given to Yŏngji (spelled Youngji in the *Huffington Post* version), the only fully developed female character in the novel, and prosecutor Pak Minuk. In both the film and the novel, Yŏngji is portrayed as a victim first of the villagers with whom she grew up and then of the men in the village taken over by Ch'ŏn Yongdŏk (Cheon Yongdeok). But in the film version, she emerges triumphant: the closing scene situates her at the railing outside the elevated home of Village

Head Ch'ŏn as she looks down at Ryu Haeguk (son of Ryu Mokhyŏng), who is about to depart, with an expression that is in turns playful, wistful, cynical, and vindictive. Pak for his part emerges in the film as much more proactive than his graphic novel counterpart, who struggles to align himself with Haeguk, whose complaint of a misdemeanor early in the novel ultimately results in Pak losing his position as a public official and being banished to private practice in a remote seaside location.

The film version of *Ikki* is significant in that it skillfully blends the Hollywood-influenced thriller genre with a social-activist approach characteristic of Korean fiction produced during the period of military dictatorship in South Korea (1961–1988). The stronger role accorded Yŏngji in the film is consistent with the increased visibility of women in Korean literature in the new millennium as well as in Korean politics and society in general. The film's portrayal of prosecutor Pak Minuk as an activist is likewise salutary in the context of Korean history, both traditional and modern, in which literary representations of the bureaucracy are rife with images of inaction, incompetence, and lack of integrity.

Ikki the literary work

As a work of literature, *Ikki* echoes both classical Korean fictional narratives in its melodrama and contemporary Korean literary fiction in its themes— the corruption of power, the sins of the fathers, misogyny exacerbated by vestiges of neo-Confucian gender role expectations and a patriarchal social structure, and the lingering effects of trauma. It is also contemporary in its psychological insight and the complexity of characterization of the protagonist and supporting characters.

More characteristic of graphic fiction but less evident in contemporary Korean fiction is the vivid presence of evil. Korean, Korean Canadian, and Korean American readers report that they are drawn to *Ikki/Moss* by its suspense and thrills. The images are in color, but with a predominance of black, brown, and gray tones. Much of the story takes place at night, indoors, or underground. Readers have remarked that author Yoon's depiction of his characters' eyes is especially effective.

The sinister mood of *Ikki* is reinforced by its setting in a village that is both familiar—in its rice paddies, tractors, greenhouses, and tool sheds— and yet strange in its remoteness from the nearest town, its lack of women, and the prominent, elevated location of the largest dwelling, that of Ch'ŏn the village head. Author Yoon Taeho reported to co-translator Ju-Chan Fulton and myself that his immediate inspiration for this graphic novel came from an automobile journey he took to the Korean countryside, in which he exited the expressway and found himself alone at night on a solitary tree-lined track with the expressway looming impossibly high above him. He was struck by the thought that if misfortune were to befall him there, he would not be found soon.

Ikki is an allegory of the abuse of power, a problem that was endemic during the period of military dictatorship in South Korea. It also incorporates strong elements of trauma as well as addressing issues of class, gender, and community. In these respects, it is reminiscent of Korean literary fiction of the 1970s and 1980s, which addresses the social, political, and historical realities of those decades. Readers of *Ikki* might see in Village Head Ch'ŏn a more twisted version of the protagonist of Yi Ch'ŏngjun's novel *Tangshin tŭr ŭi ch'ŏnguk* (1976, trans. 1986 *This Paradise of Yours*), a former military man who runs a leper colony on an island in the West Sea.

In *Ikki*, protagonist Ryu Haeguk, a young man whose obsessive-compulsive disorder has led to estrangement from his wife and child, receives word that his father has died in the remote village where he moved after serving in the Republic of Korea's forces in the Vietnam War. Haeguk journeys to the village and finds an odd assortment of men at the center of whom is the village head, Ch'ŏn Yongdŏk, a small, mousy-looking man and former police investigator, who declares to Ryu that he is the "be-all and end-all of the village." Surprised to learn that there was no medical examination of his father's body, Ryu decides to remain in the village—even though it is clear that the locals want him to return to Seoul as soon as possible—and investigate the circumstances of his father's death as he processes his father's belongings. For the time being, he is given a room at the back of the village store, which is run by Yŏngji, a young single woman who seems to be the only female resident of the village.

Exploring his father's spacious home, Ryu discovers in the basement a tunnel that leads to the home of Chŏn Sŏngman (Jeon Seogman), one of the group of men beholden to Ch'ŏn, the village head. Ryu learns from one of the other men of Chŏn's troubled past, including several suspicious deaths related to him. Upon release from prison after the most recent of those deaths, Chŏn was taken under the wing of the village head, who back when he was a criminal investigator had handled the inquiry into that death. When Ryu breaks into Chŏn's home in search of evidence that might link the man to his father's death, Chŏn surprises Ryu, stabbing him with a gimlet and then pursuing him to an overlook, where Ryu turns on him and sends him plunging to his death on the rocks below.

This chain of events is repeated with another of Ch'ŏn's henchmen, who dies in a blaze at his home, where he has kidnapped Ryu. At this point Ryu enlists the aid of former prosecutor Pak Minuk, with whom Ryu has a conflicted relationship. There follows a confrontation between Ryu and Ch'ŏn in which Ryu learns of his father's traumatized past—while in Vietnam during the war, the elder Ryu mistakenly shot and killed a Vietnamese woman at full-term pregnancy, and the woman's dying act was to release the stillborn baby. Returning to Korea, Ryu's father proceeded to abandon his wife and young Ryu and settle in the remote country village, drawn by the possibility of atonement at a prayer retreat located there. But under the influence of Ch'ŏn, who by then has retired from the police and relocated to the village, and the unscrupulous woman who directs the retreat, the residents of the retreat are persuaded to part with their money, which is used in a massive land-buying scheme. When this scandal comes to light, Ch'ŏn and accomplices react by carrying out a mass murder of the sleeping residents (reminiscent of the mass suicide at Jonestown in northern Guyana in 1978), which Ryu's father witnesses and comes to feel complicit in. With evidence of his misconduct accumulating, Ch'ŏn decides to eliminate Ryu. But Ryu, with Pak and national law enforcement personnel, strikes first, confronting Ch'ŏn. After one last lecture to his accusers, which calls to mind Lady Chang's protestations of innocence as she is forced to drink poison in the mid-Chosŏn fictional narrative *Inhyŏn wanghu chŏn* (The true history of Queen Inhyŏn) and Magistrate Pyŏn Hakto's reminder to Yi Mongnyong at the end of the ever popular *Ch'unhyang chŏn* (The tale of Ch'unhyang) (Rutt & Kim, 1974) of the importance of maintaining the social order and the laws of the land, Ch'ŏn produces a pistol, positions the barrel under his chin, and blows his head off.

Ikki in English translation

There are a variety of challenges in translating a webtoon version of a graphic novel. Whereas with a print volume one can easily go back and forth between the original text and the translation, with a webtoon we work on an online platform that presents the Korean text and images on the left and only the images on the right, to which we add the English text. In the case of *Ikki* to *Moss*, because author Yoon made changes in the webtoon version prepared for online subscription and for *The Huffington Post*, Ju-Chan Fulton and I were essentially negotiating four texts: the initial five-volume print version, the subsequent four-volume print version, Yoon's initial webtoon version, and finally the slightly modified webtoon version delivered to *The Huffington Post*.

Second, *Ikki* is not an easy story to follow. Like most good fiction, and especially works that involve political and social problems, there's a great deal of hidden meaning. Even after reading the five-volume print version twice and the four-volume print version thrice, we still generated nine pages of queries for the author, which we had an opportunity to discuss with him when he visited the University of Washington in March 2015. Questions continued to arise as we translated the entire work. Even those whose first language is Korean admit to difficulty in understanding certain areas of the story.

Third, onomatopoeia is a constant challenge. Do we Romanize sound-words (*ŭisŏng'ŏ*) or use English equivalents? For example, to represent the sound of a motor vehicle, both the engine and the wheels on the road surface, Yoon uses *boooong*. We utilized that Romanization, prompting one of my students to ask why we hadn't used the English *vroooom* instead. Good question. A similar decision is involved in translating *ŭit'aeŏ*, Korean words that represent actions rather than sounds—for example *hoek*, which indicates a sudden movement. In this case we opted for Romanization, figuring that however one pronounced this word, the aspiration required by the initial *h* might prompt readers to think of similarly aspirated words such as *whoosh* or *whirl*.

Fourth, editing a webtoon translation is more of a challenge than editing a print translation. The text has to be consistent with the images, and most of the text we are translating is dialog rather than narrative. A further complication is that typographical errors by the Rolling Story team that prepared the webtoon version of *Ikki* for translation for *The Huffington Post* proved difficult to correct. For example, in an early installment, our "attorney at law" came out as "attorney at low." We found it necessary to go through each batch of installment translations at least twice after completing a first draft, referring constantly to the images, and especially to the facial expressions of the characters—for example, to assess how strongly or how subtly to render the language in a particular dialog.

Subtext—what is implicit rather than explicit in a text—is a constant challenge in literary translation. Many of the images in a graphic novel are unaccompanied by dialog, and the translator must bear in mind a target audience that is not necessarily used to reading between the lines when encountering a work of foreign literature in translation. How much "dumbing down" (which is essentially what the pejorative term *domestication* means) should the translator do? Our approach was to add cues we believed would aid readers in understanding the basic story line—an important consideration with a graphic novel that in its first print edition ran to five volumes—as well as the cultural subtext. For example, we found the map appearing at the beginning of episode 9—a sketch by Ryu Haeguk of his father's house and its environs—to be insufficient in comparison with the narrative and dialogue provided by the author, and we augmented it accordingly.

The greatest challenge, and perhaps the part of the process that offers the most satisfaction in translating a graphic novel, is the dialog. Here, inevitably, less is more, and there has to be rhythm and movement to the language. It is essential at this stage to read the translation aloud and to hear it read aloud.

Conclusion

As a final consideration, I cite anecdotal evidence from my students at the University of British Columbia suggesting that *Moss*, the English translation of *Ikki*, has significant potential for commercial success in addition to its demonstrated appeal in the courses I offer on modern Korean literature, the modern Korean novel, and Korean popular culture. In recent years I have used episodes from *Moss* in my courses and then canvassed my students as to whether a translation of the entire novel would be economically feasible. They agree overwhelmingly that it would. Perhaps the most intriguing comment I heard was from a Korean Canadian student who is bilingual and bicultural; he argued that the parents of Korean American and Korean Canadian students are desperate for English-language materials that will offer their children a gateway to the wave of Korean popular culture that is now sweeping the globe. A colleague at Harvard commented that there is an urgent need for an English translation of a contemporary Korean graphic novel, and observed that *Moss* would be the first published English translation of an entire Korean graphic novel not limited to a specific age group. It would therefore seem that a viable literary translation could serve as more than merely a cosmopolitan dessert in a multimedia feast; building on the ever increasing sophistication of digital platforms for the delivery of cultural content, it could become the capstone of the multimedia life of a Korean graphic novel, marking a progression from *misaeng* (an incomplete life) to *wansaeng* (a complete life).

Notes

1 For the complete version of *Ikki*, see: http://blog.daum.net/_blog/BlogTypeView.do?blogid=0TCSW&articleno=26&categoryId=9&regdt=20100616123406&totalcnt=32.

2 *Moss*—the complete English translation by Bruce and Ju-Chan Fulton of *Ikki*—is no longer available at *The Huffington Post*. Selected episodes are available on a rotating basis from Spottoon, a Korean platform (as of this writing episodes 1–10 are available for free). https://www.spottoon.com/episode/2/78/MOSS/67.

References

Gong, Jiyoung. [Kong Chiyŏng] (2009). *Togani* [The Crucible]. Seoul: Ch'angjak kwa pip'yŏngsa. (Translation in progress by Bruce and Ju-Chan Fulton).

Han, Ch'angwan, and Hong Nanji. (2011). Webt'un ŭi yŏnghwahwa rŭl wihan sŭt'orit'elling yŏngu: Webt'un <Ikki> ŭi sŭt'orit'elling chungshim ŭro [Storytelling for Converting Webtoon into Movie: The Case of *Moss*]. *Hanguk k'ont'ench'ŭ hakhoe nonmunji* 11, no. 2: 186–194.

Ismail, Sherrille, and Irene Wu. (2003). Broadband Internet Access in OECD Countries: A Comparative Analysis. A staff report of the Office of Strategic Planning and Policy Analysis and International Bureau, Federal Communications Commission, Washington, DC.

Jin, Dal Yong. (2016). *New Korean Wave: Transnational Cultural Power in the Age of Social Media*. Champaign: University of Illinois Press.

Lee, Young-Hee. (2013, August 10). Internet Entrepreneur Is Serious about Comics. *Korea Joongang Daily*. Retrieved from http://koreajoongangdaily.joins.com/news/article/article.aspx?aid=2975871

Lynn, Hyung Gu. (2016a). Korean Webtoons: Explaining Growth. *Research Center for Korean Studies Annual, Kyushu University* 16: 1–13.

———. (2016b, February 23). Translating Korean Webtoons: An Interview with Bruce and Ju-Chan Fulton. *Asia Pacific Memo* 365. Institute of Asian Research, University of British Columbia.

Moura, Hudson. (2011). Sharing Bites on Global Screens: The Emergence of Snack Culture. Pp. 37–49 in Dal Yong Jin, ed., *Global Media Convergence and Cultural Transformation: Emerging Social Patterns and Characteristics*. Hershey, PA: IGI Global.

Park, Seok-hwan. (2014). "P'ot'ŏl webt'un p'ŭllaetp'om ŭi sanŏp kyumo wa unyŏng chŏngch'aek model yŏngu" (A Study on the Size of the Portal Webtoon Platform Industry and its Management Policy Models). *Aenimeish'ŏn yŏngu* (Korean Journal of Animation) 10, no. 2: 145–162.

———. (2016). Websites Offer Korean Webtoons in English. *Koreana: Korean Culture and Arts* 30, no. 1: 73.

Rutt, Richard, and Kim Chong-un, trans. (1974). *Virtuous Women: Three Classic Korean Novels*. Seoul: Royal Asiatic Society, Korea Branch.

Yi, Ch'ŏngjun. (1974–1975). *This Paradise of Yours*, trans. 1986 Chang Wang-rok and Chang Young-hee. Seoul: Crescent Publications.

"Yoon Tae-ho." (last edited May 24, 2018). *Wikipedia*. Retrieved from https://en.wikipedia.org/wiki/Yoon_Tae-ho

"Yoon Taeho on the Culture of Webtoons and *Moss*." (September 11, 2015). New York: Asia Society. Retrieved from https://www.youtube.com/watch?v=vt8EPifSdWo.

"Yoon Taeho's Discussion about Webtoon." (October 22, 2014). *Sumgyeojin Gem*. Retrieved from http://sumgyeojingem.com/yoon-tae-hos-discussion-about-webtoon/

9 Media's representation of female soldiers and their femininity

A case study of Korean webtoon *Beautiful Gunbari*

Taeyoung Kim

Introduction: publicizing the issue of women's conscription in Korea

For a long time, the strict compulsory military service has been controversial in South Korean (henceforth Korean) society. Apart from the nation's geopolitics and the issue of national security, performing military duties has long been considered as a coming-of-age ceremony in Korean society and an index of social equality and justice. In this regard, draft dodging has been considered as a more serious moral and legal action than other crimes, which made a few politicians to resign from their positions and many celebrities to leave the entertainment business.

Against such a backdrop, issues such as the introduction of a conscientious objection to conscription and a substitute military service system, which argues to employ exceptional clauses for those who have special religious or political beliefs, triggered a strong backlash from the public (Kwon, 2012). Even if the Constitutional Court of Korea ordered the Ministry of National Defense to implement an alternative service system in 2018, the government responded with a provision of a three-year alternative service at correctional facilities for those who would refuse to join the military system. Such a measure is criticized as a punitive response from human rights activists.[1] Combined with the public's strong cynicism to special measures and minorities those who demand to be exempted from the duty due to their religious or political backgrounds, controversies over conscientious objections and alternative services demonstrate how Korean society understands its military system as vital to its population.

The hostility against those who refuse or avoid conscription reflects Korea's long-standing militarism, which is built upon the country's strong nationalistic atmosphere and its modern history (Bliss, Oh & Williams, 2007; Kim, 2015). Implemented by the Japanese colonists in the early 20th century, militarist ideologies have been consolidated throughout the Korean War and the following authoritarian regimes. This even continued after the nation's democratization in the early 1990s since the militarist culture already penetrated into democratic cultures.

In a similar vein, to allow women to conduct military duties represents gender conflicts in Korean society. Since the Constitutional Court ruled that the *Support for Discharged Soldiers Act* was unconstitutional in 1999, there have been acrimonious disputes between feminists and so-called "male advocates" over this topic.[2] In the name of gender equality, the government started to accept more women in military services. In the late 1990s, the Ministry allowed female cadets to enter military academies. In 2008, the government established units of Reserve Officers' Training Corps (ROTC) in several women's universities and allowed female cadets to join all ROTC units. Despite these measures, disputes over the roles of women in the military have become more intense. For instance, when Ewha Women's University—which is the oldest female university in the nation and has functioned as a hub for the nation's feminist scholars and activists—decided to host an ROTC unit in 2016, its student council objected to the university office's plan, arguing that ROTC is an ideological state apparatus of androcentric values. In contrast, the majority of students disagreed with the student body believing that this would give more employment opportunities to women, which resulted in the council's withdrawal of its statement (Lee, 2016, February 29; Choi & Hwang, 2017, March 10). Given that serving in the military has been a common means for men to justify their dominance in a heavily patriarchal society, responses from students suggests that the issue of female conscription is still ongoing.

The media contributes to amplifying this debate. For example, Munhwa Broadcasting Corporation (MBC), which is the nation's second-largest terrestrial nationwide broadcasting company, broadcasted a reality television show called *Real Men* (*Jinjja Sanai*). Sponsored by the Ministry of National Defense, it showed how male celebrities endure tough lives in military bases. Thanks to the success of this program, producers launched special episodes and cast female celebrities, exploring how they survive in what is a new environment for many women. While the episodes received even higher viewer ratings than usual, they were criticized by liberal-progressive media in terms of their masculine perspectives in representing women's bodies and performances of female celebrities. Meanwhile, conservative media published a series of columns to demand action for supporting veterans and to discuss the necessity of publicizing the discussion of imposing military service upon women in public (Joongang Ilbo, 2014, March 14; Cho, 2015, December 16).

Considering that the exemption of women from conscription has been used by men to justify the asymmetries in gender politics and hierarchize women, such changes imply friction in the nation's gender politics (Hall & Rodriguez, 2003). Then, understanding the media's representations of female soldiers is crucial since they distort feminist ideas and instigate backlashes from men, which leads to the reconsolidation of gender hegemony

(Gibbs, 2001). As a case study, this study analyzes *Beautiful Gunbari* (*Beautiful GI* in English), a famous webtoon about the lives of female police officers.[3] Although a webtoon is based on fictional narratives, its popularity was related to the representation of female soldiers in other media products, including *Real Men*.

Such popularity as well as controversies over these media products represent how the genre of militainment is influential in Korean society. They also imply how the military system and militarism permeate daily lives. According to Payne (2016), militainment is a neologism of "military" with "entertainment." The genre promotes the military system by representing it with well-disciplined close-order drills and repackaging its activities as adventures. In conjunction with the narrative of patriotic ideologies, such representation reinforces militaristic ideologies in society (Mundey, 2001). By portraying one's military service as full of exciting and fruitful memories, the military system and media expect to disarm anti-militaristic attitudes of the public and describe the lives of soldiers as noble. Ultimately, it serves to legitimize the military system and militarism (Schaffer, 2019). As the case of *Descendants of the Sun* (2016)—a television melodrama depicted the military life—suggests, which has recorded 41.6% viewer ratings, militainment has been considered as a popular genre in the Korean cultural industries (Kim, 2016, April 15). Despite criticisms against the genre, it has gained ample success thanks to the nation's history of military dictatorship and geopolitical conditions of the Korean Peninsula.

One of the major changes that recent Korean militainment products show is the existence of female characters in uniform. In that sense, *Beautiful Gunbari* demonstrates well such a trend of representing female soldiers as it has the longest history among several militainment products produced recently about the lives of female soldiers. Moreover, considering the genre of comics, where creating their own world provides more imaginative freedom to cartoonists, a webtoon is expected to cover more stories about the lives of female soldiers compared to other militainment genres (Bukatman, 2016). Prior to the analysis, this study discusses militarism's position in Korean society as a dominant ideology. Then, based on the textual and discourse analysis on *Beautiful Gunbari*, it explores the discursive foundations of such representation of female soldiers.

History of Korean militarism and its impacts on gender politics

The birth of Korean militarism traces back to its colonial period (1910–1945, Kwon, 2001). During the colonial era, Japanese authorities ruled Korea based on militaristic measures, and mobilized their army to subjugate the Korean population's independent movements, exploit natural resources and crops, and draft military sex slaves and workers. After the defeat of Japanese imperialism, the US Army Military Government in Korea

(USAMGIK, 1945–1948) incorporated legacies of its predecessor to control the territory. Despite Korea's independence in 1948, revolts of communist guerrilla and the Korean War (1950–1953) legitimized to implement militaristic values in the fledgling nation. Then, continuing political uncertainties and corruption provoked a military coup in 1961 by Park Chung-hee, who established an authoritarian regime that ruled the nation until 1979.

Under the Park administration, militarism seized hegemony in Korean society. During his tenure, military forces were used to construct infrastructure while militarist ideas were adopted as a means to implement plans for economic development. Indeed, Park introduced a political initiative called the *Saemaul* Movement [*Saemaul Undong* in Korean], aimed at modernizing rural areas. While the movement was praised for developing the rural economy, much of its propaganda and methods of mobilizing the population derived from militarism. Alongside constructing infrastructure and housing, the state emphasized the need for mass-education to revive the spirit of the population. Park introduced the *Charter of National Education* (*Kookmin Kyoyook Hunjang* in Korean) in 1968 to reinforce the population's unquestioned loyalty and dedication to the nation.[4] Both the Charter and the *Saemaul* movement functioned as important ideological devices to construct the nation's new identity fueled by anticommunist and militaristic values (Moon & Jun, 2011).[5] After a failed raid on the presidential residence by North Korean forces in 1968, the Korean state's focus on militarism became more intensified. The government established the armed reserved forces and required all students to attend military drill and exercises. In the aftermath of the third constitutional reform called *Yusin*, the administration made it legal for dissidents to be court-martialed.

The nation's militarism became more powerful when Park was assassinated in 1979 and Chun Doo-hwan seized power in 1980 by another coup. The Chun regime introduced more militaristic measures on controlling the society, such as the *Samchung Concentration Camp* [*Samchung Gyoyukdae* in Korean] and the *Nokhwa Project* [*Nokhwa Saeop* in Korean], which both aimed at rehabilitating "troublemakers," including disorderly students, the homeless, ex-convicts, through military trainings. Although the government emphasized that military-style camps would "purify" their mentalities, the camps were abused to detain and suppress rebellious students and oppositional politicians.

Despite the growing antipathy against such oppressive acts, militaristic values became more prevalent in society. This continued even after the establishment of the civilian government in 1993 (Kim, 2016). Many conservatives argued that Park had to be considered as the architect of modern Korean society in the belief that his leadership made the nation's rapid economic growth possible, even if his presidency was accused of a totalitarian and authoritarian dictatorship. In the name of economic growth, militaristic leaderships became exonerated from its infringements of human rights and militarism continued to function as a dominant ideology in Korean society (Yap & Chu, 2015).[6]

Militaristic values are still omnipresent in Korean society. As mentioned above, serving in the military is considered as a rite-of-passage event for men, and the military is believed to be a place where boys become mature (Enloe, 2000). Indeed, military experiences become an important factor in terms of employment and marriage since they are believed to guarantee a man's health conditions and his strong mentalities. In addition to this, a number of militaristic behaviors become commonplace in civilian society, such as violence against juniors in some colleges, and strict hierarchies at work. Combined with the nation's long-standing legacies of Confucian traditions of respecting seniorities and allegiance to the organization a person belongs to, legacies of militarism are emboldened. Then, these behaviors and ideologies of militarism provide a discursive foundation of hegemonic masculinity—which refers to embedded masculine norms and imperatives for men naturalized in society (Connell & Messerschmidt, 2005). As long as militaristic norms are used to construct masculinity, both the military system and militarism reinforce the dominant position of military values in all social groups, while other types of masculinities are neglected, overlooked, and often suppressed. For instance, a common subject in Korean men's drinking parties is to compare one's military life with others, comparing whose military life was tougher. While male participants boast of their military duties depending on their specialties or units, those who are exempted from military duties or serve in the civil services are treated as second-class or invisible. Such competitions and exclusions demonstrate influences of military services upon Korean masculinity.

In response to this, feminists have continually attempted to abolish military practices in Korean society. For them, militarism was understood to strengthen hegemonic femininity in Korean society since the military system excluded women from its entry arguing that they were weak or inappropriate to serve the duty (Kwon, 2005). Considering that the military experience was regarded as a coming-of-age ritual to be treated fair among colleagues, such exemption of women meant the degradation of their status in the society. Moreover, given that feminist movements in Korea began in the early 1970s to protest against the state's militaristic measures and to demand better working conditions for female workers who had to work 15 hours per day without proper education, feminist movements in Korean society was an antithesis to the ruling ideologies—both male chauvinism and militarism. Called the People's feminism (*Minjung* feminism in Korean), labor agitators engaged in feminist movements arguing for the liberation from various types of class and gender subjugations (Louie, 1995).

For many feminists, militarism at once is embedded and reinforces patriarchal and masculine values. It often consolidates women's role as reproducing labor for the nation in the name of national strength (Yuval-Davis, 1997; Fraser, 2009). In this regard, after the nation's political democratization in the 1990s, Korean feminists began to raise their voices on negative impacts of state violence on women's rights. They also demanded apologies and reparation from the Japanese government for victims of sexual violence, known as Comfort Women during the Second World War. The constitutional appeal against the *Support for Discharged Soldiers Act* in 1999 can be explained as an extension of such movement.

Despite these efforts, social discrimination against women and those who are exempted from military duty continued in invisible ways. Combined with a harsh backlash against feminist movements, many women started to agree with female conscription. According to a public poll in 2005, 55% of female recipients agreed to expand the conscription system (Joongang Ilbo, 2005, July 1).[7] In addition, the society's conservatization after a series of nuclear and long-range missile tests of North Korea weakened the position of anti-military feminists. They were often asked to define their attitudes towards their homeland and prove how they could contribute to national security if they were against the military system (Zhurzhenko, 2012). Finally, the rise of neoliberalism in Korean society also triggered conservatization and this became a threat against feminist movements. After the nation's financial crisis in 1997 and the following neoliberal reforms, the new economic system made the population, especially young people, depoliticized and indifferent to social issues.

Therefore, despite a series of corruption scandals in the defense industries and the public's cynicism against various abuses and its hyper-bureaucratic and hierarchal structure in the military system, the military system and its militaristic ideologies are still considered as a *sine qua non* for securing the nation and consolidate hegemonic masculinity in Korean society. As long as militarism has legitimized the asymmetries in gender politics and justified a variety of gender discriminations in Korean society, the media's representation of female soldiers reflect the discursive dynamics between feminism and militarism.

Methods

Beautiful Gunbari is published serially in Naver Webtoon, Korea's largest *webtoon* platform whose market share was about 76.9% in 2017 (Korea Creative Content Agency, 2018). Thanks to the nation's high penetration of smartphones and the high-speed wireless Internet, the *webtoon* industry expanded much faster than other sectors in cultural industries recording a double-digit growth in 2013 and 2014 (Korea Creative Content Agency, 2015). Moreover, *webtoons* are considered as creative ideas and original sources for transmedia storytelling which can be easily applicable to other media genres (Jin, 2015). Indeed, a number of television series and films such as *Scholar Who Walks the Night* (2015), *Cheese in the Trap* (2016), and *Love in the Moonlight* (2016) were based on original *webtoons*.

Considering the growing impacts of webtoons on the Korean cultural industries, understanding the position of *webtoons* and their texts become
important.

Beautiful Gunbari is written by Seol-I and illustrated by Sungwon Yoon.
It has been published in Naver Webtoon every Mondays since May 2014.
It is considered as one of the most popular *webtoons* on the platform even
though its synopsis—which covers the violent reality of military lives—
is different from others which storylines are often inclined to romances,
everyday life, and fantasy tales. Although the webtoon has a strong fandom, it has provoked a series of controversies over its representation of
female soldiers and the lives of military personnel.

Throughout the analysis, this research expects to provide insights into
understanding the representation of militarism as well as its relationship
with gender politics in media.

In terms of research methods, the study analyzes the discourse of *Beautiful Gunbari* based on textual analysis. Finding meanings of the text of
fictional genres is important as it is more sensitive to the audience's psychological and emotional identities than non-fictional genres (Matanle,
Ishiguro & McCann, 2014). In detail, the research uses both literal and
visual texts of the first season's 141 episodes (from February 22, 2015, to
November 12, 2017) to explore the media's representation of female soldiers. Based on the findings from the text analysis, it compares with other
media products which covered the lives of strong women and how media
consumes them. By doing so, the study aims to find how militarism and
media consume female soldiers as a means of reinforcing the pre-existing
gender politics.

Depicting female soldiers: from a crying baby to a warrior

The storyline: rationalization and legitimization of various abuses in the military system

For a long time, soldiers have been represented through different genres in
Korean media products. As mentioned above, rather than criticizing and
re-evaluating the military system as well as its abuses, media has been criticized of romanticizing it to strengthen patriotism and militarism (Jang,
2019). Such characteristics can be also found in *Beautiful Gunbari*. It has
a main narrative as a Bildungsroman of Jeong Soo-ah, the heroine, who
serves as a female police officer.[8] The narrative is based on a hypothetical
situation that the Korean government requires women to serve in the military as men. The story begins with Soo-ah's military basic training with
some explanations why she has decided to choose the police force instead
of other military placements; a female police officer saved her life from a
criminal. This makes her think of serving as a police officer as "cool."

However, various abuses that occurred during her basic training make Soo-ah uncomfortable with the military system. Although she tries to console herself that she is under stress because she has been separated from her families and friends, she keeps experiencing physical and mental distress beyond what she has expected from basic training. This becomes worse when she finishes her basic training and is assigned to a local police unit as a private. On her first day, her seniors beat and abuse her because of her clumsiness and slow-witted attitude. She decides to report the abuse to her commander. But she realizes such disclosure will only deteriorate her position in the unit and not change the situation after meeting a whistle-blower whose life in her unit has become that of an outcast who is left alone. Finally, she understands the real meaning of "confidentiality," that any violence in the barracks should not be reported; this was the first thing she learned. Alongside Soo-ah's cases, the webtoon plainly portrays military violence against rookies.

After having private conversations with her seniors during her patrols, Soo-ah understands the roles of violence within the military system as a "necessary evil." Although she still disagrees with the violence and harassment, Soo-ah decides to become an outstanding soldier by following discipline and rules as directed by her seniors. She tries her best to memorize the unit's radio paroles faster than her colleagues and participates in the unit's talent show. Moreover, she also takes on the role of leader when the unit has to stop a protest even though she is still a private. Such efforts draw the sympathy of her seniors and build up her reputation as a good soldier. Meanwhile, she also gets used to the abuse and becomes more violent like her seniors; talking in a rough manner and using slang. While she keeps questioning the violence within the military system, her seniors continue telling her about the unavoidability of such hierarchical abuse.

In comics, violence against women is not a new phenomenon and it is often understood in a masculine context (Garland, Branch & Grimes, 2015). Likewise, in *Beautiful Gunbari*, violence is normalized within the military system and considered as a rite of passage to endure pain and become a "real" soldier. For instance, there is a cut in the webtoon where a senior of Soo-ah acknowledges her behavior as "bull-shit," but she also justifies herself because such "bull-shit" behaviors are seen and experienced throughout society. Such "bull-shits" in the military system are connived and admitted in the webtoon's storyline by showing off they are outcomes of "misbehaviors" done by rookies, and Soo-ah realizes the "uniqueness" in the military system. Then, violence and abusive language against her are translated as necessary pains and rituals one must endure to become a "real" soldier and gain recognition from seniors. Throughout the episodes, however, such a storyline results in justifying unlawful acts and structural abuses in the military system as necessary evils that soldiers have to obey and follow.

No more tears

When it comes to the storyline, tears are often used as devices for showing Soo-ah's feelings of depression, anger, and exhaustion. In many societies, crying signifies one's weakness and is considered a feminine expression of emotion. Like other institutions overwhelmed by masculine values, seniors in the military system forbid their juniors from teasing and whining arguing that such complaints make soldiers look "weak." In *Beautiful Gunbari*, Soo-ah and her colleagues hide their emotions by muffling their faces in pillows or crying in the toilet. In order to become a "real" soldier, the storyline asks women to abandon "feminine" expressions of emotion such as crying, to become tougher and more masculine. Not surprisingly, macho and boyish characters in the webtoon are depicted as successful and outstanding soldiers. They are portrayed as both physically and mentally strong, enduring all kinds of abuse and every military activity. Such a storyline, which devalues healthy expressions of a person's emotion throughout—labelling it as "feminine"—which distorts the concept of femininity, can be found in elsewhere. For instance, there is a scene in MBC's *Real Men* series when a female cast cries during the training and this makes her drill instructor furious (Sportstoday, 2015, February 23).

Despite her efforts, however, demands of seniors on Soo-ah to control her emotions and express more masculine virtues, seem impossible to achieve. This indicates that female soldiers lack "masculinity," which is considered the main requirement in order to become a "real" soldier (Enloe, 1993). This can be connected to the Korean government's measures on female military officials, as it allows women to join the military service only as non-commissioned officers or officers who are seen as merely giving orders to male soldiers—who actually perform all the physical work. Granted, these measures are often used by male-chauvinistic views to insist that women are not eligible to serve in the military because they cannot withstand hardships. Combined with these stereotypes, webtoons such as *Beautiful Gunbari* invite hegemonic femininity in representing Soo-ah and her "incompetent" colleagues.

Female soldiers as sexy ladies

As mentioned, the military system is a fundamentally masculine apparatus and functions as a "proving ground for masculinity (Carreiras, 2006, 41)." That said, the existence of female soldiers in the military system challenges fundamentals of hegemonic masculinity in society (Prividera & Howard, 2006). Indeed, when governments encourage women to join the armed forces, it is widely known that most of them are assigned to non-combat troops such as medical units and army prosecutors. Such an arrangement of female personnel in the armed forces is used as a pretext for blaming them as secondary soldiers assisting their male comrades, which is based on a conventional perspective that acts of war are perceived as masculine constructs (Herbst, 2005; Ette, 2013). Based on this recognition, *Beautiful Gunbari* portrays Soo-ah as a hardworking but still doubtful soldier. Although the character tries her best to survive harsh military life, the storyline as well as graphics emphasize her physical figure, which is not related to the actual depiction of military life.

While its storyline focuses on inconsistencies between the masculine military system and female soldiers, the webtoon tends to emphasize women's bodies. According to Marshall and Gilmore (2015), graphic images are not neutral and embed masculine gazes toward women's bodies. This implies that men's voyeuristic and fetishistic desires are also inherent when depicting and consuming women, either in real life or in media, which means female bodies are subject to the hegemonic order. In this regard, this webtoon provides off-color images of women's bodies in each episode's title page, especially with Soo-ah's figure and particularly her breasts. Furthermore, the portrayal of Soo-ah's body in certain cases explicitly projects male or homosexual imaginations towards female characters. As Gill (2007) argues, femininity is a bodily property and reflects a sexist and voyeuristic gaze. Even if Soo-ah is recognized by her seniors as an outstanding private, the physical depiction of the character remains focused on her body, as seniors and colleagues constantly marvel at Soo-ah's figure throughout episodes. Meanwhile, to recognize macho-style seniors as women, they are portrayed as boyish caricatures in title cuts that are at times irrelevant to the storyline of each episode. In this regard, title cuts are used to satisfy the masculine desires of female characters.

Therefore, characters, storyline, and texts of *Beautiful Gunbari* imply ambivalence in terms of depicting female soldiers. Throughout episodes, female soldier characters express various types of military abuse, including violence and old-style military orders, which are key components of hegemonic masculinity in Korean society. On the surface, such portrayals of female soldiers may have some effects of improving awareness of women's role in the military system as well as mandatory conscription. However, by illustrating several characters as physically and mentally weak, the webtoon satisfies the masculine gaze and reinforces the ideology that women were not suitable to serve as full soldiers. In conjunction with the growing number of female personnel in the military and contradictory representations of media on female soldiers as "weaker" than their male counterparts, the storyline—which exploits female soldiers to reassure that the military system is masculine in nature and women should remain as secondary objects—becomes more persuasive. Therefore, such narrative and characters reinforce hegemonic gender norms while they also justify hierarchical violence and abuse. Furthermore, by picturing the character's bodies blatantly, the *webtoon* sexualizes female soldiers to satisfy masculine gazes. This also consolidates stereotypes of women and ideologies of hegemonic femininity.

Strong females: another way to scapegoat females

Apart from female soldiers, Korean media have made attempts to absorb and present some ideas of gender equality and have released a few products showing off the power of female characters lately such as *Weightlifting Fairy Kim Bok-Joo* (2016) and *Strong Girl Bong-Soon* (2017). Clearly, their characters and storylines go against typical storyline and character settings of Korean media, which often depict women and their abilities as less than those of men. Such representations are different from traditional plots in Korean melodrama of describing female characters like housewives or "Cinderellas" who fall in love with rich "silver spoon" playboys. Throughout their respective storylines, both television series emphasize the physical strengths of female characters and how they bring success in the characters' careers.

On the surface, such female characters and their storylines in which they accomplish their goals through their superior physical strength—such as becoming a world champion in weightlifting (Kim Bok-joo) and joining a video game company (Do Bong-soon)—coincide with some feministic critiques that women can accomplish their professional goals by themselves. Indeed, *Strong Girl Bong-soon* seem to represent the "ideal" lives of active women since Bong-soon's physical superpower allows her to live an ordinary life as an independent subject without physical and sexual harassment and abuse from men. In a similar vein, *Weightlifting Fairy Kim Bok-joo* sheds light on the life of female weightlifters—which is often perceived as an extreme, male-dominated arena. Throughout their storylines, both series demonstrate how female characters can lead the narrative with their own abilities and bring successful results.

Despite some achievements, however, both series end up with reassuring the traditional mise-en-scène of Korean melodramas, which the future of female characters is deeply connected to their male lovers. In detail, both Bong-soon and Bok-joo have romantic ideas to live as "normal" women who fall in love and get married to charming male characters who love them in return. Since they are depicted as physically stronger than their male counterparts, such dreams are considered absurd. Granted, this is linked to a long-standing stereotype in Korean society that women are labelled as "abnormal" if their physical, mental or intellectual abilities overwhelm men, which is representative of how the patriarchy impacts gender hierarchies in society. Such stereotypes are well-represented by supporting characters in the series who do not understand why such handsome and talented men fall in love with these female characters. Then, even if Bong-soon and Bok-joo are portrayed as self-confident and independent characters, both storylines deliver messages that their ultimate happiness is found in and delivered by male characters. Otherwise, they would be left as special but "incomplete."

Such development of the storylines of both series coincides with *Beautiful Gunbari* in many ways. Like some characters of *Beautiful Gunbari*, both

Bok-joo and Bong-soon are depicted as "muscles without a brain," and this could be solved by their beloved boyfriends. While such strong female characters reproduce the preexisting gender hierarchy between men and women, media labels such as strong female characters as "unnatural." As long as their characters and their relationships with male lovers are translated as absurd, such representations result in degrading female characters and consolidating their status as subject to male characters. In spite of the depiction of female characters as strong enough to achieve their dreams by themselves, the storylines and characters of each series consolidate the preexisting gender logic that women are secondary subjects which is further in line with the findings of my analysis.

Discussion and Conclusion

In many societies, there have been attempts to victimize women as scapegoats during a nation's economic downturn (Orgad & De Benedictis, 2015). Likewise, women's exception to conscription, which has functioned as a discursive framework for men to discriminate and ignore women in Korean society—along with critiques of patriarchal systems from feminist movements, becomes another reason to blame women as "free-riders." Despite backlashes from feminists and liberal-progressive politicians, such mentalities were emboldened following a long economic recession after the late 1990s. While feminist movements are accused of selfishness by men, many women are forced to give up their feminism in reality, which results in the devaluation of their status (Hall & Rodriguez, 2003).

When the issue of female conscription opened a fault line in Korean society, the media depicted female soldiers as first-rate officers through television dramas, documentaries, films, and even television news programs. They argued that women were strong enough to carry out military duties, which contributed to the forming of public opinion that women were capable as soldiers. Meanwhile, there were fewer voices arguing for a reformation of the military system, which was still rampant with toxic expressions of masculinity and hierarchical abuse. Such depictions—which highlighted women's capacity of performing military duties as well if not better than their male comrades but neglected sexist injustices rampant in the military system—was linked to consolidating masculine backlash and distorting feminist discourses (Genz & Brabon, 2009).

The study argues that female soldiers in *Beautiful Gunbari* are considered as secondary no matter how capable or talented they are. The only possibility for them to be recognized as soldiers like their male counterparts was to eliminate all feminine characteristics. Even some seniors of the webtoon are deemed to macho and boyish without any physical and mental "weaknesses," yet they are depicted with a voyeuristic imagination so that they become objectified by male gazes. This finding reinforces the existence of the fundamental masculinity of the military system, which cannot be replaced or fixed solely by the presence of female soldiers, nor could it replace men's position. Most of all, such description means that the issue of female conscription and the existence of female soldiers is not related to the goal of attaining equality comparing to other gendered labor, such as domestic labor, reproductive labor, and childcare (Orgad & De Benedictis, 2015).

Combined with neoliberal ideas that suppress societal structural problems and reduce responsibility for social inequalities and struggles to individuals, the plot of *Beautiful Gunbari* and strong female characters in several media products show off men's interpretation of gender equality which is subject to masculine ideologies like militarism, while borrowing and reinterpreting some feminist critiques (Fraser, 2009). This explanation sophisticates distortion of feminist ideas to further reinforce and normalize hegemonic masculinity can be also observed in other media products. In these works, even if women are stronger and more competent than men in the military system, they feel uncomfortable about their "abnormal" talents and instead seek validation from men.

The media's representation of female soldiers as secondary and male-dependent furthers the idea of the hegemonic femininity as normal and natural. For instance, when Park Geun-hye, who served as the first female commander-in-chief of the nation from 2013 to 2017, several media covered her inappropriate salute. Such coverages on Park's salutes were in stark contrast to the case of her predecessor Lee Myung-bak', whose salutes were problematic, but media did not pay much attention to his hand salute. This reinforces that the military system should be considered as the exclusive territory of men, which justifies male dominance of the society.

Hence, unlike arguments of some conservative critics and male advocates, it becomes clear that female soldiers themselves cannot guarantee gender equality. This becomes clear when media portray female soldiers and relevant social issues such as the conscription. Although many male chauvinists in the society argue that women's exemption from the military duty is against gender equality, both the findings of this analysis and the way that media judge the female commander-in-chief's military salutes show that such an argument can be used as an excuse to justify the hegemonic masculinity in Korean society as long as the military system and militarism themselves are masculine in nature and their virtues are prevalent in the society. This results in appropriating female soldiers as a means of revisiting the gender hegemony with exploiting some gender-neutral languages such as gender equality.

As *Beautiful Gunbari* implies, people tend to personalize structural issues, enduring unfair, unequal, and violent treatment because it is normalized and that they are expected to do so. This can be seen in interpreting the issue of drafting women. Since the nation became more neoliberal, men began to blame women for their hard lives and argued their burdens should be shared with women. However, as the findings of this webtoon clearly point out, men still benefit from hegemonic femininity and patriarchy, and female soldiers are exploited to consolidate hegemonic power through voyeuristic gazes—sexy, boyish, masochist, sadist, crying baby, macho, etc. That said, the idea of employing female soldiers to promote gender equality becomes vague and is easily replaced by another type of objectification, with voyeuristic and sexist gazes. At the same time, the discourse of militarism, as well as hegemonic masculinity, is reinforced through the distortion of female soldiers. While female soldiers themselves are depicted as subjects of gender equality, they are interpreted through the lens of hegemonic masculinity and militarism, which are connected to fetishism and distortion. Then, female soldiers become scapegoats for another triumph of hegemonic masculinity and the nation's old militarism.

Notes

1 Human rights activists criticize that the government's measures on conscientious objectors are unduly rigorous since many countries provide alternative services whose durations do not exceed 1.5 times the length of regular service (Hankyoreh, 2018, August 23).
2 The Act required to give extra points to discharged soldiers when they applied for jobs in the public sectors. The Court declared the Act was unconstitutional because extra points for discharged soldiers mandated by the Act would violate rights of women and disabled people to serve in public service. However, the decision did not mean that all supports for veterans would be violations of the Constitution. Indeed, it stated that the government should provide alternative social and financial benefits to veterans including job placements, vocational training, discounts on educational expenses, and medical protections. (Cho et al. v. the Support for Discharged Soldiers Act, 1999).
3 "Webtoon" is a neologism combining words "web" and "cartoon." While this genre is distributed on digital platforms like webcomics, its characteristics are different from traditional webcomics because a new episode is published weekly and its frame cuts are customized for mobile devices (Jin, 2015).
4 The Charter was initially made for students. However, the government required the entire population including factory workers, civil servants, and business people to memorize it. This compulsory recitation continued until 1989.
5 Park's personal background as a Japanese army officer contributed to praising militaristic values along with patriotism and nationalism. Indeed, Park and his colleagues justified their coup in 1961 by comparing to a failed coup attempt in 1936 by a handful of Japanese young loyalist officers, arguing that their depositions were to rescue the nation from incompetent and corrupted politicians and to transform their nation into a wealthy state (Henderson, 1968).
6 In a similar vein, a number of conservative critics blamed the Democrats who came to power in 1993 during the nation's financial crisis in 1997. They believed that incompetent politicians ruined the fruits of economic development achieved by Park administration.
7 In contrast, only 24.9% of male recipients agreed to female conscription.
8 A Bildungsroman refers to a literary genre which focuses on the protagonist's moral, physical, psychological growth from youth to adulthood.

References

Bliss, S. Oh, E. J., & Williams, R. (2007). Militarism and sociopolitical perspectives among college students in the U.S. and South Korea. *Peace and Conflict: Journal of Peace Psychology, 13*(2), 175–199.

Bukatman, S. (2016). *Hellboy's world: Comics and monsters on the margins.* Los Angeles: University of California Press.

Carreiras, H. (2006). *Gender and the military: Women in the armed forces of western democracies.* Abingdon: Routledge.

Cho et al. v. the Support for Discharged Soldiers Act (1999). Retrieved from: http://search.ccourt.go.kr/ths/pr/ths_pr0103_P1.do?seq=0&cname=%ED%8C%90%EB%A1%80%EC%A7%91&eventNum=3675&eventNo=98%ED%97%8C%EB%A7%88363&pubFlag=0&cId=010300&page=&qrylist=98%ED%97%8C%EB%A7%88363%7C98%ED%97%8C%EB%A7%88363&selectFont= (accessed June 27, 2018).

Cho, S. (2015, December 16). 여군 예능으로 본 "여자도 군대가라"는 심리 [Mentalities of people who argue "women should join the army" represented from televised entertainment shows starring female soldiers]. *Kyunghyang Shinmun.*

Choi, G. Y., & Hwang, H. R. (2017, March 10). 잃어버린 캠퍼스의 봄, 입학하자마자 취업 스펙 쌓기 경쟁 [First-year university students are forced to build a career for their future employment, without enjoying their first Spring]. *Dong-A Ilbo*, A12.

Connell, R., & Messerschmidt, J. (2005). Hegemonic masculinity: Rethinking the concept. *Gender & Society, 19*(6), 829–859.

Enloe, C. (1993). *The morning after: Sexual politics at the end of the cold war.* Berkeley: University of California Press.

Enloe, C. (2000). *Maneuvers: The international politics of militarizing women's lives.* Berkeley: University of California Press.

Ette, M. (2013). Gendered frontlines: British press coverage of women soldiers killed in Iraq. *Media, War & Conflict, 6*(3), 249–262.

Fraser, N. (2009). Feminism, capitalism and the cunning of history. *New Left Review, 56*, 97–117.

Garland, T., Branch, K., & Grimes, M. (2015). Blurring the lines: Reinforcing rape myths in comic books. *Feminist Criminology, 11*(1), 48–68.

Genz, S., & Brabon, B. (2009). *Postfeminism: Cultural texts and theories.* Edinburgh: Edinburgh University Press.

Gibbs, N. (2001). The war against feminism. *Time.* Retrieved from http://content.time.com/time/magazine/article/0,9171,159157,00.html (accessed June 27, 2018).

Gill, R. (2007). Postfeminist media culture: Elements of a sensibility. *European Journal of Cultural Studies, 10*(2), 147–166.

Hall, E., & Rodriguez, M. S. (2003). The myth of postfeminism. *Gender & Society, 17*(6), 878–902.

Hankyoreh (2018, August 23). Defense ministry considers 1.5 to 2 times length of regular service for conscientious objectors. *Hankyoreh.* Retrieved from http://english.hani.co.kr/arti/english_edition/e_national/858931.html

Henderson, G. (1968). *Korea: The politics of the vortex.* Cambridge, MA: Harvard University Press.

Herbst, C. (2005). Shock and awe: Virtual females and the sexing of war. *Feminist Media Studies, 5*(3), 311–324.

Jang, K. (2019). Between soft power and propaganda: The Korean military drama *Descendants of the Sun*. *Journal of War and Culture Studies, 12*(1), 24–36.

Jin, D. Y. (2015). Digital convergence of Korea's webtoons: Transmedia storytelling. *Communication Research and Practice, 1*(3), 193–209.

Joongang Ilbo (2005, July 1). 여성 56% "여자도 군대에 가야" [56% of women answers "Women should join the military". *Joongang Ilbo*. Retrieved from http://news.joins.com/article/1626864 (accessed July 3, 2018).

Joongang Ilbo (2014, March 14) 여성 징집, 이제 공론화를 고민해야 한다 [It is time to publicize women's conscription]. *Joongang Ilbo*, 30.

Kim, D. (2015). Nationalist technologies of cultural memory and the Korean War: Militarism and neo-liberalism in "The Price of Freedom" and the War Memorial of Korea. *Cross-Currents: East Asian History and Culture Review, 4*(1), 40–70.

Kim, J. (2016, April 15). '태양의 후예', 숱한 화제 낳고 대단원의 막 [*Descendants of the Sun* ended after leaving the talk of the town]. Retrieved from http://news.kbs.co.kr/news/view.do?ncd=3264792&ref=A (accessed February 7, 2020).

Kim, S. (2016). Crossing borders: A feminist history of "Women Cross DMZ". *The Fletcher Forum of World Affairs, 40*(1), 133–156.

Korea Creative Content Agency (2015). 웹툰 산업 및 실태 조사 [A survey study on the webtoon industries]. Retrieved from http://www.kocca.kr/cop/bbs/view/B0000147/1825421.do?menuNo=201825 (accessed June 27, 2018).

Korea Creative Content Agency (2018). 2017 만화산업백서 [Annual white paper on the animation industries 2017]. Naju: KOCCA.

Kwon, I. (2001). A feminist exploration of military conscription: The gendering of the connections between nationalism, militarism and citizenship in South Korea. *International Feminist Journal of Politics, 3*(1), 26–54.

Kwon, I. (2005). How identities and movement cultures became deeply saturated with militarism: Lessons from the pro-democracy movement of South Korea. *Asian Journal of Women's Studies, 11*(2), 7–40.

Kwon, I. (2012). Gender, feminism and masculinity in anti-militarism: Focusing on the conscientious objection movement in South Korea. *International Feminist Journal of Politics, 15*(2), 213–233.

Lee, H. (2016, February 29). 여대 ROTC 3호 이화여대, 대놓고 좋아하지 못한 사연은? [Why Ewha women's university could not celebrate the hosting of the 3rd ROTC unit among women's universities]. *Hankook Ilbo*.

Louie, M. (1995). Minjung feminism: Korean women's movement for gender and class liberation. *Women's Studies International Forum, 18*(4), 417–430.

Marshall, E., & Gilmore, L. (2015). Girlhood in the gutter: Feminist graphic knowledge and the visualization of sexual precarity. *Women's Studies Quarterly, 43*(1–2), 95–114.

Matanle, P., Ishiguro, K., & McCann, L. (2014). Popular culture and workplace gendering among varieties of capitalism: Working women and their representation in Japanese Manga. *Gender, Work & Organization, 21*(5), 472–489.

Moon, C., & Jun, B. (2011). Modernization strategy: Ideas and influences. In B. Kim & E. Vogel (Eds.), *Park Chung-hee era: The transformation of South Korea* (pp. 115–139). Cambridge, MA: Harvard University Press.

Mundey, L. (2001). *American militarism and anti-militarism in popular media: 1945–1970*. Jefferson, NC: McFarland & Company.

Orgad, S., & Benedictis, S. (2015). The 'stay-at-home' mother, postfeminism and neoliberalism: Content analysis of UK news coverage. *European Journal of Communication, 30*(4), 418–436.

Payne, M. (2016). *Playing war: Military video games after 9/11*. New York, NY: New York University Press.

Prividera, L., & Howard, J. (2006). Masculinity, whiteness, and the warrior hero: Perpetuating the strategic rhetoric of U.S. nationalism and the marginalization of women. *Women and Language, 29*(2), 29–37.

Schaffer, L. (2019). Recovery of the soldier and the necropolitics of peace in *Descendants of the Sun*. *Journal of Popular Film and Television, 47*(1), 48–55.

Sportstoday (2015, February 23). 진짜 사나이 여군 특집 이다희, 훈련 도중 눈물 흘린 사연 [Why Lee Da-hee cried in *Real Men?*]. Retrieved from http://stoo.asiae.co.kr/news/view.htm?idxno=2015022307012736237 (accessed July 3, 2018).

Yap, O., & Chu, H. (2015) Military support of citizens' challenge in the Asian industrialized countries. *Journal of East Asian Studies, 15*(3), 391–422.

Yuval-Davis, N. (1997). *Gender and nation*. London: Sage.

Zhurzhenko, T. (2012). Feminist (de) constructions of nationalism in the Post-Soviet Space. In M. Rubchak (Eds.), *Mapping difference: The many faces of women in contemporary Ukraine* (pp. 173–192). New York, NY: Berghahn Books.

Part III
Platform politics and media convergence

10 Managing the media mix
Industrial reflexivity in the anime system

Marc Steinberg

Since the turn of the millennium, Japanese anime, manga, light novels, and games have taken a *managerial turn*. These and other works within Japan's franchising or "media mix" model of its media industries have taken to weaving stories, unfolding anime, or making games that put the reader, viewer, or player in the role of the manager. Not only do media franchises unfold in intensified transmedia fashion, with a multiplication of media forms providing for an intensified media mix, they also feature narratives and games about the management of these transmedia properties, idol groups, or stars. This is particularly pronounced in idol management games and anime, cultural products that feature the management of an idol group, from its beginnings into stardom, with the *Idol Master* games and media mix most famous for this game and narrative form. But these also include games within the simulation game genre (Leblanc 2018), including convenience store management simulation games like *Konbini*. Perhaps most explicit in its managerial focus is the improbable hit media mix about a high school baseball club manager who applies lessons from management guru Drucker's classic book, *Management: Tasks, Responsibilities, Practices* (1974) to guide her high school baseball team to the playoffs. This is of course Iwasaki Natsumi's 2009 best-selling novel turned into manga and anime media mix, known as *Moshidora* or: *Moshi Kōkō Yakyū no Joshi Manager ga Drucker no "Management" wo Yondara* (What If the Female Manager of a High School Baseball Team Read Drucker's "Management"?), which showed the incredible thirst for media thematizing management. Who would have imagined that Drucker could be narrativized and turned into one of the bestselling fiction books of the year? And yet the concept was genius: merging the popularity of business books and how-to literature with a very readable novel format and subsequent anime development. Of course, this list should also include works that are about *media work*, from the *Shirabako* series that displays and narrativizes anime production in minute detail (Suan 2018), to the *Bakuman* manga and live action film about the manga industry (Hartzheim 2019), to episodic considerations of how the anime industry works in relation to its most ardent fans like *Genshiken*. Also worthy of mention are *The Devil is a Part-Timer!*

(Naoto Hosoda, 2013), a series about the Devil from another world who is suddenly transported to our world without his powers, and who plans to rule the world by working his way up the management chain of Mc-Donalds); *Sekko Boys* (Tomoki Takuno, 2016), a series about an idol unit managed by a young, somewhat inexperienced woman; and *Girlish Number* (2016, dir. Shōta Ihata), *Seiyuu's life!* (2015, dir. Hiroshi Ikehata), and *Rec* (2006), all of which are about the anime industry in particular, through the eyes of *seiyū* voice actors. Finally, the "meta" gag manga and anime *Pop Team Epic* makes most of its jokes about manga-anime-game genres and their production processes, including highlighting complaints of animators and voice actors in various episodes.[1]

That Japanese media industries are staging media operations and media management for the pleasure of viewers, players, and fans is perhaps no great surprise. This reflexivity is not new, however. Japanese media industries are famously self-reflexive. Television in particular has been noted for its self-reflexive qualities. Kitada Akihiro, in his analysis of Japanese television, notes how self-reflexivity was, for television and popular culture, one way of performatively escaping the "trap" of Marxist ideology and practice that was seen as the culprit for the lynchings by extreme leftists in the early 1970s (Kitada 2005, 2012). Aaron Gerow (2010) notes the reflexivity of television in his important analysis of the "telop" text-over-image commentary of Japanese television. Alexander Zahlten (2017), for his part, describes the reflexivity of Japanese media in the 1980s, as does Misono (2017) in the 1980s and 1990s.

The so-called "subcultural" contents of anime-games-manga-etc. are particularly prone to self-reflexive meta-commentary, and reflexive staging of their own media strategies. These are media associated with what I've elsewhere termed the "anime system," a transmedia combine or comics-animation-merchandise alliance that in Japan is termed the media mix (Denison 2016; Lamarre 2018; Ōtsuka 2014, 2018; Steinberg 2012a). Indeed, there is perhaps no industry more self-reflexive of its own industrial conditions and practices than anime and its associated media, a reflexivity which has only intensified with the rise of digital media and the corresponding destabilization of boundaries between media.

One of the ways we might understand this reflexivity is through John T. Caldwell's (2008) concept of "industrial reflexivity," wherein workers auto-theorize their conditions of work; in this case, however, it is the *works* rather than the *workers* that theorize their own transmedial conditions of production. Bryan Hikari Hartzheim (2019) uses this framework of industrial reflexivity effectively to analyze works like *Bakuman*. Another is through Thomas Lamarre's recent proposition that we term reflexive objects "meta-models" or the "metastory" (Lamarre 2018, 293; 304; see also Boluk & Lemieux (2017) on "metagaming"), which we might understand as media (or media franchises) reflecting on and staging their own *relations to other media*, potentially through a single medium, such as television animation. Michelle Cho (2017) in turn calls these "metatexts" in her analysis of television shows representing the K-pop industry. That is to say, we should regard works that theorize management in relation to the media industries in particular as being auto-theorizations of the media industries, through the media industries, with film, comics, and television being especially hospitable environments for this self- or auto-theorization (Steinberg & Zahlten 2017, 13).

This article proposes to critically reflect on such *meta-modeling* and *auto-theorization*, asking to what degree these audiovisual experiments of auto-theorization push media mix theory or transmedia theory in new directions, and to what degree they repeat known or existing paradigms. What does this reflexive performance of anime or media mix self-knowledge produce? And what, if anything, can it teach those who inquire about transmedia in Asia? To answer this question and address these issues in a concrete manner, this chapter will offer a close reading of the recent anime series *Re:Creators* (dir. Aoki Ei, 2017), which stages the collision of multiple fictional words within the "real" world, and the bleed between fictional and real universes. As such it is one of the best candidates to assess whether a self-reflexive series can teach us something about transmedia in Japan.[2] While self-referentiality within anime series is frequent, and while reference to managerial practice by no means rare, this series is unique in engaging with the management of anime franchises themselves. This makes it the ideal site for inquiry here.

Re:Creators stages battles between characters from multiple distinct manga, anime, and video games who have appeared in the real world, thereby engaging with theories of world-creation and world-building central to media mix industry practice. This chapter will suggest that with series such as *Re:Creators* industrial meta-modeling has itself become a genre (or meta-genre) within the incredibly dense universe of Japanese franchising, all the while offering a novel site for the theorization of Japan's and East Asia's transmedia practices. In other words, this article follows work such as Lamarre (2018), who examines animation and game works to discover their models of media systems contained therein. This chapter unpacks the series to see what it teaches us. And yet it also treats this series symptomatically, paying close attention to the manner in which it singles out the government as having a unique role in the management of media practice. The role of the government here is part fantasy, insofar as it imagines the government to be an effective responder to moments of crisis, a role the government failed spectacularly to do in the face of the March 11, 2011 earthquake-tsunami-nuclear disaster. On the other hand, it is part reality, insofar as it reflects the Japanese government's Cool Japan initiative that aims to support Japanese contents. Yet in a third moment this government involvement usefully shines a light on the committee-based management of a media mix franchise common within Japanese media mix practice.

In other words, this chapter offers a close reading of *Re:Creators* in order to unpack the narrative and medial aspects of the most explicit auto-theorizations of the production of a transmedia narrative. In doing so it examines the meta-model of the media industry, government, and consumers it presents. This meta-model, I will argue, must be treated as both a useful modeling of existent practices around transmedia, and as symptomatic or fantastical in its imagination of the positive role the government plays in the promotion of these franchises. In what follows I will analyze both the nature of the meta-model sketched by *Re:Creators* and the fantasies about the media industries that it builds into its narrative and visual unfolding. Before turning to *Re:Creators*, however, it is worth pausing to appreciate the wider, recent turn within film and media studies to the analysis of management as a site of media work. It is in relation to this critical turn to the analysis of the media industries that I wish to also situate *Re:Creators* as offering a poignant intervention into the theorization of contemporary Japanese media industries.

Management theory and managing media

Film and media studies have recently committed themselves to analyzing management as a crucial locus of media work. Within an industry context, this question of management is often addressed as how to manage creativity—for, on the surface of things, creativity and management are fundamentally oppositional concepts. Creativity should be unconstrained, open, unbounded. Management on the surface appears its polar opposite: bounded (by time and money), rationalizing, ordering. After all, management theory emerges from what Walter Kiechel (2010) in his book on the management consulting industry calls an impetus toward "greater Taylorism"—the expansion of the Taylorist idea of rationalizing production from the production process narrowly defined to the entire firm or corporation. As expanded Taylorism, management would presumably crush all forms of deviation from routine—the very definition of creativity and creative work. In fact, though, creativity and disorder have been features of managerial discourses since at least the 1990s, when a series of widely read popular management books hit the shelves (Micklethwait & Wooldridge 1996). These popular management texts pushed companies to embrace uncertainty, chaos, unpredictability, and disorganization. It seems fair to say that this emphasis on disorganization is the very opposite of what management books traditionally preached (Beyes, Conrad, & Martin 2019). These works also introduced a new term and tendency into managerialism: the network. As Luc Boltanski and Eve Chiapello detail in *The New Spirit of Capitalism* (84), the metaphor of the network becomes a master metaphor in management literature of the 1990s. For them, this is significant, as "management literature is a medium offering the most direct access to the representations associated with the spirit of capitalism in a given era"; it is also "one of the main sites in which the spirit of capitalism is inscribed" (57). If indeed management literature offers both direct access to representations of capitalism, but also thereby inscribes capitalism and its operations, we must ask after the role of media texts that engage media mix management. What does it mean that media texts are exploring the role of media management—is this, then, a site wherein the spirit of media capitalism is inscribed?

Recent work in media industry studies offer some inroads into answering this question. A particularly notable work is Derek Johnson, Derek Kompare, and Avi Santo's edited collection *Making Media Work*, which has led the way in arguing for the need to pay attention to practices of management and managerial discourse. As contributor Amanda Lotz writes, the relation between creation and management is increasingly blurred: "Industry managers are distinct from the individuals responsible for actual creative work such as writing or directing—although this, too, isn't always a hard and fast distinction; contemporary media industries increasingly feature a blurring of 'creative' and 'managerial' roles" (2014, 26). This blurring of the boundaries is seen particularly clearly in the context of transmedia storytelling in Japan. Within the media mix, the creator often takes on the role of the producer of the series (Steinberg 2017a); although this role is sometimes taken up by the publishing house, or the production committee (on which more below).

Finally, Melissa Gregg points to the necessity of paying close attention to business texts as crucial sites of analysis of the construction and regulation of work in the contemporary knowledge economy. As she points out, "In cultural studies, it is characteristic to draw on popular texts to understand the reproduction of ideology, even if the field has shown reluctance to apply this principle to popular genres of business" (2018, 159). Consequently, Gregg pays close attention to the overlooked genres of the airport business bestseller or the "self help instruction book." While not self-help or time management per se, or a theorization of capitalism in the precise manner Boltanski and Chiapello describe, *Re:Creators* functions in a manner similar to such offerings: it is a vernacular and popular account of contemporary media mix practices. At the same time, it's a popular text that advances a particular portrait of the managing of creativity that is fascinating for what it tells us about an idealization of how media can be managed, and how the government can intervene in this media management that fits neatly within the ideological framework of the Cool Japan campaigns around anime. It furthermore offers a glimpse into media mix planning that is as much fantasy as reality. But this is precisely the point; much as self-help books about productivity are symptomatic encapsulations of the transformations of capitalism and offer panaceas to the intense uncertainty this produces (Gregg 74–75), the model of the media mix featured in *Re:Creators* is also symptomatic of changes to the management of media mix practice and offers the industry assurance that they remain in firm control during times of media change.

Re:Creators

Re:Creators is a rare example of a media mix that started from the anime, with a manga version following subsequently. It is interesting not as a media mix project itself, but rather as a meta-model or meta-theorization of the media mix, which gives us a window into a media mix thinking through a close analysis of the anime alone. As such the anime alone is the focus here. I adopt a close reading practice, similar to other such analyses of meta-modeling (including Cho 2017; Lamarre 2018; Steinberg 2012b). While textual readings alone have their limits, here I connect textual reading and analysis of the formal media techniques deployed within it to industry analysis and cultural-historical conditions, which ground the analysis of *Re:Creators* that follows.

The narrative of *Re:Creators* is as follows. The human world is the world of *creators* who spawn character *creations* that inhabit fictional worlds in different media, from anime to manga to games to light novels—to mention only a few of the media featured here. Yet something goes wrong, and one of the creations (named Altair) manages to escape her world. Not only this, Altair has the power and the will to infiltrate other fictional worlds, and bring the characters that dwell within distinct fictional worlds into *our* world, the world of the creators. Suddenly, knights, giant mechanical robots, magical girls, and other character creations come to coexist with humans—bringing their extraordinary powers to bear on the human world. Except this coexistence isn't peaceful or harmonious. Ripping a page from philosopher Leibniz's theory of monads and the compossibility or incompossibility of worlds that accompany them, these characters bring pieces of their worlds with them into the human world. The danger in all of this is that the human world cannot accommodate these competing fictional worlds. The characters' multiple fictional worlds collide within our world and threaten the ability of our world to accommodate these competing realities. The endgame of this is the self-destruction of the world of the creators through a kind of overload of other distinct, colliding worlds. This is indeed Altair's aim: to provoke the destruction of our world by introducing too many competing realities.

Worlds are *colliding*. Thus explains one of the fictional characters who entered the human world, Meteora Österreich, a mage and librarian from a PlayStation Vita video game, who figures as a decoder and analyst of the events of the series, who offers expository explanations of events throughout. The powers of the real world to contain all the disruptions to everyday space and time brought by each of the fictional characters, each of which bring pieces of their worlds and worldviews with them, lead to a state wherein the contradictions of the world threaten to literally destroy the actual world—the land of the creators. As Meteora explains things in Episode 4: "This world contains forces that try to make things make sense in order to maintain order." The world is elastic, she continues, but not elastic enough to contain hundreds of "story worlds." "The coefficient of elasticity will eventually reach its limit, and the equilibrium mechanisms governing the laws of this world will be damaged." In the worst-case scenario, if too many worlds collide, "Everything will be reset, including this world, the foundation for creating other worlds." This "reset" is what Meteora terms "the great destruction."

Putting the great destruction aside, the principle of the incompatibility of worlds and indeed the whole premise of *Re:Creators* appears to borrow from the philosophical tradition of multiple possible worlds. Represented by the thinkers Gottfried Leibniz or his 20th-century interpreter Gilles Deleuze, they refer to the composssibility as a condition when all things from a given world fit logically together, and to incompossibility as the mutual contradiction of worlds, events, or people. In the case of *Re:Creators*, the coexisting worlds are colliding, and this collision of incompossibles threatens to destroy the fabric of the existing world. It also draws on Japanese world theory developed around subcultural media by critics like Otsuka Eiji (2010), Azuma Hiroki (2009), Komori (2009) and beyond who were directly or indirectly impacted by Leibniz's world theory.

Given the crucial character of Leibniz's philosophy to understanding the conceptual framework of *Re:Creators*, I would like to briefly go over Leibniz and his relation to the media mix's world building.[3] Leibniz is the philosopher of multiple possible worlds, of which our actual world is only one (albeit the *best* one). According to Leibniz, God creates the world before he creates the monads which exist therein (not so different from some contemporary media industry practice, wherein Henry Jenkins (2006) notes a tendency for the world to come prior to narrative or character development). Conversely, each monad contains within itself the entirety of the world in which it exists. Two monads can be said to exist in the same world insofar as they reflect the same series of events or circumstances which make up this world, each from its own perspective (Leibniz, *Monadology*, §18). Each monad contains the world in its entirety; since monads "have no windows through which something can enter into or depart from them," (Leibniz, *Monadology*, §7) they cannot be causally affected by any other monad, except when they are preprogrammed from the beginning of time. While the monad cannot be causally affected directly, it is in fact a reflection of the entire universe; each monad is a "perpetual living mirror of the universe" (Leibniz, *Monadology*, §56) such that any change in one part of the world would require a change in all the reflecting monads that inhabit it. The consequence of this double presupposition of closure and reflection is that a monad—or individual—is assumed to have an essential connection to its world.

It is around this essential, predetermined relation between a monad and its world that Leibniz develops the key concepts of compossibility and incompossibility. Two persons are said to exist in a *compossible* or convergent world insofar as a series of events in one person's world matches the other's.

Two persons are said to exist in *incompossible* worlds if within one person's world events exist which do not exist in the other's. As Deleuze (1993, 60) formulates it: "Compossibles can be called (1) the totality of converging and extensive series that constitute the world, and (2) the totality of monads that convey the same world" (Deleuze 1993, 60). "Incompossibles," on the other hand, "can be called (1) the series that diverge, and that from then on belong to two possible worlds, and (2) monads of which each expresses a world difference from the other" (Deleuze 1993, 60). God, according to Leibniz, is the guarantor of compossibility and the harmony of all within each world.

Like the narrative worlds of contemporary media, a world is defined by the series of events that inflect them, and the kinds of individuals that inhabit them. A given world is defined by the events or individuals within it, and which the monads reflect in their being. The addition of a new term to this world would, then, offer up two possibilities. The first is that the term will add to the definition of the existing world, prolonging a given series. This would be the media mix equivalent of building the picture of a world piece by narrative piece. The second is the possibility that the addition of a new term will force a branching of the series, introducing a divergence that will ultimately lead to the generation of a new world.

The relation of Leibniz's theory to transmedia practice should be evident: it provides the contours of an understanding of the consistency of a world, and the conditions and basis upon which a world might fracture, should enough inconsistencies emerge. The addition of narrative pieces (events, terms, or singularities, in Deleuze's formulation) do not merely add to an existing narrative, nor do they necessarily instigate a "breaking point," as Henry Jenkins (2006, 127) has written, "beyond which franchises cannot be stretched." They do however, present the possibility that a narrative world fragments, such that the only way to reconcile the inconsistencies is by recourse to tropes such as time paradox, or parallel worlds theories.

I have argued in earlier work (2012a and 2012b) that the particularity of the Japanese media mix and transmedia practice lies in its general amenability (of both industry and fans) to the neo-monadological project of generating bifurcating series, and to deploying multiple, incompatible, incompossible worlds. If, as Ōtsuka Eiji (2010) argues, world-building is crucial to the media mix, the production of incompossible worlds is equally part of the media mix practice. This is seen most clearly in time travel narratives, loop narratives, and narratives that branch off into multiple possible narrative forks—and also explains the widespread use of these narrative tropes within Japanese media mix productions. This is a general tendency, rather than an essential attribute of the media mix; nonetheless, this tendency is found in fan practices of reimagining narrative worlds (with fans creating the narrative world equivalent of counterfactual histories); and it has been a trend since the late 1980s within the media industries, as they responded to and incorporated fan practice into official media productions.

Kawasaki Takuto and Iikura Yoshiyuki (2009) for instance define the media mix in these terms, noting the frequency of incompossibility, and the equally frequent use of narrative devices such as time loops, multiple parallel narratives, and other tropes to make sense of narrative non-cohesion. Fans, readers, or viewers respond to the "contradictions that arise from each medium's distinct narratives... by treating them as 'parallel worlds'; by ignoring them; or by using these contradictions as the ingredients for readers' 'deep readings,' 'documentation' or 'play with the setting'" (Kawasaki and Iikura 2009, 25). In short, contradictions are embraced as industry strategy met by fan productivity in response to this.

It's this neo-monadological project that *Re:Creators* takes up on a narrative level. In doing so, *Re:Creators* goes one step further than earlier narratives (which revolved around time travel or loop structures), by exploring in depth the consequence of incompossibility *on our world*, the world of the viewers, readers, and players. What happens, the series asks, if these are not simply contradictions requiring reading techniques by active audiences, but rather worlds that encroach on and threaten the consistency of our very own world? *Re:Creators* is a 22-episode narrative and visual exploration of the consequences of media industries' embrace of the incompossible on the world from which these narratives are emitted, the creators' world—which is to say, our world. It's a thought experiment on the question of what happens if the boundaries between created worlds and the world of the creators break down, not simply as a question—often asked by media of obsessive fans—what happens when fans take works too seriously. No, this time, as a moment when the stability of the seemingly ontological boundaries between fiction and our world melt away, and the fictions come to haunt the world of the creators. The danger posed within the real world is that the fictional works infiltrate the creators' world to such a degree that the real world itself threatens to collapse under the weight of the contradictions introduced by these multiple incompossible worlds. For in a truly Leibnizian manner, each character brings with it a whole world; and the incompossibilities or contradictions these multiple characters and their worlds smuggle into our world becomes the real threat to our world.

Instead of appearing as a media mix commercial strategy that would allow for the proliferation of objects and media forms, incompossibility instead appears as an existential threat to the world of the creators. And the media industries (or their creators) are shown to virtuously operate not as capitalist enterprises colonizing the minds of their readers-viewers-players but rather as forces of good trying to contain this chaos. Indeed, the media industries in the series work to generate their multiple iterations of characters and spin-offs *in order to maintain the existing world*, rather than as a means of simple commercial gain. Neo-monadological incompossibility is presented as a narrative threat of chaos, with the creative work of creators trying to maintain the order and consistency of worlds. The hard (over)work of the creative workers is here shown to be all about total mobilization in order to prevent the catastrophic collapse of our world. But they don't do so alone, or in isolation. The government is there to help.

Governing production, administering the media mix

What makes *Re:Creators* particularly unique in part for making the mixing of worlds—so much a part of fan practice—into an official production. As, Gabriella Ekens, in *Anime News Network*, writes: "*Re:Creators* is a copyright-safe version of that fanfiction every otaku has wanted to write at some point in their lives: a metatextual crossover showdown between characters from all the biggest genres in anime." And yet *Re:Creators*' crossover is of nominally fictional creations; creations made for this particular anime, and yet reminiscent of characters and genres from established manga, games, or anime. Moreover, perhaps more important still, the perspective offered on the series is not that of fans (who, as we will see, are treated as those who must be governed), but rather of the media mix producers. The point of view of the viewer is aligned with the creators, the media mix managers, and one aspiring media mix creator who is the protagonist of the series. The media mix producer-in-chief in this case is not the creators themselves or the companies for whom they work, but rather, in a crucial if symptomatic twist, the Japanese government. Depicted as a benevolent force for good, the government steps in to make sure things don't go too far, and the world isn't destroyed by the collision of multiple incompossible worlds. As of episode 5, the anime focuses on the interventions by a government agency, which takes stock of the situation, and later organizes the creators into a massive, unprecedented media mix alliance to create another world-reality (including a set of cross-over characters and trans-world experiments) that would prevent the collapse of our reality through the weight of contradictions that are accumulating via the creations.

Like many other media texts that represent the operations of the media industries themselves, *Re:Creators* tell us stories about the media industries, that must be treated as media industry fantasies; capital dreaming of its own idealized operations. More interesting still, these operations involve the close collaboration with the Japanese government, which is here figured as uniquely benevolent and in control. (Here collaboration is completely absent of its more sinister meaning that Ian Condry (2013) points our attention to, in the sense of collaborating with enemies.) The image of a government in control can be read in two ways, here: first, as fantasy of competence that covers over the Japanese government real incompetence in the face of recent natural and human-made disasters; and second, as an idealized reflection of the Japanese government's actual implication in the creation and promotion of Japanese contents in Japan and outside Japan.

First, in the fantastic mode, the government as image of competence would seem ironic in the face of the still searing image of a government completely out of its depths and ineffective in the face of the country's largest postwar crisis, the March 11, 2011 earthquake-tsunami-nuclear disaster known as 3.11. During 3.11 the government's incompetence in the face of the nuclear radiation leakage that continues today was on full view. It is this very governmental incompetence that forms the ground for the brilliant Anno Hideaki Godzilla film, *Shin-Godzilla / Godzilla Resurgence* (2016), where bureaucratic bungling is as great a threat to Japan as Godzilla.

In the fictional telling of *Re:Creators*, however, the government is the paradigm of competence in the face of a world-threatening crisis. Not only that, the government harnesses the power of corporations in organizing and managing creative workers, focusing their attention on creating fictional works that are aimed at staving off the destruction of the world. This creative work is fundamentally organized to the ends of media mix creation. In short, the government agency titled the "Cabinet Special Situations Countermeasures Council" (embodied in the person of its director Kikuchihara Aki) takes the place of the real-world "production committee" (*seisaku iinkai*) within the media mix system, dictating in this case not only the development of a single franchise, but of multiple franchises. In actual industry practice, the production committee or production consortium is a funding format which sees the collaboration of multiple different industry stakeholders in the production of a given anime series or film (Steinberg 2012a; Tanaka 2009; Wakabayashi, Yamada, & Yamashita, 2014). Typically, these committees are composed of magazine and book publishers, video software distributors, film or animation production and distributors, television broadcasters, advertising agencies, game companies, and toy makers. The collaboration usually involves some degree of financial commitment, and a coordination in order to promote the work as well. The actual production committee for the *Re:Creators* anime is composed of Aniplex (a music and anime company owned by Sony), Shogakkan (a major publishing house), and ABC Animation (an animation company which is a consolidated subsidiary of the Asahi Broadcasting Network Holding Company).

Yet within the fictional world of *Re:Creators*, the production committee is headed by the government, in the figure of the impressively capable bureaucrat, Kikuchihara. This brings us to the second reading of the government's role in *Re:Creators*, as reflection of a particular reality of the government involvement in the promotion of Japanese media mix contents, via its Cool Japan policy framework. While in the real world, the government is never a part of the production committees, it has since the early 2000s had a policy of supporting the diffusion of contents, under its Cool Japan policy. In the fictional world of *Re:Creators*, the government plays a crucial organizing role in the management of the media industries. That the government is shown to be all-powerful and efficient can be read as a symptom of the proximity between government and media industries today. Indeed, the very narrative figuration of the government in this role of control is an ambivalent reflection of its actual role in the Cool Japan strategy of promoting Japanese "contents" around the world (Choo 2012). Cool Japan is at base the government-supported export of Japanese manga, anime, and games (so-called "subcultural contents") to other countries, and the use of these properties as the basis for tourist attractions to Japan, or corporate platform building, among other activities (Hernández 2018; Seaton & Yamamura 2015; Steinberg 2019). The policy has had multiple stages and incarnations, depending on the favor of the government in power, and has been criticized at various moments as being ineffective in realizing its goals of increasing the export of Japan's cultural content. For this reason the effectivity of the government in *Re:Creators* is part fantasy of effectiveness, and part reality of its real implication in the contents industry in contemporary Japan. Moreover, *Re:Creators'* figuration of the Japanese government in a military relation to contents production is also reminiscent of the militarized use of anime contents or characters for the purpose of military recruitment and making war palatable that Akiko Sugawa-Shimada (2018) has drawn attention to.

In *Re:Creators*, military intervention is on a continuum with cultural production. This also recalls recent work by Ōtsuka Eiji (2018) in which he argues that we should consider Japanese domestic wartime propaganda as a precursor to media mix production. Framed in a decidedly more optimistic light, within the narrative world of *Re:Creators*, the defense of the world comes by way of media mix production. Altair, the creation who aims to provoke the destruction of the world, can only be defeated by the fictional creations she brings into the world. These fictional creations in turn must be given the powers they need to defeat the seemingly unbeatable Altair. These powers can only be given through an elaborate media mix narrative. The Japanese government, in the form of bureaucrat extraordinaire Kikuchihara, takes control of the narrative and the production of texts, creating a media mix of massive proportions. The fictional Japanese government thereby enacts on a narrative level a heavy-handed version of the role the actual Japanese government has played in cultural promotion over the last two decades, and indeed becomes reminiscent of the military mobilization through the media mix under wartime conditions, and during the Pacific War. In *Re:Creators*, the government brings together artists and mid-level managers of the media franchise to create a meta-work or a total work of media mix, somewhat ironically admonishing the creators and *Re:Creators'* viewers not to underestimate government projects.

Gathering first corporate executives of anime production companies, publishers, events producers and so forth and lecturing them on the need to cooperate, Kikuchihara speaks to a room full of creators, offering them a timeline for the creation of a media mix production of unprecedented proportions; one that crosses worlds, and incorporates the Creations who have crossed into the creators' world. Accompanied by a PowerPoint presentation that features a media mix production timeline, Kikuchihara mobilizes the defense of Japan. With detailed information about which work comes out when, and leading up to a massive "season finale" or final battle, this series takes the viewer behind the scenes of a typical media mix production (which often includes such production organization timelines), albeit with the pretense of a world-saving anime. At the narrative level, this is a collaborative work of previously impossible proportions, involving dozens of artists in the co-creation process. This ultimately aims at the staging of a massive public (yet mediated) final battle, which is to be presented in a live venue as an anime work. When the creators complain about the impossible timeline, reflecting a widely known sense of already unreasonable expectations of animation workers in particular, who work in underpaid and overworked conditions (Lewis 2018; Okeda & Koike 2011), Kikuchihara tells them to "shut up"; and that "the government will not accept any delays on this project." "To put it simply," she continues, "I'm telling everyone to die." By government executive order, Kikuchihara intensifies the already deplorable working conditions of the creators.

The unruly audience

If the hierarchical control structure is relatively clear, with the government taking the lead role here, the position of the audience is equally interesting, insofar as it is figured as a passive, or reactive entity which must be placated. In order for this final battle and massive collaboration to work, readers and viewers within the anime world must be convinced of the possibility of such a world-crossing narrative. In a unique twist on the incompossible worlds theme, it turns out that part of the challenge within *Re:Creators* is for the government and its creative workers to convince its fictional readers' and viewers' in the transformations in the text or character. In short, the fictional audience must *believe* in the changes to the characters, for these changes to actually have their desired effect. What this means is that a character designer can modify one of the in-world characters all they want on paper, but these modifications only take effect in fact once the reader/viewer/player believes in the modifications made. The fictional viewers inside the narrative must *ratify* the changes in order for them to take effect. Here *Re:Creators* figures its fictional audience according to a form of democratic participatory culture that functions according to a viewer consent model, or viewer belief model. Changes only take effect once a sufficient number of viewers are convinced of the changes to the characters or their settings. This is why the government must coordinate with the creators— not only to help stave off the invasive characters and the potential destabilization of the world, but also to convince the readers/viewers/players in the narrative that the changes that will enable the ultimate overpowering of the rogue character *make sense*. Consent (as well as content creation that produces this consent) is the crucial element of this scenario.

In *Re:Creators'* presentation, then, there is no contradiction between industry and culture, or management and creativity for that matter.

The government and its creator proxies cooperate smoothly to merge creativity and its management. This coincidence of creativity and its management is at the heart of *Re:Creators*, where creators—novelists, animators, manga writers, game creators—are all assumed to function within constraints. The greatest of these constraints is in fact the fictional audience must be fully convinced of changes made to the narrative or setting. Receivers are the final arbiters of value in a creative work, and are in some senses the true managerial force here. Powerful as the government is, it is ultimately up to viewers to accept the modifications made to a story for it to take root.

This audience reception is judged by two means. The first is a fictional device that Meteora creates to measure audience reception to a given narrative line. This is a "magic survey device" as Kikuchihara puts it, reminiscent of the Nielsen ratings system, but capable of monitoring and displaying audience reactions in real time. Second, and this time in the background rather than foregrounded by the narrative, the comments of the audience are seen throughout the series, displayed on a Niconico Video style video platform and interface. Known as a video sharing platform particularly frequented by enthusiasts of anime, games, and manga, Niconico Video (Niconico dōga) also delivers and mediates comics and games, creates a market for buying and selling goods, and hosts a site for its own Wikipedia-style user-produced encyclopedia. Niconico differs from most U.S. streaming platforms in the formal manner in which it mediates content: it allows users to comment on top of videos, and these comments stream over the top of the video being viewed. It's one of the main platforms for watching and commenting on anime in Japan (Hamano 2008; Jin 2017; Johnson 2013; Li 2017; Steinberg 2017b; Steinberg 2019).

Not surprisingly, then, the Niconico Video interface is adopted and presented as the interface of choice of the fictional viewers within the world of *Re:Creators*. The comments that stream over the image allow the government to monitor crowd reactions in real time, producing something reminiscent of a monitoring of the general will of the people, which Azuma Hiroki controversially outlined in his manifesto for a new, internet-mediated, real-time polling of the populace, as a new form of democratic politics (Azuma 2014; Looser 2017). Crowd reactions are in turn monitored in a control room setting which features multiple monitors tracking user reactions in real time—in a set-up reminiscent of the convergence between aesthetic experiment and social control that Yuriko Furuhata (2014) finds in the form of the control room. Indeed, much like Furuhata's argument about Expo '70 in Osaka, which she describes as "a laboratory for testing and experimenting with networked systems of governance as much as it was a platform for showcasing artworks based on multiple screen projections" (2014, 58), the control room in *Re:Creators* combines the monitoring of crowds with the display of media mix art. This monitoring and display works in the service of governance.

Finally, despite the indication that the audience has a will of its own, the narrative of the series asks the real viewer (you or I) to identify with the government and with the creators, not with the audience. The onscreen audience is shown to be a stubborn entity which the government must carefully manipulate to properly save the world. The crowds of viewers are entropic, slow-responding, and sometimes intransigent masses who must be coerced. In other words, this is a very governmental, top-down view of the crowds as a mass. Indeed, the crowds are almost always visually depicted as a mass, usually a non-individualized group of people in the auditorium, or people watching it via the Niconico-like interface on the web, often seen from behind (and therefore depersonalized). In either case, the audience is merely an unruly accumulation of emotional investment—as Altair memorably puts it in Episode 20. The crowd's investment in the antagonist, Altair, who threatens the destruction of the world is precisely what keeps that character alive. It is the affective investment in Altair, expressed in part by crowd sentiment and the virtual crowd on the Niconico-like video platform that keeps the character alive, despite the government and creators' best efforts.

Fictional creations, digital world

This interface level at which the audience is read and evaluated links to the next issue I'd like to address: the *mediality* of the characters in the series. Thus far I've paid attention principally to narrative development and reflexivity at the level of agents in this narrative. Here I'd like to turn to an analysis of the medial form this world takes. This is particularly pertinent since this is an anime about anime characters entering the real world. The series must hence solve the problem of how to treat such transgressive phenomenon visually. How should fictional anime characters which appear within the real world look (especially when the "real" world within *Re:Creators* is of course itself animated)? These are crucial issues, since while occasionally heavy on didactic exposition, the series takes the visual composition of the anime series quite seriously.

The visual complication of the series revolves around the need to represent fictional characters in the diegetic world of the narrative. How this is done, and what tropes are used in the production of creations within the "real" world is the visual challenge of the series. Indeed, the series is "meta" not only on the narrative level, but also in its visual and aural levels as well. Early on the series establishes that although the creations come from fictional works, they look like flesh and blood humans.

The technique by which the anime series establishes the distinction between "real" humans within the anime and creations from other worlds is to mark the creations by their associated anime genre (Denison 2015). The "real" humans are shown as ordinary, or messy, or afraid, whereas the creations are marked by their behavior and their visual look as distinctly "anime"-style. Additionally, the series uses generic, medial, and textural differences to establish distinctions between the creations within their created worlds, and the creations as they exist within the creators'/our real world. In terms of genre, these characters are coded as "anime" character of a particular genre formation, with different characters belonging to distinct generic formations—from the magical girl genre, to the mecha giant robot genre, to the detective noir genre, to the fantasy swordplay genre—each of which have distinct and different generic parameters and representational traits. The creations appear in costume and stand out in comparison to the ordinary world around them. These are then collectively counterposed to the "regular" human creators, who are depicted in (often equally generic) "otaku" fandom genres of depicting characters, or government operatives—both of which nonetheless are distinct from the created characters in having a realism that the "creations" do not.

The medial distinctions form another, more important manner of distinguishing the creations/characters from the creators/humans. An early sequence where one of the main creations, Selesia Upitiria, sees herself on the website associated with her anime production is one example of this. The two are differentiated by an emphasis on the mediality of the latter. The website Selesia is a pixelated and degraded image, a clearly mediated image, unlike the non-pixelated "real life" Selesia, who is now part of the real world. The real world Selesia is markedly less posed, more naturalistic, and more relaxed, whereas the image from the screen is posed, tense, hair floating in the air, posed against a background of stars, with a slight halo around her character. In other words, the latter image is a promo still, heavily designed, and shown to be pixelated, as if we're looking at the image through an old monitor, whereas the real Selesia is blended into the real (creators') world, clearly emotionally distressed by having to confront her fictional portrayal. This shot-reverse-shot of the two Selesias is one of the mediated moments of the series, preceded by a capture of the website in its entirety, complete with cursor, a menu on the left side of the screen followed by a Twitter-like thread on the bottom, as well as share icons on the top right of the screen. In short, it is designed to look like the typical interface for an anime promotion website.

This emphasis on a generic interface is found throughout the series. Indeed, the series excels at foregrounding the interfaces through which consumers engage with fictional texts. The opening sequence of the first episode of the series is itself a sequence of shots of the characters who would become central narrative drivers of *Re:Creators*, in their mediated forms. A giant poster in a public venue resembling the Akihabara district of the mecha Monomagia from the mecha anime *Infinite Divine Machine Mono Magia*. A close-up of someone holding a smartphone with a tweet displaying a cropped screen capture or photo of a single frame from the cyberpunk anime and manga *Code·Babylon*, which features Blitz Talker. The manga frame features the onomatopoeia as well as the moire "screentone" pattern of manga background. A series of hanging train posters of princess and knight, Alicetaria February, from the fantasy epic manga and anime franchise *Alicetaria of the Scarlet*, advertising its newest manga magazine serialization. A Niconico Video-style interface complete with onscreen comments over a video featuring Mamika Kirameki from the magical girl anime series *Magical Slayer Mamika*. A *New Type*-like anime magazine (titled *Ani Type*) with *Elemental Symphony of Vogelchevalier* protagonists Selesia and her partner Charon. Notable about each of these is how they foreground the layer of *mediation* and platform *interface*: public billboard, smartphone screen and social media as well as manga print screentone, train poster and manga magazine promotion, computer video streaming platform, magazine cover. These are the mediated ways that anime and manga appear, showing the crucial function of promotional media in the consumption of these narratives. It is also crucial that it is through these paratexts—as Jonathan Gray (2010) has termed them—that they are shown to the viewers of *Re:Creators* that these are indeed fictional characters, from meta-fictional franchises. These paratexts display these creations as always-already mediated, fictional characters. These include both digital and physical media, from print- to screen-based mediations of the characters.

If remediated print is one of the ways these characters appear, the digital form seems to be their "native" format, and their ur-medium. The characters are *born digital*. They also die digital. This is witnessed most clearly in moments where these characters disappear from sight, or die in the world of the creations. At these moments they dissolve into what appears to be their physical world building blocks: polygons. This is visible in the first episode as the human protagonist Sōta Mizushino dives into the world of Selesia. Here a blue digital light of 2D pixels and 3D pixelated cubes opens up in the floor in front of him; he falls through this digitalized floor into the world of Selesia, before being pulled back into his own world, the "real" world of the creators. Throughout the series, when Altair disappears, she does so by dissolving into pixels as she goes. We see the same 2D and 3D pixilation at work, albeit with more finality, in Episode 9 when Mamika dies—first bleeding, then ultimately disappearing into floating blue three-dimensional cubes, cubic 3D pixels that ascend into the sky—a three-dimensional variant of the pixel, the basis for raster images that are the building blocks for these characters. Accompanying this cubic-pixel disintegration is the sound of a low pitch digital glitch, a kind of granular hum that vibrates the character out of existence.

The physical being of the character beyond the blood that comes out at first is digitality, then. Their flesh and their ontological is digital, which here stands in for the fictional world in toto. These characters are born digital, and return to the digital upon death in the creators' world. This "born digital" and more specifically "born raster" nature is further emphasized in the end credit sequence starting in the second season of the show, beginning in episode 14. This sequence foregrounds the real or fictional production of these creations themselves (whether by character designers in our world, or by fictional character designers in the *Re:Creators* world is purposefully unclear). While opening with a series of rough drawing of the characters, presumably in the phase of character design, these sketches themselves are made in what appear to be a raster graphics or pixel-based program like the industry standard Photoshop. We see this most clearly in an image of Selesia. Here we have a preliminary sketch of Selesia bent over looking down on something, with the image slightly pixelated, and clearly a draft sketch. This is followed by a very pixelated, zoomed in version of this same image, this time further along in the production process, cleaned up, with the animator methodically coloring the image alongside a color reference version of the character. This sequence can be read as much as a nod to the production process of *Re:Creators* the anime series the viewer is watching, as to the production process of the fictional anime *Elemental Symphony of Vogelchevalier* from which Selesia originates, within the *Re:Creators* storyworld. This tension between the two is at the heart of the meta series that *Re:Creators* represents. The subsequent appearance of photographic human hands makes it likely that this should be seen as part of the production process of *Re:Creators*, rather than the fictional shows within the series. Yet the initial ambiguity is crucial to the experience of the series as itself meta-reflection or a meta-modeling of the anime system itself. This meta-modeling includes the production process, from the planning stages featured in the main narrative to the design and coloring process we see in the end credits.

Moreover, the sequences noted above reinforce the anime's theme: these characters are born digital, and that their being and building blocks are pixels. Finally, they are only experienced through layers of mediation that themselves are predominantly digital, rather than analogue. This is in turn confirmed by the very model of the world of the creators offered in the series. The in-series creators' world is itself informed by a digital epistemology. The reality of the fictional world of *Re:Creators*, the world of the creators, is itself figured as a kind of information processing machine. This world has a certain degree of elasticity that can accommodate for aberrations in world consistency. But, as I've noted above, too many inconsistencies and the world collapses, unable to *process* the aberrations and the worlds they imply. This figuration of the in-series world in terms of a computational logic of information processing or information overload is not unique; an epistemology of computation informs many disciplines, areas of study, and analyses of our world as well. So it is fitting that the world of *Re:Creators* also bears the imprint of a cultural logic of computation. The world itself is subtly figured as a computer, or computational, reflecting the larger digital shift that David Golumbia (2009) notes in *The Cultural Logic of Computation*. There Golumbia (2009, 1–2) sets out to "question not the development of computers themselves but the emphasis on computers and computation that is widespread throughout almost every part of the social fabric." This computational logic appears to inform not only the representational logic of the fictional characters within the "real" of *Re:Creators* who are born and die digital; it also appears that the real world of *Re:Creators* is itself computational in nature, a vast information processing machine wherein incompossibility is figured not as logical con-tradiction but as system failure brought about by the inability of the world to process the information generated by inconsistencies. Leibniz returns, then, this time as father of cybernetics, rather than thinker of incompossi-bilites (Furuhata 2017; Liu 2010).

Conclusion

As this chapter has argued, *Re:Creators* stages the management of media industries. The series stages management of the media industries as the management of (1) media; (2) narrative worlds; (3) characters; (4) con-tinuity of worlds. But in an expansion of usual figurations of the media mix in academic work, it's not just the media industries and media worlds that are managed here. The series also frames the management of the me-dia industries as the management of (5) audiences, including fans; (6) of mediation and the materialities of interface; (7) of people in general, the general populace whose belief in the fiction must be sustained—and ascer-tained in real time. The management of the media mix coincides with the management of the social fabric, of the people. It is truly a management of the social whole, not simply of a media franchise.

If this is something of a hyperbolic presentation, it is also a fascinating one; one that coincides with a turn toward an analysis of the government of the people by Azuma, on the one hand, and an analysis of the use of the media mix as a mode of governing or social control by Ōtsuka and others, on the other hand. Management here coincides with governmental or me-dial management, insofar as populations are figured as under control via the media they consume. This sees government expanding the true meaning of management today; an expanded Taylorism to follow Kiechel's formula-tion that takes the entire social fabric as its object of governance—much as platforms do today (Steinberg 2019). The government benevolently protects a prone and powerless populace via effective media management that staves off the threatened implosion of the world from forces unseen by most. Or rather, forces that are *seen* by everybody but thought *fictional* by all but the very few tuned into the real crisis the world is undergoing in *Re:Creators*. In deceiving as much as it enlightens, *Re:Creators* is nonetheless a fasci-nating example of the self-reflexive meta-modeling of the contemporary Japanese mediascape by Japanese media.

To be sure, part of this meta-modeling of the media industries is a fan-tastic presentation of the power of the media industries and a truly fictional portrait of a wished-for (but as yet unattained) efficiency and causal effi-cacy of the government. In short this is the dream of Cool Japan, realized in *Re:Creators* in a way it hasn't yet been in our world. And yet in its fan-tasies of total media management, *Re:Creators* does foreground a tendency within the increasing government engagement with media industries that should be taken seriously. While presented as a utopian moment wherein the government intervenes for the greater good, we should read this series as calling attention to the truly dystopian possibility of ever greater government involvement in the media mix. Moreover, in bringing to light some forms of governmentality, and foregrounding the grueling process of production within the anime and manga industries (albeit presented here as a state of emergency), the series subtly calls attention to the truly deplorable work conditions under which media workers operate in Japan. The incessant labor under conditions of precarity framed as "out of the ordinary" and due to a state of emergency in *Re:Creators* in fact points to something closer to the actual conditions of media workers in Japan; conditions that have only worsened in the new platform era (Hernández 2018).

In its refusal of the habitual opacity of media mix planning—planning that is conducted behind closed doors and in the secrecy of non-disclosure agreements—*Re:Creators* promises and delivers on a view into the inside of media mix planning, and the development of cross-world franchises. On the one hand it presents fantasies about the efficacy of the Japanese government in the face of crisis. On the other hand, it suggests the continuum between government planning on Cool Japan and military response to national emergency, reminding viewers of the link between government intervention and militarization; and it also draws our attention to real problems within the media industries today—notably the overwork and conscription-like circumstances of the animation laborers today. This last theme of overwork in particular threatens to result in what Meteora warns of as "the great destruction" of media workers and media industry alike. As such—and to return to one of this chapter's opening questions around the effectiveness of self-reflexive media productions today, and whether it contributes to the production of knowledge about the media mix operations—the meta-modeling and auto-theorization found within *Re:Creators* does in fact produce some crucial knowledge about media work today, as it dramatizes and thereby calls attention to the management of the media industries and transmedia projects today.

As such, *Re:Creators* is not only part of a body of works within the managerial turn of anime noted in the opening to this chapter; it also joins a small, if growing, list of productions that are about the media mix, and are theorizations of it from within it. From the media mix art project Tamala2010 (Raine 2011), to Murakami Takashi's character-based art projects, to the Persona series (Lamarre 2018), to projects like *Sword Art Online* (as analyzed in this book), media mix projects can be the site of knowledge production, or creative dramatization of their own conditions of production. *Re:Creators* hence is part of a longer history of meta-modeling and auto-theorization. What sets *Re:Creators* apart, however, and makes it a unique work worthy of our critical attention, is its focus on the crucial intersection between media mix planning, franchise management, and government control, an intersection of topics that will only require more attention as the Japanese government plays an increasingly large role in the distribution (and perhaps in the near future, the production) of media mix properties.

Notes

1 I thank Victoria Berndt for drawing my attention to *Pop Team Epic*, about which she is writing. I also thank Jacqueline Ristola for her RA work in compiling a list of self-referential and/or managerial manga and anime.
2 For the sake of expediency, I will use the terms transmedia and media mix interchangeably here. Elsewhere I have argued for the importance of separating these terms and their histories (2012a; 2015). In particular, while transmedia assumes a relation to storytelling (its most common formulation being *transmedia storytelling*), the media mix need not be narrative.
3 This section draws on my earlier work in *Anime's Media Mix* (2012a) and particularly from "Condensing the Media Mix" (2012b).

Works cited

Azuma, H. (2009). *Otaku: Japan's database animals*. Minneapolis: University of Minnesota Press.

Azuma, H. (2014). *General will 2.0: Rousseau, freud, Google*, translated by J. Person. New York: Vertical.

Beyes, T., Conrad, L., & Martin, R. (2019). *Organize*. Minneapolis: University of Minnesota Press.

Boltanski, L., & Chiapello, E. (2005). *The new spirit of capitalism*. London: Verso.

Boluk, S., & LeMieux, P. (2017). *Metagaming: Playing, competing, spectating, cheating, trading, making, and breaking videogames* (Vol. 53). Minneapolis: University of Minnesota Press.

Caldwell, J. T. (2008). *Production culture: Industrial reflexivity and critical practice in film and television*. Durham: Duke University Press.

Cho, M. (2017). Domestic *Hallyu*: K-Pop metatexts and the media's self-reflexive gesture. *International Journal of Communication, 11*, 2308–2331.

Choo, K. (2012). Nationalizing 'cool': Japan's global promotion of the content industry. In N. Otmazgin & E. Ben-Ari (Eds.), *Popular culture and the state in East and Southeast Asia* (pp. 85–105). London: Routledge.

Condry, I. (2013). *The soul of anime: Collaborative creativity and Japan's media success story*. Durham: Duke University Press.

Deleuze, G. (1993). *The fold: Leibniz and the Baroque*. Translated by Tom Conley. Minneapolis: University of Minnesota Press.

Denison, R. (2015). *Anime: A critical introduction*. London: Bloomsbury Publishing.

Denison, R. (2016). Franchising and film in Japan: Transmedia production and the changing roles of film in contemporary Japanese media Cultures. *Cinema Journal, 55*(2), 67–88. doi:10.1353/cj.2016.0006

Drucker, P. F. (1974). *Management: Tasks, responsibilities, practices*. New York: Harper & Row.

Ekens, G. (2019). The real anime inspirations behind the creations of *Re:Creators*. Retrieved from https://www.animenewsnetwork.com/feature/2017-07-28/the-real-anime-inspirations-behind-the-creations-of-re-creators/.119444 (July 28, 2017) (Consulted on March 2019)

Furuhata, Y. (2014). Multimedia environments and security operations: Expo '70 as a laboratory of governance. *Grey Room, 54*, 56–79.

Furuhata, Y. (2017). Architecture as atmospheric media. *Media Theory in Japan*, 52–79. doi:10.1215/9780822373292-003

Gerow, A. (2010). Kind participation: Postmodern consumption and capital with Japan's Telop TV. In M. Yoshimoto, et al. (Eds.), *Television, Japan, and Globalization* (pp. 117–150). Ann Arbor: Center for Japanese Studies, the University of Michigan.

Golumbia, D. (2009). *The cultural logic of computation*. Cambridge: Harvard University Press.

Gray, J. (2010). *Show sold separately*. New York: New York University Press.

Gregg, M. (2018). *Counterproductive: Time management in the knowledge economy*. Durham: Duke University Press.

Hamano, S. (2008). *Ākitekucha no seitaikei: Jō kankyo wa ikani sekkei sarete kita ka* (Ecosystems of architecture: How do information environments come to be planned?). Tokyo: NTT Shuppan.

Hartzheim, B. H. (2019). Making of a mangaka: Industrial reflexivity and Shueisha's weekly Shônen jump. *Television & New Media*, 1–18. https://doi.org/10.1177/1527476419872132

Hernández, Á. (2018, 08). The anime industry, networks of participation, and environments for the management of content in Japan. *Arts, 7*(3), 42. doi:10.3390/arts7030042

Iwasaki, N. (2009). *Moshi koko yakyu no joshi maneja ga dorakka no inobeshon to kigyoka seishin o yondara*. Tokyo: Daiyamondosha.

Jenkins, H. (2006). *Convergence culture: Where old and new media collide*. New York: New York University Press.

Jin, D. Y. (2017). *Digital platforms, imperialism and political culture*. New York: Routledge.

Johnson, D. (2013). Polyphonic/pseudo-synchronic: Animated writing in the comment feed of nicovideo. *Japanese Studies, 33*(3), 297–313.

Johnson, D., Kompare, D., & Santo, A., eds (2014). *Making media work: Cultures of management in the entertainment industries*. New York: New York University Press.

Kawasaki, T., & Iikura, Y. (2009). Ranobe kyara wa tajû sakuhin sekai no yume o miru ka? (Do light novel characters dream of a world of multiple works?). In I. Hirotaka & K. Yoriko (Eds.), *Raito noberu kenkyû josetsu* (pp. 18–32). Tokyo: Seikyusha.

Kiechel, W. (2010). *The lords of strategy: The secret intellectual history of the new corporate world*. Boston: Harvard Business Press.

Kitada, A. (2005). *Warau nihon no "nashonarizumu"*. (Japan's sneering 'nationalism'). Tōkyō: NHK Books.

Kitada, A. (2012). Japan's cynical nationalism. In M. Ito, D. Okabe, & I. Tsuji (Eds.), *Fandom unbound: Otaku culture in a connected world* (pp. 68–84). New Haven: Yale University Press.

Komori, K. (2009). Monodorogii kara mita Maijō Ōtarō (Maijō Ōtarō seen from the perspective of monadology). In G. shōsetsu kenkyūkai (Ed.), *Shakai wa sonzai shinai: Sekai-kei bunkaron* (pp. 197–218). Tokyo: Nan'undo.

Lamarre, T. (2018). *The anime ecology: A genealogy of television, animation, and game media*. Minneapolis: University of Minnesota Press.

Leblanc, D. (2018). *The only game in town: Simulators and the circuits of capitalism* (MA Thesis, Concordia University).

Leibniz, G. W. (1991). In *The monadology: An edition for students*, Nicholas Rescher (Ed.) & Trans.) London: Routledge.

Lewis, D. W. (2018, 01). Shiage and women's flexible labor in the Japanese animation industry. *Feminist Media Histories*, 4(1), 115–141. doi:10.1525/fmh.2018.4.1.115

Lotz, A. (2014). Building theories of creative industry managers. In D. Johnson, D. Kompare, & A. Santo (Eds.), *Making media work: Cultures of management in the entertainment industries* (pp. 25–38). New York: New York University Press.

Li, J. (2017). The interface affect of a contact zone: Danmaku on video-streaming platforms. *Asiascape: Digital Asia*, 4(3), 233–256.

Liu, L. H. (2010). The cybernetic unconscious: Rethinking Lacan, Poe, and french theory. *Critical Inquiry*, 36(2), 288–320.

Looser, T. (2017). Media, mediation, and crisis. *Media theory in Japan*, 347–367. doi:10.1215/9780822373292-015

Micklethwait, J., & Wooldridge, A. (1996). *The witch doctors: Making sense of the management gurus*. New York: Random House.

Misono, R. (2017). Critical media imagination: Nancy Seki's TV criticism and the media space of the 1980s and 1990s. In M. Steinberg & A. Zahlten (Eds.), *Media theory in Japan* (pp. 221–249). Durham: Duke University Press. doi:10.1215/9780822373292-003

Okeda, D., & Koike, A. (2011). Working conditions of animators: The real face of the Japanese animation industry. *Creative Industries Journal*, 3(3), 261–271.

Ōtsuka, E. (2010). World and variation: The reproduction and consumption of narrative. *Mechademia*, 5, 99–116.

Ōtsuka, E. (2014). *Japan becomes 'media-mix (media mikkusu-ka suru nihon)*. Tokyo: Īsuto shinsho.

Ōtsuka, E. (2018). *Taishō yokusankai no media mikkusu: "Yokusan ikka" to sanka suru fashizumu* (The media mix of the imperial rule assistance association: The "Yokusan ikka" and participatory fascism). Tokyo: Heibonsha.

Raine, E. (2011). The sacrificial economy of cuteness in Tamala 2010: A punk cat in space. *Mechademia*, 6(1), 193–209.

Seaton, P., & Yamamura, T. (2015, January). Japanese popular culture and contents tourism–Introduction. *Japan Forum*, 27(1), 1–11. Routledge.

Steinberg, M. (2012a). *Anime's media mix: Franchising toys and characters in Japan*. Minneapolis: University of Minnesota Press.

Steinberg, M. (2012b). Condensing the media mix: Multiple possible worlds in The Tatami Galaxy. *Canadian Journal of Film Studies*, 21(2), 71–92.

Steinberg, M. (2015). 8-Bit Manga: Kadokawa's Madara, or, the Gameic media mix. *Kinephanos: Journal of Media Studies and Popular Culture*, 5, 40–52.

Steinberg, M. (2017a). Platform producer meets game master. In M. Boni (Eds.), *World building transmedia, fans, industries* (p. 143). Amsterdam: Amsterdam University Press.

Steinberg, M. (2017b). Converging contents and platforms: Niconico video and Japan's media mix ecology. In J. Neves & B. Sakar (Eds.), *Asian video cultures* (pp. 91–112). Durham and London: Duke University Press.

Steinberg, M. (2019). *The platform economy: How Japan transformed the consumer Internet*. Minneapolis: University of Minnesota Press.

Steinberg, M., & Zahlten, A. (2017). Introduction. In M. Steinberg, & A. Zahlten (Eds.), *Media theory in Japan* (pp. 1–29). Durham: Duke University Press.

Suan, S. (2018, 07). Consuming production: Anime's layers of transnationality and dispersal of agency as seen in Shirobako and Sakuga-Fan practices. *Arts*, 7(3), 27. doi:10.3390/arts7030027

Sugawa-Shimada, A. (2018, 03). Playing with militarism in/with Arpeggio and Kantai collection: Effects of shōjo images in war-related contents tourism in Japan. *Journal of War & Culture Studies*, 12(1), 53–66. doi:10.1080/1752627 2.2018.1427014

Tanaka, E. (2009). Industrial structure of 'Japan Cool': Co-existence of media-mix and diversity of contents by production commission systems in Japan (Kūrujapan no sangyō kōzō: seisaku iinkai hōshiki ni yoru mediamikkusu to tayō-sei no heison). *Journal of the Japan Association for Social and Economic System Studies*, 30, 45–52 (in Japanese).

Wakabayashi, N., Yamada, J., & Yamashita, M. (2014). The power of Japanese film production consortia: The evolution of inter-firm alliance networks and the revival of the Japanese film industry. In R. DeFillippi, & P. Wikstrom (Eds.), *International perspectives on business innovation and disruption in the creative industries: Film, video and photography* (pp. 50–65). Cheltenham: Edward Elgar Publishing.

Zahlten, A. (2017). 1980s Nyū Aka: (Non)Media theory as romantic performance. In Steinberg, M., & Zahlten, A. (Eds.), *Media theory in Japan* (pp. 173–200). Durham: Duke University Press.

11 *Yōkai* monsters at large
Mizuki Shigeru's manga, transmedia practices, and (lack of) cultural politics

Shige (CJ) Suzuki[1]

The specters of *yōkai* are haunting Japan

This article investigates the ubiquity of *yōkai* in postwar and present-day Japanese mediascapes. In Japan, *yōkai* are largely understood as preternatural creatures found in ancient folklore and legends, often translated in English as "monsters," "spirits," "goblins," "specters," "shape-shifters," and the like.[2] They are routinely compared with spirits of the natural world, similar to the fairies of England and the kachina of the Pueblo, but not ghosts (Alt, 2015). In contemporary Japan, one encounters *yōkai* as characters not only in popular manga, anime, or video game titles but also in other media forms such as toys, magazines, TV commercials, advertisement posters, and other character-themed merchandise. They are also embodied as statues on streets in cities all over Japan.[3] Although the Japanese public seems to embrace *yōkai* characters, it would be reductionistic to ascribe this to Japan's Shinto-inspired animistic beliefs. Such a view would invite an Orientalist frame from outside and cultural nationalism from within, both of which we want to avoid. Instead, the proliferation of *yōkai* in present Japan is rather, I would argue, a product of previous and ongoing practices of the cross-media adaptations and transmedia storytelling called "media mix," or something analogous to what Henry Jenkins (2006) has called "media convergence."

Jenkins' (2006) concept of "media convergence" has multiple meanings, but one of its more focused ideas is that it encompasses, according to him, "the flow of content across multiple media platforms, the cooperation between multiple media industries, and the migratory behavior of media audiences who would go almost anywhere in search of the kinds of entertainment experiences they want" (Jenkins, 2006, p. 2). In this statement, Jenkins refers to two major actors who play an important role in forming this new media culture: corporations and fans. At variance with this, the Japanese-coined term "media mix" originally referred more to a type of corporate market strategy, for the term itself has been informed and popularized by the Japanese media company Kadokawa and other media corporations since the late 1970s, although similar media franchises and market strategies existed much earlier. The term "media mix" has been also used in English language academia when discussing contemporary Japanese media culture or popular material culture (Allison, 2006; M. Itō, 2005; Steinberg, 2012) in more nuanced ways. In this article, I will use "media mix" in a way almost equivalent to Jenkins' concept of "media convergence," primarily because the article's focus is on *yōkai* and Japanese media contexts; however, I offer further clarification of the term whenever necessary to address certain aspects of Japan's media mix, or to compare it with an English-language concept of media convergence.

Perhaps one of the most utilized *yōkai* "source materials" in Japan's media mix is the array of *yōkai* characters depicted in manga by Mizuki Shigeru (1922–2015). Mizuki is one of the most well-known manga creators in the modern history of manga. From the 1950s, he produced several manga titles featuring *yōkai* characters, most famously *GeGeGe no Kitarō*, which was recently translated into English as the *Kitarō* series (2013–2016). Since the 1960s, the *Kitarō* series has been repeatedly serialized, reprinted in book format, and adapted into TV anime series and other media forms, strongly associating the name of Mizuki with *yōkai* monsters.

This article engages in a discussion of *yōkai* manga characters in Mizuki Shigeru's manga and their transmedia expansion, not as an expression of Japanese cultural tradition, but as an outcome of previous and ongoing transmedia practices by media companies and other social agents. Whereas media scholars and cultural critics such as Marc Steinberg and Ōtsuka Eiji have discussed and conceptualized Japan's "media mix" as business and marketing strategies (Ōtsuka, 2014; Steinberg, 2012), this study focuses on another aspect of transmedia adaptions and/or storytelling that is not fully addressed in previous scholarship; that is, the transmedia migratory potential of the media-specific form of manga—especially the specific style of character design employed in mainstream manga that is well-suited to transmedia versatility—and the problems that result from current corporate-led media mix practices. This article argues that recent Japanese transmedia practices are propelled by the iconic drawing style used for manga characters and the character-centric multimedia production scheme, which makes manga(-originated) characters—including Mizuki's *yōkai* characters—versatile with regard to moving across different media platforms. Although transmedia practices can enhance the potential for generating synergies among previously discrete cultural industries and, in the case of media companies, for attaining more profits, such a close relationship undermines the autonomy of each media industry and/or company, which can in turn attenuate any social critique or cultural politics previously exercised through storytelling in manga, including Mizuki's works. By analyzing the transmedia practices that have used Mizuki's *yōkai* manga as "original" sources, this article addresses what has been gained as well as what has been lost when *yōkai* are migrated into different media platforms.

The media mix of *Yōkai*

The proliferation of *yōkai* characters from Mizuki's manga titles in the Japanese mediascape has reached an extent that, for many Japanese, it is difficult to recall images of *yōkai* without visualizing Mizuki's *yōkai* drawings.[4] Such a strong visual connection has been shaped not only by his serialized *yōkai* manga published and republished in magazines and book formats over the past several decades, but also by continual adaptations of his manga into anime series. The first anime series based on Mizuki's *yōkai* manga was broadcast in 1968. Historically speaking, the swift economic recovery and subsequent rise of a middle class led to exponential growth in homes with black-and-white TV sets after the technology's introduction in 1953, and by the time this anime appeared in the late 1960s, there was an explosion in color set ownership. Along with Mizuki's *yōkai* manga, this anime series brought about the first so-called "*yōkai* boom" in postwar popular culture.[5] Since then, anime series based on *GeGeGe no Kitarō* have been produced and broadcast in every decade to date. The newest iteration, *GeGeGe no Kitarō* (sixth series), was broadcast in 2018. Constant transmedia adaptations over the past five decades from manga to anime have prompted republications of Mizuki's manga, with new episodes and stories added. Mizuki himself has become sort of a media celebrity; *GeGeGe no Nyōbō*, the TV dramatization of Mizuki's wife's life with him (including fantasy moments with his characters) that aired over six months in 2010 and became one of the highest rated programs of that year, contributed to the revival and a new generation of interest in his *yōkai* manga. These reiterations have generated readers and audiences for Mizuki's *yōkai* stories and characters across different generations while creating a shared world in which consumers and audiences—both parents and children—can interact and converse through popular cultural media iterations of Mizuki's *yōkai*.

The transmedia migration of Mizuki's *yōkai* characters has expanded beyond typical media platforms as well. Mizuki's *yōkai* characters have also been used in the character merchandizing business, turning them into toys, plastic dolls, cellphone cases, advertisement posters, collectables, video-game characters, designs for other everyday objects like beverage and food product packaging, and even statues lining streets. The physical manifestation of Mizuki's *yōkai* characters—what media scholars Scott Lash and Celia Lury (2007) call the "thingification of media"—in these physical objects, no longer limited to manga pages or TV screens, has transformed everyday objects and their mundane environments into multiple points of entry into the transmedia(ted) world of Mizuki's *yōkai* manga and his *yōkai* world. This in turn gives fans and consumers a sense of intimacy with his *yōkai* characters. The affective nature of *yōkai* has been intensified by these and similar media mix practices, which have simultaneously created a synergy that serves increased financial gains for media corporations.

There's no doubt that Mizuki's *yōkai* manga function as urtexts for the contemporary derivative transmedia works and products, but it should be noted that Mizuki's *yōkai* manga characters are, in fact, a result of recurrent, historical *yōkai* transmedia adaptation practices. Although *yōkai* can be traced back to ancient folkloric beliefs and oral stories that existed in different parts of Japan, Mizuki's *yōkai* manga are "influenced by *yōkai* imagery created in the Edo to Meiji periods" (Papp, 2010, p. 2). Among them, Toriyama Sekien (born Sano Toyofusa, 1712–1788), an Edo period painter and illustrator, in particular has had a considerable impact on depictions of *yōkai* by postwar war manga creators, including Mizuki.[6] Sekien was one of the first artists to popularize *yōkai* monsters by visually rendering the imaginative world of *yōkai* in illustrations and publishing them in a bound book format. Unlike prior (often colorful) *yōkai* paintings (*yōkai-ga*), Sekien's visual rendering of *yōkai* focuses on the visual figuration of individual *yōkai*, drawn in simplified black-and-white illustrations with no or minimal explanatory text. Sekien's first book, *The Illustrated Demon Horde's Night Parade* (*Gazu Hyakki Yagyō*, 1776), became popular and spawned three sequels, in which he even added his own *yōkai* and spirit creations. It was in the late Edo period—also called the "early modern" (*kinsei*) period in Japanese periodization—when society witnessed the rise of commercial culture with the advent of mass production and mass distribution, including book publication through woodcut print technology. Sekien's books were mass produced and circulated (sometimes through book-lending shops) among middle-class urban residents with varying degrees of literacy—the books were mainly illustrations. In this regard, Sekien's *yōkai* books emerged at a historical juncture in which local, folkloric tradition and (early) modern, urban technology encountered each other. It is important to note here that Sekien's illustrated *yōkai* books contributed much to the discursive shift in the status of *yōkai*. Previously, *yōkai* existed mostly in oral narratives; therefore, they were largely invisible, mysterious, and unknown, save for in medieval paintings or illustrated scrolls, where *yōkai* were often drawn as a group without names. In contrast to these precursors, Sekien's focus was not on narratives, but on pictorial images of individual *yōkai* compiled through a process of collecting, sorting, and labeling each *yōkai* being. In Sekien's books, *yōkai* became constantly visible, divorced from local storytelling traditions and contexts. Michael Dylan Foster describes Sekien's renderings as an "encyclopedic mode" which transformed *yōkai* into more accessible catalogues for readers. Foster (2009) states that Sekien "extract(ed) *yōkai* from a narrative context, transforming them into iconographic entities" (p. 169).

In her discussion of *yōkai* characters in contemporary anime and manga, Deborah Shamoon (2013) claims that Mizuki's *yōkai* manga are part of the tradition of *yōkai* visualization, produced in the "continuation of the encyclopedic mode since the Edo period" (p. 281). Using Japanese critic Azuma Hiroki's postmodern theory that understands *otaku* as "database animals,"

Shamoon (2013) argues that *yōkai* characters, presented in the encyclopedic mode, are structurally similar to the *otaku*'s postmodern consumption
of information (pp. 277–278) in that they are not concerned with "grand
narratives," a typical postmodern condition, à la Jean-François Lyotard.
Individual *yōkai* compiled into encyclopedic compendia (or "databases,"
in the contemporary vernacular) have been available for modern authors,
audiences, and other users for either their own transmedia(ted) storytelling and/or pleasurable consumption. Indeed, popular culture scholar Zília
Papp traces the genealogy of *yōkai* figurations in contemporary anime and
manga and identifies the visual and formal similarities between them with
those of the Edo period or earlier visual culture. Papp (2010) points out that
several *yōkai* characters and drawings in Mizuki's manga titles are visually
similar to—and almost direct copies of—the ones in Sekien's books.[7] Given
the status of the discursive formation of *yōkai* in the modern and postwar
periods—in the encyclopedic or database mode—Mizuki's manga can be
considered a transmedia adaptation from preexisting databases of *yōkai*
figures from the Edo period into manga, a popular medium that is viable as
a commercial force as well as a vehicle for narrative expression in the postwar period. After all, *yōkai* in the encyclopedic mode from the Edo period
existed before the idea of copyright and are available to modern authors
without restrictions for use in their creations. Yet it should be noted that
Mizuki's contributions to the *yōkai* discourse served to renarrativize *yōkai*
figures by placing them in modern, postwar settings in his story manga
(narrative comics), and even by adding his own invented *yōkai* characters
(just as Sekien did). In short, Mizuki's *yōkai* manga can be seen as transmedia storytelling in the longer tradition of transmedia adaptations and
intertextuality.[8]

Character-centric media mix

In his book *Anime's Media Mix,* Marc Steinberg (2015) contrasts American transmedia practices with Japanese media mix by highlighting this
distinctive difference: Whereas the American transmedia strategy has
gravitated toward sustaining a unified worldview across different media
platforms, Japanese media mix is centered around characters, allowing
them to exist in different, transmedia(ted) worlds, even those containing
narrative contradictions among derivate narratives or worlds (Steinberg,
2015, p. 334). Although this view might be a sweeping generalization, it
has been observed that recent Japanese media mix franchises are centered
on characters, not storytelling (Condry, 2018, para. 5). Based on his eth-
nographic research on the contemporary anime industry, cultural anthro-
pologist Ian Condry (2013) argues that in the current anime production
system, character building is far more important than storytelling or world
building (p. 56). Previously, animated film production began with a script
or overall planning, but Condry documents and analyzes the present anime

industry, especially the "production committee" (*seisaku iinkai*) system, a joint venture by multiple different companies and stakeholders (such as music companies, TV broadcast companies, publishers, toy companies, and advertisement agencies), that often begins with character building.[9] Since the decline of the studio system in the Japanese film industry, many cinematic and TV anime have been planned, backed, and made through the production committee system to share costs and reduce the financial risk of any single agent. This is also due in large part to the fact that a single anime studio company often cannot expect full compensation for a work's production costs merely by selling broadcast rights; instead, a studio works with other companies. Thereby, they rely on and resort to character merchandizing and other transmedia-derivative products in different industries—Jenkins' (2006) sense of convergence. Although this kind of marketing scheme is not specifically unique to Japan, it is important, in recent anime production, for the production committee to carefully craft the appeal of characters first—assigning a sort of brand image to them—while narrative elements and the fictional world are scripted and developed afterward. This character-centric mode of production enables more potential for cross-media adaptations because each character has its own autonomous status (*jiritsu-sei*) that can be easily divorced from a narrative world and moved to other media platforms. In regard to the Japanese media mix, Condry (2013) argues that "rather than transmedia storytelling, we witness a kind of transmedia *character* telling" (p. 57).

Both Steinberg and Condry discuss the Japanese media mix by focusing on the medium of anime and anime production (Condry & Steinberg, 2013). Yet I would like to pay attention to manga and its media specificity: the hand-drawn nature of manga and characters drawn in a cartoony way. This is partly because manga as a medium seems to still play a central role in the current form of media mix more than anime.[10] In his discussion on manga characters, Japanese manga critic Itō Gō proposes the concept of *kyara*, separating it from a typical sense of character or "round character," in E. M. Forster's classification on characters in novels (Forster, 1985). According to Itō, *kyara* is something ontologically prior to character—a sort of "proto-character"—which gives a "sense of existence" and a "sense of life." For Itō (2006), *kyara* (i.e., proto-characters) are shaped by visual images, whereas characters are "shaped by narrative action" (p. 107). Media studies scholar Thomas LaMarre (2011) comments on Itō's theory of *kyara* by saying that "the pared-down design of *kyara* allows it not only to move across different narrative worlds, but also to generate new worlds wherever its users see fit" (p. 129). Though manga as a media form can have diverse styles and forms, both Itō and LaMarre seem to identify the power of manga characters for transmedia migrations in manga's cartoony character design. Japanese critic Odagiri Hiroshi more carefully interprets this discussion of Itō, and devises a triad scheme of analyzing character in visual media (manga, anime, and video games, etc.). According to him, a character has a combination of three elements: meaning, interiority (*naimen*), and icon/image (Odagiri, 2010, p. 119). If a character is dominantly defined by meaning, it is a flat character; if a character is defined by interiority (or the conscious self), it can be a round character.[11] If character is defined by image, it is what Itō calls *kyara*. To put it plainly, *kyara* is an iconic image drawn in a simplified form, whereas a character is defined by narrative and a sense of selfhood (interiority of a character). Itō's concept of *kyara* points to the force of iconic character design that appeals to those who can identify it without any context or narrative background. In other words, the transmedia migratory capability and versatility of manga-originated characters—including Mizuki's *yōkai* characters—derive from their cartoony iconicity.[12] Unlike a photo-realistic character with distinctive visual details, an iconic, often caricature-derived, cartoony style of character allows itself to be identified as the "same" character, regardless of each individual (nuanced) visual difference—insofar as it carries specific identifiable iconic resemblance—even when adapted into different media platforms.[13] Although not limited to Japanese manga character design,[14] this iconic, cartoony drawing style can be most readily observed in postwar mainstream story manga, possibly due to the intense labor typically required in producing the same main characters repeatedly in manga pages while completing each serial installment within a relatively short period of time. While drawing manga, a cartoonist has to draw, by hand, the same protagonist repeatedly in different panels and pages throughout the story, and each image may have slight differences (i.e., postures, angles, facial expressions, etc.), but the visual resemblance of each drawn image—the iconic elements of the character drawing—guarantees the recognition of the character's identity. Also, American comics artist/critic Scott McCloud (1994) argues that, in contrast to naturalistic drawing, greater abstraction in character drawing invites cognitive and affective investment from readers (p. 36). Iconic, hand-drawn character design in the form of manga is the key—or at least, one of the keys—to understanding the character-centric media mix. In short, the autonomy of *kyara* with its cross-media, expansive capabilities emerge from the cartoony iconicity that has been practiced by mainstream manga authors, which escapes from being bound to narratives or specific media platforms.[15]

Contents tourism and cultural politics

A recent development of the Japanese media mix surrounding *yōkai* involves local governments and communities as important actors—no longer limited to the private sector. As many villages and towns in rural Japan have suffered declines in their economies and populations since around the 1970s, several municipalities, in cooperation with local chambers of commerce, have initiated "village-revival" or "town-revival" movements, known as *mura okoshi* and *machi okoshi*. These local revitalization movements were initially developed to support local businesses, industries, and communities to maintain or increase population through the promotion of local products, traditional festivals, and performances for domestic and international tourists. Since the 1990s, however, several local governments have begun to use anime and manga characters and settings to promote local tourism. In 1993, the municipal office in the small town of Sakaiminato, Tottori Prefecture, created a tourist attraction called "Mizuki Shigeru Road," where more than 100 bronze statues of Mizuki's *yōkai* characters stand, lining the sidewalk of the main street from the train station through to the township center. Using the fame of Mizuki Shigeru—who spent his childhood there—the municipality has attempted to promote tourism in the town, even targeting foreign tourists by creating a tourist website in English, Chinese (both Traditional and Simplified), Korean, and Russian. In 2003, the Mizuki Shigeru Memorial Museum was built, followed by the construction of a Yōkai Shrine, along with a constant stream of planned *yōkai*-themed festivals, exhibits, and other events. Large images of Mizuki's *yōkai* were used to decorate local trains and busses, and *yōkai*-themed souvenirs and products are sold at vendors and shops on the main streets of the town. Sakaiminato's campaign was recognized as a "successful case" of town-revival movement through its leveraging of Mizuki's *yōkai* characters to steadily increase local tourism while regentrifying and populating previously deserted streets and local stores in the town (Sawada, 2009). In 2005, the national government reported that Sakaiminato's case was an ideal model for what they called "contents tourism,"[16] and encouraged other municipalities and local governments also facing socioeconomic decline to follow suit.

Since then, the term "contents tourism" has attracted considerable attention from Japanese mass media outlets, local officials, media companies, and even academics. Similar to the English-language counterpart of film-induced tourism or media-induced tourism, Japanese contents tourism is driven by popular media, especially manga, anime, TV dramas, and games (Seaton & Yamamura, 2015). In this type of tourism, manga/anime fans visit the locales depicted in their favorite manga or anime. One well-known example is the Washimiya district of Kuki City in Saitama Prefecture. The town was used as the setting for the anime series *Lucky Star,* broadcast in 2007. The anime's opening sequence features a shrine based on the real-life Washinomiya Shrine. Fans *of Lucky Star* suddenly flocked to Washimiya to visit the shrine, take photos, and explore. The activity of visiting a place modeled or featured in anime or manga is now called *seichi junrei,* meaning "pilgrimage to a sacred site."[17] This media-hyped fandom activity has become prominent since the case of *Lucky Star,* and similar "pilgrimages to sacred sites" (para. 6) have taken place all over Japan. In 2017, the Japan Anime Tourism Association, supported by the Kadokawa Corporation and others, announced a list of 88 sacred anime sites located all over Japan (Nagata, 2017). Local communities have responded to fans' expectations by media mixing local products with images and characters from manga and anime. The main streets of the Washimiya district, for instance, are full of manga/anime-themed products, cafés, souvenirs, flags, and posters. Tourism studies scholar Takayoshi Yamamura (2014) describes Washimiya as a successful example of contents tourism due to the "collaboration between the local community, the fans, and the copyright holders" (p. 64). Contents tourism is viewed as another expression of media mix, involving the public sector and local communities.

While contents tourism has the potential to boost the economic well-being of local businesses and communities, problems and concerns have emerged when a local community faces a sudden influx of fans roaming through their township. Also known as "*otaku* tourism" (Alexander, 2017), local governments and commerce associations have become aware of the need to appeal to young (or adult) male *otaku* fans of anime and manga, sometimes opting for risqué images and designs of anime/manga characters in their media mix collaborations. In 2014, the city of Shima, in Mie Prefecture, announced the anime *moe* (adorable/cutie) character Aoshima Megu as the official mascot for the city.[18] The idea for this character was taken from the local traditional seafood industry, which uses "sea women" (*ama*) who dive, in time-honored fashion, without the aid of modern scuba gear, and for whom the region is well known. Yet the character they announced was a 17-year-old, long-haired, anime-like diver with overemphasized, large breasts. The sexually suggestive character swiftly caused controversy, and more than 100 professional female divers criticized the character design, demanding the withdrawal of the character (Osaki, 2015b).[19] In 2013, the popular anime series *Silver Spoon* (based on the serialized manga of the same title) was broadcast. The series depicted a real-world agricultural facility in Hokkaido. Fearing an intrusion of fans into the facility that could potentially spread diseases among livestock animals, the production company inserted a message in the closing credits requesting that viewers refrain from visiting the facility and the vicinity. These cases reveal some of the unexpected and—at times—unwanted results, as well as the chasm between what some local communities originally intended and what the media mix actually brought to them.

All in all, contents tourism as a tool of the media-mixed local revitalization movement has delivered varied results. It is, moreover, important to also consider what kinds of power relationships are at work in this media-mixed cultural activity called contents tourism. It is apparent that local communities attempt to capitalize on the enthusiasm of manga and anime fans, but in doing so, they fashion themselves after images mediated through manga or anime. Anime and manga fans, on the other hand, driven by the narrative of anime or manga, come to these "sacred sites" with preconceived notions about the local towns or places. Encounters and interactions between local residents and visiting fans are structurally similar to those that take place in the "contact zone." Scholar Mary Louise Pratt (1992) uses the term "contact zone" to refer to "social spaces where disparate cultures meet, clash, and grapple with each other, often in highly asymmetrical relations of domination and subordination" (p. 4). Although contents tourism does not take place in colonial spaces (which is Pratt's concern), similarly uneven power relationships are at work between localities and the media industry with its accompanying consumers. In the case of contents tourism, power is assigned and owned more on the side of media companies and industries— after all, it is a media event—not on the side of the locality. In other words, a local community transforms itself into satisfying images for tourists from outside, not the other way around. The encounters in this "contact zone" seem to share a common problem with modern tourism. Yet the level of simulation is intensified by the media mix, as it generates a novel type of "virtual reality" or "augmented reality" tourism. Although visitors can explore and enjoy a series of simulacra, with media-mixed images superimposed onto local places, residents live dual lives: a self-exoticized, simulated life and a quotidian one. This kind of consumption, exemplified in contents tourism, is what Japanese critic Azuma Hiroki (2009) calls "database consumption" (p. 54), a mode of consumption in which *otaku*—as postmodern animals—are concerned with small narratives or appealing details. Fans have little interest in local history or reality—and if they are at all, it is of secondary importance to them—and come to a local town or place solely to confirm what they are already familiar with through anime or manga, or to look for *moe* characters deployed in the media mix of local scenery and products. In the case of contents tourism based on Mizuki's *yōkai* in Sakaiminato, the local government and business owners have retroactively exploited the popularity of Mizuki's *yōkai* and local ties for the propagation of the simulated image of locality, rather than locality as it is.[20] In such a simulated space, *yōkai* are commodified, standing by the roadside only to entertain visitors without unsettling or intervening in their preconceived ideas of the locality or *yōkai*.

Absence of narrative

Although the abundance of transmedia-derivative products of manga-originated characters testifies to their adaptability across different media platforms, it should be noted that there are a few of more problems and even dangers in the current form of Japanese media mix. First, the convergence of different media platforms ensures a closer relationship or even interdependency among different media industries, as the "production committee" system exemplifies. In the Japanese media mix, such a convergence of different media industries can undermine the autonomy of each different company, industry, or other social agents, resulting in the conscious avoidance of controversial issues. More specifically, whereas print publishers, including manga publishers, have traditionally functioned as an outlet for diverse and even alternative voices in contrast to mainstream media or those who are in power, large media corporations such as TV broadcast stations and radio, both of which have to be licensed by the state, often hesitate to deal with certain controversial issues—for instance, the post-Fukushima disaster situation (Suzuki, 2016). Second, as discussed above, current corporate-led media-mix strategies tend to reduce or disregard narrativity by prioritizing characters, instead producing their characters as nonnarrative media forms (i.e., illustrations or designs) or commodities (i.e., character merchandise). Such an orientation in the current media-mix approach (to manga-originated characters) can undercut or attenuate social critique or political edge that would previously have been exercised in the narratives of manga, not characters.

As previously mentioned, *yōkai* originated from ancient, folkloric beliefs that were shared within a community through oral storytelling. This oral and communal nature of *yōkai* storytelling possessed social functions that conveyed collective wisdom, social order, or cultural values, including morality, life lessons, and forewarnings about possible individual and social dangers, with strong psychological appeals and impacts.[21] Mizuki's story manga retains—or, more correctly, reactivates—this rich narrative potential in the popular medium of manga in the postwar context. Mizuki's (2012) autobiographical manga *NonNonBā*, for instance, narrates Mizuki's upbringing in a rural town in Tottori and his interaction with an elderly woman named "NonNonBa" who tells *yōkai* stories to a young Mizuki. The manga highlights the emotional impact of *yōkai*, emphasized by *NonNonBā*'s storytelling, showing that *yōkai* appear only when the young protagonist Mizuki (as a character) believe their existence—often guided by NonNonBa, an elderly *yōkai* storyteller. In the manga, *yōkai* are not always visible, as they appear only at specific times and places, unlike contemporary *yōkai* characters in the media mix. The manga depicts a *yōkai* named *Betobeto*, who only appears when a person is walking through dark mountains to warn of danger, and another named *Akaname*, who appears in the bathroom to offer life lessons to children about cleaning the places they use. Both of these also suggest a larger relationship among humans, nature, community, and the (otherworldly) world in Mizuki's deanthropocentric world (see Suzuki, 2011). Though taking *yōkai* images from Sekien's *yōkai* catalogue books, Mizuki never fails to assign social, cultural, and moral functions to his *yōkai* through storytelling in his manga.

Furthermore, in Mizuki's manga, *yōkai* often demonstrate a critique of industrial capitalism, human greed, and anthropocentrism as exemplified in otherworldly *yōkai* monsters. Mizuki's *Mammoth Flowers* (*Manmosu furawā*; 1968), for instance, depicts the titular, enormous *yōkai* monster as emerging from Tokyo's infamous landfill island, causing destruction to Tokyo. Set in a Japan in the midst of the postwar economic boom, this reflects the reality of when the manga was published, since the rapid economic rise also brought about enormous industrial and commercial waste that filled up landfills, polluting air and water. Japan experienced

unprecedented levels of pollution and other environmental problems, causing health issues and becoming a major social concern. At the end of the
story, the *yōkai* flower only disappears, undefeated, when the government
decides to change the goal of the country from achieving economic success
to guaranteeing the "right to maintain the minimum standards of whole-
some and cultured living," a phrase taken from Article 25 of the postwar
democratic Japanese Constitution. The inserted narration at the end of the
story explains the nature of this *yōkai*: "For the poor, it was a flower for
salvation; for the rich, it was a curse" (Mizuki, 1968, p. 62). In his edited
book *Monster Theory*, Jeffrey Jerome Cohen (1997) states that the "monster is born only at this metaphoric crossroads, as an embodiment of a
certain cultural moment—of a time, a feeling, and a place" (p. 4). Mizuki's
yōkai takes on this kind of monstrosity and "reveals" and "warns"—as the
etymology of monster (*monstrum*) suggests—of a possible danger or crisis
of human society or civilization.

   To be fair, Mizuki is also partially responsible for the current,
information-centric, consumptive mode of media mix. Along with *yōkai*
story manga, Mizuki has published several "encyclopedic books" about
yōkai. In Mizuki's career, the shift from *yōkai* narratives to *yōkai* characters
(or character merchandizing) can be observed when Mizuki's character Kitarō became visually attractive (*kawaii*) in the first TV series (1968–1969).
However, in Mizuki's earlier Kitarō manga—titled *Hakaba Kitarō* (*Grave-
yard Kitarō*), Kitarō was depicted as a ghastly figure associated with ugliness,
grotesqueness, and liminality.[22] In the first episode of the manga *Hakaba
Kitarō*, he was born from the grave of the last surviving member of a tribe
(called *yūrei-zoku*) that was marginalized and driven away by humans. Kitarō's birth scene depicts him as a baby with one eye missing. Adopted by a
human couple, he is marginalized in the human world. The narration says
about his condition as a child: "NOT HUMAN. UGLY FACE. OTHER
CHILDREN ARE REPULSED BY HIS APPEARANCE. THEY REFUSED
TO PLAY WITH HIM, AND HE IS ALWAYS ALONE" (Mizuki, 2016,
p. 49). The story ends when Kitarō, who feels no liberty in the human world,
embarks on a journey in search for a better place. In this first episode, Kitarō
is presented as a marginalized figure in an anthropocentric society, possibly
influenced by Mizuki's own experience of the war and postwar marginalization (disabled soldiers were marginalized as they were unwanted visible
reminders of the past war in the midst of the country's recovery). It is not
difficult to see a reflection of Mizuki himself (who had lost one arm in the
war) in the figuration of one-eyed, marginalized Kitarō. Yet, when adapted
for the TV series, Kitarō on the TV screen appears as a cool hero who fights
with good *yōkai* members against evil *yōkai* monsters. This shift of Kitarō
from a ghostly *yōkai* to a TV hero was not only aesthetic but also political,
as Mizuki's manga—in particular, the ones from his earlier period (from the
1950s to 1960s)—demonstrate the monstrosity and liminality of *yōkai* that
"warn" of the hubris of human civilization and critique the darker side of
industrial capitalism in the middle of Japan's economic advance.

To further consider the divorce of *yōkai* from the storytelling tradition, it is useful to consult Frankfurt School Marxist scholar and literary critic Walter Benjamin's distinction between information and storytelling. In "The Storyteller" (1936), one of his most well-known essays, Benjamin (2002) claims that the importance of storytelling is in its "ability to share experiences" in contrast to the information from new media—the "newspapers" in his age (p. 143). In contrast to the information that does not survive its moment, Benjamin values the importance of storytelling. In opposition to information, he states that "the story form is different. It does not expend itself. It preserves and concentrates its strength and is capable of releasing it even after a long time" (Benjamin, 2002, p. 148). Benjamin praises the craft of storytellers who are capable of reviving (or retaining the ideal form of) precapitalist "mouth-to-mouth" communication and the collective nature of sharing experiences through storytelling. It is perhaps not coincidental that Benjamin pays attention to the power of storytelling by ascribing it to folkloric collectivism (remember that this is where *yōkai* stories emerged, historically). For Benjamin, storytelling has a power to cogently retain wisdom produced, narrated, and shared by a community, whereas information is transient, individual, and quickly forgotten. Following Benjamin's distinction, Mizuki's story manga, I would argue, retains the collective wisdom and shared experiences of ordinary people through storytelling. On the other hand, the decontextualized and denarrativized *yōkai* "characters" in the current Japanese media mix make *yōkai* monsters into consumable, transient objects.

Conclusion: media mix and neoliberal society

As discussed above, the abundance of *yōkai* characters in the current Japanese mediascape is an outcome of both historical transmedia practices by modern manga authors and transmedia practices by the alliance of media companies and industries. Along with books about *yōkai*, the existence of *yōkai* compendia compiled in the encyclopedic/database mode have allowed modern authors, producers, and media companies to take advantage of *yōkai* characters as inspirational sources for creating new stories and/or to capitalize on them for transmedia business purposes. In addition, in the current media mix, one can hardly ignore manga's media-specific element: the iconic drawing of characters. This convention, required by the intense labor and economy of drawing, equips characters—including Mizuki's *yōkai* characters—with the versatility of transversal movement across different media platforms and everyday objects through character merchandizing and other transmedia adaptations. Although such media convergence has created a potential for substantial financial gain for corporations, it undermines the traditional nature of *yōkai* stories. The present-day Japanese media mix, which prioritizes character building over storytelling, diminishes the folkloric, collective, and critical nature of *yōkai* that was exercised in their narrative forms. On the other hand,

Mizuki's *yōkai* manga—in particular, those from his earlier period (from 1950s to 1960s)—still address the monstrosity and liminality of *yōkai* that retain the potential for conveying shared knowledge and critiques. Yet, just as we have seen in the case of contents tourism, it is hard to identify such a critical potential in *yōkai* in the current media-mix derivative products that are only owned, consumed, and forgotten without any narrative or critical traces in a neoliberal society. Jenkins' concept of "transmedia storytelling" has addressed the flow of content across multiple media platforms in an increasingly media-saturated environment, and also emphasized valuable contributions to our understanding of the world (Jenkins, 2006, pp. 154, 459). In view of the latter, Mizuki's *yōkai* story manga are an example of transmedia storytelling, while corporate-led media mix(ed) *yōkai* are merely a product of transmedia adaptations for consumption

Given this context, it is instructive to think about one of the recent "successes" of the media-mix project, the Yo-kai Watch franchise. This mixed-media franchise, modeled on the success of the Pokémon franchise, revolves around a plot in which the main character/player collects friendship medals with which the character/player can summon *yōkai*. In this plot, the majority of *yōkai* exist only to be collected and owned by the player. From the beginning, this project was planned as a media-mix project, starting with a manga serialization before selling a video game for Nintendo consoles (Pokémon was originally an RPG video game for a hand-held console). The success of the anime adaptation prompted an upsurge in the production of other media products, such as subsequent video games (Level-5 for Nintendo 3DS game console), toys (Bandai), and animated films (OLM, Inc.). The anime begins with the boy protagonist in a forest stumbling upon a capsule-toy vending machine, like the ones found in Japan's game arcades and shopping malls. Following a mysterious voice, the protagonist throws a 100-yen coin into the vending machine and encounters his first *yōkai* emerging from the capsule. The act of purchasing, depicted in the anime's first episode, simulates consumption and even conditions young audiences to become consumers, modeling how they are supposed to behave when they encounter capsule-toy vending machines in social reality. In a recent essay, Marc Steinberg (2017) discusses the "priming" strategy exemplified in the Yo-Kai Watch franchise that conditions the audience toward total consumption (p. 253). This is a sign of what Michael Sandel (2013) describes as a drift from a market economy to a "market society," where even people's civic lives—and their decisions and behaviors, as well—are penetrated by the logic of the neoliberal market, while social and communal morality declines. The Yo-Kai Watch media-mix disciplines kids in the direction of conforming to such a market society.

Last, as Jenkins' (2006) concept of media convergence also points to fans activities, there is still a possibility that new *yōkai* narratives—even socially and politically critical ones—might emerge from fans' derivative narrative works (possibly found in *dōjinshi*/fanzine activities). However, we would need another study to explore this potential.

Notes

1 This article was supported by the Academy of Korean Studies Grant (AKS-2018-C01). Notes on Japanese names: This article uses Japanese names in the Japanese convention—that is, a family name (surname) first, followed by a given name. If a Japanese person has written or is quoted in English language articles, I use the order of the names as they originally appear.

2 The term yōkai seems to resist a simple translation. Michael Dylan Foster (2009) notes that yōkai is "variously translated as monster, sprit, goblin, ghost, demon, phantom, specter, fantastic being, lower-order deity, or more amorphously, as any unexplainable experience or numinous occurrence" (p. 2).

3 Most famously, there is a street called "The Mizuki Shigeru Road" in the city of Sakaiminato, Tottori Prefecture, where more than 100 yōkai statues line the street, which will be discussed later in more detail. Also, in the city of Fuchū, in Tokyo Metropolis, has a street featuring yōkai characters from Mizuki's GeGeGe no Kitarō. A recent addition was in the city of Fukusaki, Hyogo where yōkai statues sit on benches for the entertainment of tourists and pedestrians.

4 Folklore Studies scholar Michael Dylan Foster (2009) confirms this by saying that "for almost anybody who grew up in postwar Japan, the word yōkai conjures up an image created by Mizuki Shigeru" (p. 164).

5 Along with Mizuki, Tezuka Osamu and other manga creators have published yōkai manga in the late 1960s. Some Japanese critics claim that Tezuka decided to create a manga series Dororo, featuring yōkai characters from a sense of rivalry of Mizuki's increasing popularity in the manga scene (Kurosawa, 2013).

6 Other writers and critics who have influenced Mizuki's yōkai imagination include writer/educator Inoue Enryō (1858–1919) and folklorist Yamagita Kunio (1875–1962).

7 This calls into question the authorship of Mizuki and is, therefore, related to another thread of postmodern discussion on the death of the author à la Roland Barthes.

8 I will discuss what kind of narratives Mizuki's yōkai manga convey in the Absence of Narrative section.

9 See more on this in Condry and Steinberg's (2013) conversation, "Media Mix Is Anime's Life Support System."

10 In her book review, sociologist Casey Brienza (2013) critically comments on Steinberg's Anime's Media Mix by stating that it misses the central role of manga. She notes, "Categories of print, particularly manga and increasingly light novels, are where so many media mixes originate and they, not their animated adaptations, remain, from a Japanese perspective, at the center" (para. 6).

11 The term "interiority" (naimen), used by Japanese critics, is inherited from Japanese literary scholar Karatani Kōjin's sense of the conscious self as a modern discovery. See "The Discovery of Interiority" in Katarani's Origins of Modern Japanese Literature (1993).

12 By "cartoony," I am following the distinction used in comics scholar Joseph Witek's (2012) essay. Although acknowledging a wide array of diverse styles in comics, Witek separates two modes: the cartoon and the naturalistic mode. Witek sets up a binary in drawing styles: iconic, minimalist, and cartoony versus realistic, literal, and representational (p. 42). In postwar mainstream story manga, Tezuka-inspired cartoony drawing has been influential in defining mainstream cartooning style—for example, a clear-lined, abstract drawing style for character design, exemplified by Astro Boy (Tetsuwan Atomu) or Doraemon.

13 In Japan, one can also find merchandise and products based on real-life figures, such as celebrities and tarento (media personalities), as well. Yet this kind of character, merchandise based on real-life figures has less transmedia migratory capabilities compared with fictional manga/anime characters.

14 Certainly, the iconic designing of characters is not unique or limited to Japanese comics. Some notable examples in American comics include comic-strip-originated Snoopy and Popeye. Still, compared with other realistically drawn characters, these characters share the cartoony drawing style with that employed by Japanese mainstream manga.

15 The historical fact that anime used to be called manga eiga (manga movie or manga film) before the 1970s suggests the centrality of the manga medium in transmedia adaptations—called "media mix" after the late 1970s—since Japanese animators tried to "animate" static manga image/icons initially.

16 Yamamura (2014) notes that the first public use of the term "contents tourism" (was in this report, which was written by three governmental organizations, the Ministry of Land, Infrastructure, Transport and Tourism (MLIT); the Ministry of Economy, Trade, and Industry (METI); and the Agency for Cultural Affairs (p. 61). I use the term "contents tourism," instead of "content tourism" following the usage argued for by Seaton and Yamamura (2015) in that it better reflects not only the dynamic plurality of the industry, but also Japanese pronunciation.

17 Since the 1980s, more manga and anime have begun depicting ordinary people in real-world settings, often based on a local town or village, in contrast to previous depictions of heroes and heroines set in fantasy worlds. This change has contributed to a rise of contents tourism behind the scenes.

18 The term "moe," initially derived from otaku culture, referring to a fan's strong affection toward a female manga/anime character. See Azuma (2009) for details.

19 In the same year, the city of Minokamo, in Gifu Prefecture, adopted another buxom anime character as its city mascot, tied in with the anime series Nō-Rin, which is set in an agricultural high school based on a light novel. A wave of protest followed the official selection of the sexually suggestive character (Osaki, 2015a).

20 It should be noted that Mizuki is strongly associated with this local town through his autobiographical titles both in prose and manga. He was born in Osaka, but spent his childhood there in Sakaiminato.

21 Etymologically, the term yōkai can also mean "eerie phenomena, feelings, or sound." As a psychological response to a mysterious occurrence or feeling, ancient people gave shapes with specified names—as Papp (2010) writes, yōkai are "the form given to change and the anxiety, uncertainty, fear and awe associated with it" (p. 12).

22 The prototype for the Kitarō character may be traced back to slightly ambiguous *kamishibai* (paper theater on the streets) narratives for which Mizuki drew illustrations. See Kan (2007, pp. 131–142).

References

Alexander, L. (2017, June 3). "Contents tourism in Japan": How popular narratives drive people to "sacred sites." *The Japan Times*. Retrieved from https://www.japantimes.co.jp/culture/2017/06/03/books/book-reviews/contents-tourism-japan-popular-narratives-drive-people-sacred-sites/#.W4oLPZNKh-U

Allison, A. (2006). *Millennial monsters: Japanese toys and the global imagination.* Berkeley: University of California Press.

Alt, M. (2015, December 10). Shigeru Mizuki's war-haunted art and life. *The New Yorker*. Retrieved from https://www.newyorker.com/culture/culture-desk/shigeru-mizukis-war-haunted-creatures

Azuma, H. (2009). *Otaku: Japan's database animals.* Minneapolis: University of Minnesota Press.

Benjamin, W. (2002). The storyteller: Reflection on the works of Nikolai Leskov. In H. Eiland & M. W. Jennings (Eds.), *Walter Benjamin: Selected writings Volume 3 1935–1938* (pp. 143–166). Cambridge, MA: Belknap Press.

Brienza, C. (2013, January 12). *Anime's media mix: Franchising toys and characters in Japan* by Marc Steinberg [Book review]. *LSE Review of Books*. Retrieved from http://blogs.lse.ac.uk/lsereviewofbooks/2013/01/12/book-review-animes-media-mix-franchising-toys-and-characters-in-japan/

Cohen, J. J. (1997). *Monster theory: Reading culture.* Minneapolis: University of Minnesota Press.

Condry, I. (2013). *The soul of anime: Collaborative creativity and Japan's media success story.* Durham, NC: Duke University Press.

Condry, I. (2018). Teaching anime: Exploring a transnational and transmedia movement. *About Japan: A teacher's Resource.* Retrieved from http://aboutjapan. japansociety.org/teaching_anime__exploring_a_transnational_and_transmedia_ movemen#sthash.zDAIjFHX.dpbs

Condry, I., & Steinberg, M. (2013). *Media mix is anime's life support system* [Web log post]. Retrieved from http://henryjenkins.org/blog/2013/11/media-mix-is-animes-life-support-system-a-conversation-with-ian-condry-and-marc-steinberg-part-two.html

Forster, E. M. (1985). *Aspects of the novel.* Orlando, FL: Harcourt, Inc. (Original work published 1927).

Foster, M. D. (2009). *Pandemonium and parade: Japanese monsters and the culture of yōkai.* Berkeley: University of California Press.

Itō, G. (2006). Manga history viewed through proto-characteristics. In P. Brophy (Ed.), *Tezuka: The marvel of manga* (pp. 107–113). Melbourne, Australia: National Gallery of Victoria.

Itō, M. (2005). Technologies of the childhood imagination: Yugioh, media mixes, and everyday cultural production. In K. Karaganis & N. Jeremijenko (Ed.), *Structures of participation in digital culture* (pp. 88–110). Durham, NC: Duke University Press.

Jenkins, H. (2006). *Convergence culture: Where old and new media collide.* New York, NY: New York University Press.

Kan, J. (2007). *Kamishibai to bukimi na monotachi no kindai* [Kamishibai and the modernity of those deemed "uncanny"]. Tokyo, Japan: Seikyūsha.

Karatani, K. (1993). *Origins of modern Japanese literature.* Durham, NC: Duke University Press.

Kurosawa, T. (2013). *Yōkai būmu no aranami ni idonda "Dororo" no chosen* [A challenge of *Dororo* to the rough wave of the *yōkai* boom]. *Mushi-n-bo.* Retrieved from https://tezukaosamu.net/jp/mushi/201303/column.html

LaMarre, T. (2011). Speciesism, Part III: Neoteny and the politics of life. In F. Lunning (Ed.), *Mechademia Vol. 6: User enhanced* (pp. 110–136). Minneapolis: University of Minnesota Press.

Lash, S., & Lury, C. (2007). *Global culture industry: The mediation of things.* Cambridge, UK: Polity Press.

McCloud, S. (1994). *Understanding comics: The invisible art.* New York, NY: Harper Perennial.

Mizuki, S. (1968). *Manmosu furawā: Kyodai na hana* [Mammoth flowers]. In T. Yoshihiro (Ed.), *Gekiga daigaku* (pp. 48–62). Tokyo, Japan: Hiro Shobō.

Mizuki, S. (2012). *NonNonBa.* Montréal, Canada: Drawn & Quarterly.

Mizuki, S. (2016). *Shigeru Mizuki's Kitaro: The birth of Kitaro*. Montréal, Canada: Drawn & Quarterly.

Nagata, K. (2017, August 26). Anime group launches tourism pilgrimage inspired by Shikoku Henro. *The Japan Times*. Retrieved from https://www.japantimes.co.jp/news/2017/08/26/national/anime-group-launches-tourism-pilgrimage-inspired-shikoku-henro/#.W4oLOJNKh-U

Odagiri, H. (2010). *Kyarakutā towa nanika* [What is a character?]. Tokyo, Japan: Chikuma Shobō.

Osaki, T. (2015a, December 2). Gifu city's sexually suggestive tourism promotion sparks Twitter outrage. *The Japan Times*. Retrieved from https://www.japantimes.co.jp/news/2015/12/02/national/social-issues/citys-sexually-suggestive-tourism-promotion-sparks-twitter-outrage/#.W4ot2pNKh-U

Osaki, T. (2015b, August 11). "Ama" divers denounce "obscene" city mascot, demand its withdrawal. *The Japan Times*. Retrieved from https://www.japantimes.co.jp/news/2015/08/11/national/ama-divers-denounce-obscene-city-mascot-demand-withdrawal/#.W4othpNKh-U

Ōtsuka, E. (2014). *Media mikkusu-ka suru nihon* [Media-mixed Japan]. Tokyo, Japan: Īsuto Puresu.

Papp, Z. (2010). *Anime and its roots in early Japanese monster art*. Folkestone, UK: Global Oriental.

Pratt, M. L. (1992). *Imperial eyes: Travel writing and transculturation*. London, UK: Routledge.

Sandel, M. J. (2013). *What money can't buy: The moral limits of markets*. New York, NY: Farrar, Straus & Giroux.

Sawada, T. (2009). *Sakaiminato-shi no "Mizuki Shigeru Road" seibi to shōtengai no henyō ni kannsuru kōsatsu* [A study on the "Mizuki Shigeru Road" project to change of the shopping district in Sakaiminato city]. *IATTS Review, 34*(1), 68–76.

Seaton, P., & Yamamura, T. (2015). Japanese popular culture and contents tourism. *Japan Forum, 27*(1), 1–11. doi:10.1080/09555803.2014.962564

Shamoon, D. (2013). The yōkai in the database: Supernatural creatures and folklore in manga and anime. *Marvels & Tales: Journal of Fairy-tales Studies, 27*(2), 276–289.

Steinberg, M. (2012). *Anime's media mix: Franchising toys and characters in Japan*. Minneapolis: University of Minnesota Press.

Steinberg, M. (2015). *Naze nihon wa 'media mix suru kuni' nanoka* [Why is Japan a "media mixing" nation?]. Tokyo, Japan: Kadokawa gakugei shuppan.

Steinberg, M. (2017). Media mix mobilization: Social mobilization and *Yo-Kai watch*. *Animation: An Interdisciplinary Journal, 12*(3), 244–258. doi:10.1177/1746847717739565

Suzuki, S. (2011). Learning from monsters: Mizuki Shigeru's yōkai and war manga. *Image [&] Narrative, 12*(1), 229–224.

Suzuki, S. (2016). Reviving the power of storytelling: Post-3/11 online "amateur" manga. *The Japan Studies Review, 20*, 71–92.

Witek, J. (2012). Comics modes: Caricature and illustration in the crumb family's *Dirty Laundry*. In M. J. Smith & R. Duncan (Eds.), *Critical approaches to comics: Theories and methods* (pp. 27–42). New York, NY: Routledge.

Yamamura, T. (2014). Contents tourism and local community response: Lucky star and collaborative anime-induced tourism in Washimiya. *Japan Forum, 27*(1), 59–81. doi:10.1080/09555803.2014.962567

12 Transmedia as environment

Sekai-kei and the social in Japan's neoliberal convergence

Brett Hack

In his ethnological study *The Soul of Anime*, Ian Condry sets his research on anime's transmedia production apart from scholarly works which "begin by explaining the story of a particular series or film and then analyze how it reveals something about Japan or gives us insight into cultural politics" (Condry, 2013, pp. 56–57). Condry makes the remark in passing, but it seizes on an important fact: transmediation does something to fiction which complicates narrative sociological readings. The representationalism prevalent in cultural-studies approaches too often attempts to draw direct lines between single texts and large-scale sociocultural conditions, ignoring the "communicational infrastructure established between media and things" (Steinberg, 2012, p. 91). The connections of media ecologies, as Marc Steinberg terms such infrastructures, enable or inhibit different kinds of expression. Excluding these dynamics in an analysis of social representation amounts to misunderstanding the text. However, the industrial focus in transmedia studies often makes its own exclusions. If cultural studies sometimes lose sight of the material connectivity of media systems, transmedia studies sometimes lose sight of texts' potential as imaginative experience, either closing up fictions' specificities to observe their circulation as commodities within media capitalism, or treating texts as mere reflections of their own transmedia conditions of production. Then again, transmedia texts do exhibit a tendency to become obsessively "self-conscious about their own world making and expansion," and thus more expressive of their consumption process than their stories (Saito, 2015, p. 144).[1] This ambivalence of transmedia fictions mirrors the duality of media systems at large. On the one hand, they are opaque self-referencing assemblies reproducing narcissistic logics of consumption; on the other hand, they are communicative and expressive conduits for human social imagination. Engaging both aspects of transmedia stories therefore invites an inquiry into the representation not only of a particular social condition but the very concept of *the social*—the production of a meaningfully ordered world grounded in human reciprocity—as it can be conceived through the exigencies of media networks.

This chapter will attempt such an inquiry by investigating the sociality of one of the most well-known examples of transmedia storytelling: the ecology of Japanese popular fiction associated with the so-called otaku subculture, including anime, manga, light novels, and video games.[2] I will focus on the subgenre known as *sekai-kei* or "world-type," which enjoyed a controversial period of fame in the early 2000s. Though their moment has since passed, *sekai-kei* fictions remain relevant thanks to their implication in two roughly concurrent media-cultural "convergences," to loosely apply Henry Jenkins's term, occurring in Japan during the late 1990s and early 2000s (Jenkins, 2006, p. 2). First, *sekai-kei* fictions are early examples of the convergence by which the codes of established otaku media (anime and manga) blended with those of youth-oriented novels (dubbed "light novels" afterward) and the newer form of narrative *bishōjo* (beautiful girl) games to form an integrated "environment of imagination" (Azuma, 2007, p. 64). Second, *sekai-kei*'s traumatized characters and melancholic narratives of world-annihilation are very much products of the economic and social destabilization accompanying millennial Japan's integration into global neoliberal capitalism. However, although *sekai-kei* fictions hint of recession, globalization, and ruptured national identity, they do not productively "represent" the conditions of Japan's neoliberalization, and therefore frustrate a straightforward sociological reading. Like most otaku media (and indeed like most media in the 21st century) *sekai-kei* fictions work as "machines for generating affect" (Shaviro, 2010, pp. 2–3). They produce pathos through virtual experiences assembled from the codes of their transmedia environment of imagination. But this does not necessitate, as is often claimed, a retreat into transcendent solipsism or self-gratifying media consumption. *Sekai-kei* fictions—and, I argue, the entire gamut of fictions influenced by them—are imaginative exercises in visualizing the social world *through conditions of transmediation*.

Crucial here is the concept of a *media environment*, which Steinberg defines as "both media ecology as a system and its lived experience by human subjects" (Steinberg, 2012, p. xi). While Steinberg concentrates on the anime media mix's environment of affective consumption, we should recognize that such networks fit within a larger "array of possible technologies, delivery systems, platforms, discourses, texts, modes of address," as well as patterns of usage which "define a space that is increasingly mutually referential and reinforcing" (Silverstone, 2007, loc. 191–199). The larger media environment, which includes fiction, entertainment media, advertisements, news sources, public institutions, and the manifold communicative forms of the internet, is the means by which we gain access to the space beyond our immediate perception and attempt to chart our location within it. For better or for worse, environmental networks of media allow us to see the world. But these networks threaten to overwhelm as well, dissolving meaningful representations and situated social subjects within recursive flows of stimulation. *Sekai-kei* fictions instructively engage with this dilemma, since they gaze out onto the world through *both* this larger media environment *and* the expressive network of otaku imagination, collapsing their myriad nodes into a single phenomenal experience. In doing so, they produce sensory articulations of disorder characteristic not only of their own sociohistorical moment but of all media-saturated, precarious, and globalized societies. Positioned directly on the cusp of neo-Marxian and interactionist views of the 21st-century mediascape, they speak to the difficulty of imagining location and relation within its dizzying movement. However, *sekai-kei* fictions retain a concept of the social, not in terms of a rational subjectivity, but in terms of the interplay between the world-cohering power of fiction and the ordinary affects of the everyday. These imaginative dynamics have become fundamental to the transmedia environment of otaku culture, and therefore are indispensable for understanding the latter's potential for social cognition within the larger environment of advanced capitalism.

Sekai-kei and neoliberal convergence

Economic, political, and social destabilization during the late 1990s and early 2000s put an end to Japan's postwar self-image as a uniquely stable society and fully exposed its population to the globalized insecurities of the new millennium. Yoshimi Shun'ya poignantly summarizes the emotional climate of the post-Bubble recession as "a universally depressive mood across all society," with phrases like 'failure' 'crisis' and 'collapse' repeated throughout the media" and "all the while multileveled processes of neoliberal globalization enacting historic structural change" in the background (Yoshimi, 2009, p. 169). The "neoliberal turn" Yoshimi evokes here, in which government and corporate power renders a society compliant for integration into the global flows of free-market capitalism, inevitably proceeds through the deconstruction of social collectivity on both institutional and cognitive levels. Japan's case is unique mainly in the speed and severity with which neoliberalism's undermining of the social proceeded (Watanabe, 2007, pp. 325–327). The large-scale casualization of Japan's labor force during the second half of the 1990s paved the way for a rapid increase in precarious part-time workers, escalating into a widespread insecurity about "work" as a whole (Genda, 2005). Fluidization of the job market opened up new divisions along gender, age, and class lines (Ueno, 2013, pp. 25–27), while national crises appeared to testify to a rapidly decaying public sphere. The Kobe earthquake in January of 1995 was followed by the grisly spectacle of the Ōm Shinrikyō cult's sarin gas attack on the Tokyo subway in March of the same year. News coverage of violent youth crimes solidified a panicked image of the domestic field as a shadowy space of incomprehensible violence (Kotani, 2017). National destabilization was compounded by the loss of Japan's secure geopolitical position due to the end of the Cold War and the rise of other East Asian economies, accompanied by a public re-interrogation of

Japan's colonial legacy in Asia (Yoshimi, 2009, pp. 223–225). It was also a time of increased awareness of large-scale dangers like war, terrorism, and environmental disaster (Fujiki, 2019, pp. 398–405). Increasingly atomized by the government's neoliberal discourse of "self-responsibility" (*jiko sekinin*), Japanese citizens were forced to "reorganize their everyday lives, as with Alice in the looking-glass world," amid the chaotic environments of post-Cold War geopolitics and economic globalization (Hook & Takeda, 2007, pp. 122–123).

All the insecurities birthed by Japan's neoliberal turn were intimately bound up with the rise of new media-communication technologies. The internalization of global risk, for example, was accelerated by the expansion of international visibility through increased media resources; on the one hand the globalization of Japan's television news networks, including the legalization of global satellite channels in 1994, and on the other hand, the proliferation of alternative news sources thanks to the advent of the internet in the late 1990s (See Hagiwara, 2007; Iwabuchi, 2007). The characteristic "risk consciousness" of late capitalist societies grew throughout the 1990s in a positive feedback loop with increased media coverage of the domestic and international calamities described above, weaving a simultaneously globalized and privatized sense of risk into daily life (Fukuda, 2010, pp. 51–52). The uneven penetration of the internet into the "nighttime region" of private consumption forged the image of a reclusive and "post-social" (*datsushakaiteki*) space distinct from the "daytime region" of public life (Hamano, 2014, pp. 440–444). Japan's neoliberal turn thus constituted a kind of large-scale media "convergence." The separate experiences of job casualization, market globalization, geopolitical insecurity, and social atomization were interwoven and amplified through their visibility within expanded media networks, normalizing feelings of distrust and producing forms of subjectivity conducive to the new capitalist regime of globalized and privatized risk. Zygmunt Bauman's (2000, p. 8) now-classic formulation describes this as "liquid modernity," a privatized experience of instability characterized by simultaneous "remoteness and unreachability of systemic structure" and an "unstructured, fluid state of the immediate setting of life-politics." *Sekai-kei* fictions arise out of this techno-social convergence of neoliberal insecurity.

Originating on the website *Prunie Bookmark* in late 2002, the term "*sekai-kei*" or "world-type" was invoked to describe a new story conceit in which the budding romance between an ordinary boy and a mysterious girl is directly implicated in some apocalyptic conflict, the sociopolitical specifics of which are left unknown (Maejima, 2010, p. 27). As I will detail later, the term quickly gained popularity through the efforts of a network of otaku-culture critics, many of whom were associated with the philosopher and cultural theorist Azuma Hiroki. They were for the most part non-academic writers and fans, often also creators themselves, and their analyses sometimes suffer from their own self-positioning as participant-intellectuals.

However, they were prescient in recognizing *sekai-kei* as indicative of both aesthetic and social shifts. Azuma himself, assimilating *sekai-kei* into his own theories of Japanese postmodernity, characterized *sekai-kei* as "small-scale relations…directly connected to large-scale drama…without practical intermediary institutions" (2007, pp. 96–97). This complex phrasing simply refers to the fact that plot events take place either in the confines of school and neighborhood routines or on cosmic or apocalyptic battlefields. The supposed absence of "mid-level" social relations like economics or politics led to a conception of *sekai-kei* as a solipsistic male fantasy where obtaining the heroine's affections guarantees a transcendental connection with "the world" (Satō, 2004).

Novelist Kasai Kiyoshi, one of the most active proponents of *sekai-kei* as a literary and cultural form, clarifies that *sekai-kei*'s absent "social region" is not sociality itself, but the enabling institutions which would allow for an agentic social subject. As Kasai notes, *sekai-kei* texts give the pervasive image of a "society in ruins" and a "scattered disorderly space of representation" (Kasai, 2009, p. 22). In other words, *sekai-kei* reflects the breakdown of Japan's stable postwar system and its forced entry into global competition. The three recognized "core" *sekai-kei* fictions: Takahashi Shin's manga *Saishū Heiki Kanojo* (*She, the Ultimate Weapon*, 2000–2001, hereafter *Saikano*), Akiyama Mizuhito's novel *Iriya no Sora, UFO no Natsu* (*Iriya's Sky, Summer of the UFOs*, 2001–2003), and Shinkai Makoto's self-produced anime *Hoshi no Koe* (*Voices of a Distant Star*, 2002) certainly support such a connection. Their similar narratives depict the female lead forced to fight in a brutal global-scale war while the male lead impotently looks on. In *Iriya no Sora*, the entire romance between Asaba Naoyuki and UFO-pilot Iriya Kana, including her eventual self-sacrifice, is revealed to have been orchestrated by Kana's military supervisors in order to motivate her to continue fighting. *Saikano*'s female lead Chise is altered by the Japanese Self-Defense Force into a biological weapon whose evolving fighting capacity gradually warps her body and personality into a monstrous godlike form. Finally, in *Hoshi no Koe*, classmates Nobu and Mikako are forced to communicate across the endless gulfs of space when Mikako is drafted into an intergalactic mission against a hostile alien species. The minimal social worlds against which these narratives are set effect a sense of isolation from empowering networks of social action, while clipped representations of the larger society hint of a violent and conspiratorial global space acting on the bodies and minds of the young lovers.

Although *sekai-kei* fiction is saturated with the feelings of atomized insecurity reflective of its sociocultural context, it does not convincingly engage with any of the social conditions themselves. Elements like corporate Japan's abandonment of youth workers or expanded military participation hover in the background but remain unfocused. In one scene in the *Saikano* manga, an old soldier admonishes a new recruit shocked at a pile of bodies: "Don't say you didn't know. You're a culprit too." The interchange conceivably nods to the legacy of Japanese war crimes, which were being interrogated in the years preceding *Saikano*'s publication. Likewise, in a scene from *Iriya no Sora*, Naoyuki admonishes one of Kana's supervisors for forcing Kana into "a fight you adults started," perhaps a veiled jab at the older generation of business leaders for their relegation of youth workers to casualized positions in order to protect the lifelong employment of senior managers during the "hiring Ice Age" of the 1990s. However, the indistinct nature of these representations disallows any pretensions to materialist critique, and their anecdotal location within their stories prevents them from contributing to any major thesis of the text itself. These fleeting perceptions are affective rather than representative, moments of shock or angry outbursts which give the impression of flailing at some ugly and dimly understood social reality.

The *sekai-kei* critics read these moments as further instances of *sekai-kei*'s "absence of the social," which they sublimate into abstract existentialist readings of the *sekai-kei* dynamic as alienated postmodern subjectivity, a kind of "liquid modernity" tailored for millennial Japan (Bauman, 2000). Uno Tsunehiro, for example, portrays *sekai-kei* as an imaginative withdrawal from the post-Bubble world's "disorder and impenetrability." For Uno, *sekai-kei* reacts to new social complexity with a "reclusive psychologism" (*hikikomori/shinrishugi*) in which the (male) subject "retreats inward in search of validation for their own self-image" through the divinely empowered female character loving them "as they are"" (Uno, 2008, p. 41). Uno criticizes this inactive self-searching as a transitory style which he claims gives way to neoliberal narratives of "decisionism" (*ketsudanshugi*) featuring immoral but active subjects in survival situations. In his own existentialist reading, Kasai criticizes Uno's arbitrary distinction between *sekai-kei* psychologism and the later decisionism. For Kasai, these are simply two complimentary "*sekai-kei*-esque" reactions to the failure of the postwar social order. Drawing on the political philosophy of Carl Schmidt and Giorgio Agamben, Kasai argues that *sekai-kei* represents nothing less than the collapse of the "social contract" of postwar civil society into a wartime "state of exception" where legally mediated subjectivity breaks down into a "naked" subject forced to make arbitrary decisions (Kasai, 2009, pp. 30–33). Uno's and Kasai's readings correctly seize on *sekai-kei*'s subjective experience of global disorder, and are astute in linking it to the background of Japan's neoliberalization. However, the dearth of social specifics within *sekai-kei* texts forecloses the possibility of a detailed coordination with material conditions. Consequently, these critics' search for social relevance is forced to lean on prepacked "grand narrative" theory, leading to their ultimately unsatisfying descriptions of *sekai-kei*'s social imagination in terms of a bodiless postmodern condition. Furthermore, their narrow focus on narrative and character dynamics obscures the wealth of sensory experience offered by *sekai-kei* fictions' combination of literary and visual techniques of imagination. The omission is especially disappointing because the very possibility of their discussing *sekai-kei* as a unified body of fiction emanates from a cultural development with which they themselves were involved: the integration of new modes of otaku expression into an intensified transmedia environment.

Sekai-kei and the transmedia environment of imagination

While anime and manga ostensibly define the contemporary ecology of otaku media, many of its central conceits come from other media forms. Satomi Saito (2015) offers an insightful corrective to anime-centric models of Japanese transmedia by elaborating the crucial role played by narrative-based light novels in generating original content for contemporary multimedia franchises. Focusing on the hugely influential *Suzmiya Haruhi* franchise, Saito explains how its "character movement across media" is made possible through a "curious primacy of narrative" in Tanigawa Nagaru's original light novel *Suzumiya Haruhi no Yūutsu (The Melancholy of Haruhi Suzumiya, 2003*). Saito explains that the narrative-based transmedia model exemplified by the *Haruhi* series "reflexively mimics the way consumers explore multiple story worlds" (Saito, 2015, pp. 156–157). He emphasizes that this highly successful model relies on the detachment of creativity from established institutions of production; the biggest hits are often produced by first-time novelists coming out of amateur writing communities. Light-novel fiction is itself made possible by collective recognition of common motifs, characterizations, and narrative expectations which amateur creators can creatively reassemble. Saito recognizes this shared stock as the "grand nonnarrative in Azuma Hiroki's term, or the database of endless derivative simulacra that does not belong to a single franchise but is open to multilevel user participation," less like Jenkins's industry-based model of transmedia production and more "akin to a collaborative storytelling" (Saito, 2015, pp. 159–160). Saito conceives the wellspring of this collaborative storytelling according to Azuma Hiroki's influential theory of database consumption. Azuma himself has updated his theory to account for the representational properties of light novels and related media, describing how the database enables an "environment of imagination" (*sōzōryoku no kankyō*) based on the dominance of anime-style characters (Azuma, 2007, pp. 61–64). Storytelling within this environment of imagination utilizes the total expressive universe of otaku media as a base of understanding for transmitting characters' identities and experiences in narrative form, producing a realism which takes the transmedia system as its referent (Steinberg, 2014). The transmedia dynamics Saito describes began to converge in the late 1990s, stimulated by new platforms, changes in modes of expression, and by an ongoing discussion of these changes into which *sekai-kei* figured heavily.

In his detailed history of *sekai-kei*'s role within otaku culture, Maejima Satoshi characterizes the period as a shift in viewing patterns resulting from the paradigm-shifting success of the series *Neon Genesis Evangelion*

(1995–1996). The popular reception of *Eva's* psychological angst-ridden worldview among young adults catalyzed an increased demand for self-reflexive narratives over the older trend of anime and manga based on detailed consumable worlds. As Maejima describes it, *Eva* shifted the nature of anime from "media for otaku" to "literature about otaku" (Maejima, 2010, p. 44). As the paradigmatic "post-*Eva*" fiction, *sekai-kei* became the object of controversy regarding the changing meaning of "otaku culture" taken as a whole. Critical to this shift was the rise of light novels and *bishōjo* games as central modes of otaku expression, including a self-described "*bishōjo* game movement" which proclaimed a new literariness for what had therefore been simple erotic simulations (see Azuma, 2004). Maejima goes so far as to claim that the "center of otaku culture in the early 2000s was not image but text" (Maejima, 2010, p. 58). This is certainly an exaggeration, not least because both light novels and *bishōjo* games centrally rely on images to move their narratives forward. It would be more accurate to say that the rise of these forms added a *literary* layer—first-person reflexive narrative voice from light novels—and a *ludic* layer—spatial unfolding and branching plotlines from *bishōjo* games—to the *visual-chronological* expression of anime and manga. These additions also enabled new character types, world-settings, and plot devices which intermingled with established ones to create an exponentially complex database of expression.

Like other examples of transmedia convergence, the intensified database was inextricable from its recognition by "migratory" media audiences (Jenkins, 2006, p. 2). Enabled by the rapid spread of internet availability in the late 1990s, evolving debates via online bulletin boards exponentially compounded links between fans, producers, and media themselves within a loosely unified discussion about changes in the subculture. Links to old media developed as well, since producers and critics associated with studios, publishing houses, and literary journals also participated in these discussions. Such interactions gave rise to a kind of "otaku criticism" carried out by self-identifying otaku fans and creators who also read literature and literary theory and were invested in legitimating their favored forms as valid modes of cultural expression. This process involved perceiving all related media forms as aspects of a unified environment of imagination. Perhaps the most edifying portrayal of this urge comes not from any of the innumerable idiosyncratic essays but from Satō Shin's "Bishōjo Game Perfect Map," (in Azuma, 2004, pp. 5–6). Satō's "map" is a graphic visualization of cultural practice from the early 1990s through 2004, organized according to the central categories of "literary imagination" and "narrative consumption." Individual works, including not only *bishōjo* games but also manga, anime, light novels, and literary fiction, are arranged on the table according to their relation to the two central categories, while circles and shading group various subgenres and crossover commonalities. Whether or not one agrees with its specifics, Satō's map beautifully visualizes the transmedia imagination as an integrated and collectively shared environment.

A common environment makes possible the deployment of images and issues across media boundaries, as individual texts "twist and contort their respective mediums to perform similar anime-esque elements and thus produce the image of inter-relatable media" (Suan, 2018, p. 208). Early products of the convergence, *sekai-kei* works exhibit this internal trans-mediation, and not merely in the obvious clue that the expressive core of *sekai-kei* is comprised of texts from three different media. The reading of *sekai-kei* as a narrative representation of postmodern discontent misses the intense transmedia visuality in even the printed forms. Volume 1 of the *Iriya no Sora* novel replaces a table of contents with illustrated mock-ups of movie posters which situate the chapters according to cinematic genres of "youth love story," "suspense," and "spy drama" while grouping the char-acters as "actors" according to their role within the chapter. In addition, Naoyuki's internal monologue is regularly interspersed with real-time de-scription of his field of vision as he encounters dramatic events in the story. The 2005 original video animation (OVA) actualizes the latent visuality of the text (Itō 2005). Conversely, Takahashi's original *Saikano* manga is su-perlatively narrative; the male lead Shūji's painful self-examinations often span several pages of text set on blank panels. These moments give way to a versatility of manga styles: romantic close-ups composed of sensual lines reminiscent of *shōjo* manga, mecha anime-style biomachinery and body horror drawn in realistic detail, and comedic moments in the bubbly style of gag manga. The anime version mimics these forms while capitalizing on movement and sound to emphasize the physicality inherent in the manga's themes of intimacy and trauma (Kase 2002). Within a single *sekai-kei* text, one gets a sense of an encounter with the entirety of otaku culture's inten-sified media ecology at the turn of the millennium.

However, Maejima is correct in characterizing *sekai-kei* as essentially bildungsroman-style "narratives of self-consciousness." The vast array of science-fictional tropes all serve this primary impetus. For example, in *Iriya no Sora*, Naoyuki daydreams about the newly matriculated Kana:

> There's no doubt about it; that girl is an alien.... It's the same in all the books you read...They've put agents in countless places in human society disguised as regular people....Definitely. This girl called Iriya is one of those agents, in charge of junior high schools.
> I didn't remember anything about class.
> (Akiyama, 2001, pp. 80–81)

The novel is full of such hackneyed flights of imagination tethered to Naoyuki's humdrum experience of adolescence. In this "post-*Eva*" brand of fiction, the "fantastical gadgets" of anime, manga, and science fiction are evoked not for themselves, but as tools to situate the vicissitudes of youth subjectivity in such a way that the reader/viewer gains an awareness of their relation to the whole of the integrated media environment (Maejima,

2010, pp. 110, 151). Azuma describes this style of narration as "half-clear" (*hantōmei*), meaning that it seeks to depict natural or social reality but uses the conventions of anime-related media to do so (Azuma, 2007, pp. 96–101). *Sekai-kei* fictions do not function as "clear" windows to Japan's neoliberal turn. Yet neither are they an opaque "meta-commentary format for the participatory culture" as Saito says of the *Haruhi* series (Saito, 2015, p. 157). Their "half-clear" approach orients them toward the social—here, a coming-of-age story in the midst of social breakdown—through a reflexive invocation of their transmedia environment of imagination. What makes *sekai-kei* fictions unique is their extension of this approach to the entirety of Japan's neoliberal convergence. As the remainder of this chapter hopes to make clear, *sekai-kei* reproduces an experience of the world within the to-talized media environment through which the atomized subject is forced to process the dislocating conditions of globalized neoliberal risk. The result is a horizon of undifferentiated media images without distinction between fictional and nonfictional genres. *Sekai-kei* perceives that in the 21st century, globalization, destabilization, and mediation form a mutually constitutive environment, a network that almost—but not quite—obliterates the social.

Sekai-kei and the horizon of mediated vision

According to the narrative readings discussed earlier, *sekai-kei* seeks to imagine "the world" as an abstract concept, retreating from social en-gagement toward transcendental validation. As visual transmedia, how-ever, *sekai-kei* fictions contain an earnest and embodied intention toward visualizing social experience. Simultaneously evoking social climate and transmedia networks, *sekai-kei*'s affective machinery generates a simula-tion of "what it feels like to live in the 21st century," engulfed within the globalized media environment. (Shaviro, 2010, p. 2). Figures 12.1 and 12.2 show two scenes from *Saikano* which assemble two very different scales of mediated visuality. In Figure 12.1, Shūji and his mother watch footage of the war. Their figures are repeated inside sparse white backgrounds with the television image as the focus, while Shūji's narration remarks how the broadcast contains "no voiceover or caption, just the image of war." This is the vulnerability in *sekai-kei* which Kasai notices, a moment of encoun-ter with grand and terrible events encroaching on your everyday existence via the access points made available by media networks. The spread cul-minates with the close-up of Shūji crying, combining the war image with its affective response framed inside the image of a character witnessing it. Figure 12.2 shows an analogous yet radically different mediated vision through the eyes of *Saikano*'s "ultimate weapon" Chise, whose biotechni-cal systems have begun to automatically access global satellites to spy on Shūji. Tightly packed panels crowd the page with tactical maps, a picture of the globe from space, and overlapping lines of code. The images close in around her, culminating in the same close-up, this time a moment of

Figure 12.1 Shūji and his mother catch a glimpse of war in *Saikano* (Takahashi 2001). © 高橋しん/小学館 © Shin Takahashi/Shogakukan Inc.

moral crisis as she attempts to reject what she sees. Here the triangulation of mediated visuality, affective response, and viewing subject are united inside an excess of information showing Chise more than she can handle. These scenes exemplify how *sekai-kei*'s images of intimate trauma and global chaos are articulated through shifting scales of mediated perception, in which invested subjectivities are brought to precipices of dissolution.

Sekai-kei thereby stands at the crux of the duality of media systems mentioned in the introduction, balancing two different visions of how media environments affect human life in the age of globalization. In the neo-Marxian model Steinberg (2012, pp. 188–193 *et passim*) draws on, environmentalization of media entails the subsumption of even the most intimate spheres of human life into networks of post-Fordist consumption and, in some interpretations, the production of subjectivity according to the logic of capital. Contrarily, in the interactionist model of liberal social theory and globalization studies, media environments enable subjects to imagine a global web of relations around their local existence. As Roger Silverstone describes it, "the media are becoming environmental, but not in the Baudrillardian sense of the media as generating a distinct

Figure 12.2 Chise's systems begin spying on Shūji in *Saikano* (Takahashi 2000). © 高橋しん／小学館 © Shin Takahashi/Shogakukan Inc.

sphere…more a sense of the media as tightly and dialectically intertwined with the everyday" (Silverstone, 2007, loc. 191). Silverstone's "everyday" means to preserve not only face-to-face social relations but the entire potential space of human encounters. Media representations enable the extension of these encounters toward large-scale social life by providing "symbolic resources" for situated subjects to construct broader narratives around the locus of the self (Orgad, 2012). However, they also act as conduits through which images of global dislocation enter local contexts (Tomlinson, 1999). This latter experience better describes *sekai-kei*'s endlessly telescoping and overdetermined yet also blocked and fragmented gaze. As outlined earlier, the social crises of the 1990s and early 2000s were processed and amplified through the consumption of continuously publicized media spectacles, resulting in a widespread and multifaceted risk consciousness (Fukuda, 2010). Enabled through expanded media access, Japan's public descent into neoliberal risk made visible a new network of dangers and responsibilities. *Sekai-kei* fictions construct series of audiovisual events which crystallize the feelings of dislocation within this simultaneously isolated and exposed environment.

Sekai-kei's fluctuations of sensory experience on a disorganized and globalized scale are enacted through numerous media forms: satellites, televisions, hand-written diaries, CG renderings. Their movements almost reproduce the modulations of what Gilles Deleuze calls the control society: the dissolution of subjectivity into flows of information governed by capital (Deleuze, 1995). As in the above scenes, however, affective moments are always rendered through a triangulation of subject, vision, and pre-emotional reaction. In *sekai-kei* there is always a pair of eyes somewhere, deeply (if also futilely) invested in constructing of some order of meaningful social relationships. Both the male and female characters act as viewing subjects, providing different scales of visuality with their own problems of intimacy and connection. *Hoshi no Koe*'s Mikako is the focal point for the anime's grandiose scenes of space travel and alien landscapes. However, outside of battle scenes she is usually shown wistfully holding her cell phone inside in the transparent cockpit of her fighting robot, framed against her marvelous surroundings yet isolated from them by screen-like glass augmented with data (Figure 12.3). Criticizing the lack of science-fictional rigor here would be a misrecognition of the images' goal: the vicarious experience of a subject with technologically enabled cosmic vision who is at the same time hermetically alone. *Saikano* associates its expansive moments with feelings of guilt and fear directed toward an undisclosed other. After she destroys a city, Chise's image is set against the annihilated landscape as she undergoes contradictory moments of hysterical breakdown, first pleading "Kill me!

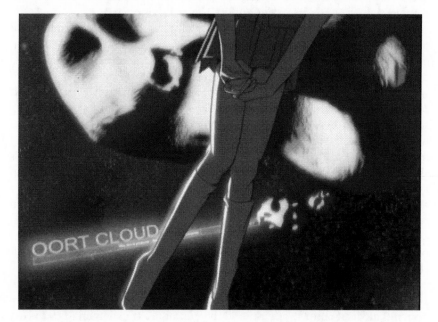

Figure 12.3 Mikako floats alone in the depths of space in *Hoshi no Koe*.

Figure 12.4 Chise breaks down after destroying a city in the *Saikano* anime.

I don't want to be like this anymore!" then screaming "No! I don't want to die! I know I've killed many people but I want to live! (Figure 12.4). Building toward their different thematic goals, the female characters' viewpoints in *Hoshi no Koe* and *Saikano* enact a fearful mediated global vision that overpowers the emotional intelligence of the subject, disordering but not completely dissolving its intentionality toward the social.

In contrast, the vantage points of male characters tend to be cramped and paranoid. The young soldier's reaction in *Saikano* and Naoyuki's confrontation with the military supervisor in *Iriya no Sora* exemplify this limited and context-poor vision which is nonetheless aware of its own engulfment within the disordered and violent global space. Mediation penetrates experience right down to the hormones; the lovers' sexualities are repeatedly scrutinized and even facilitated through surveillance and communication networks. In one scene from *Saikano* Shūji moves in to kiss Chise but she informs him that "about 900 people" are observing her. Much to Shūji's shock she adds, "You've got twelve on you." A switch in drawing styles between the two moments—from the sensual realism of a hand on a shoulder to the semiotic shapes of gag manga—actualizes this abrupt shift from touch to sight. In one rather incriminating scene from *Iriya no Sora*, Kana lies unconscious in a military bunker, with Naoyuki receiving phone instructions on how to revive her from the military aide, Enomoto (Figure 12.5). Told that he must inject medicine into her heart, Naoyuki struggles with the teenage awkwardness of touching a female body as Enomoto upbraids him. Naoyuki steels himself to plunge the phallic syringe only to be rescued by an arriving medical team. Naoyuki and the viewer are thusly treated to the experience of being guided through a sexual encounter by the communicative

Figure 12.5 Naoyuki's phallic attempt at resuscitating Kana in the *Irya no Sora* OVA.

armature of the military industrial complex. Again we find ourselves at the limit point between the media environment as an enabler of mutual experience and as subsumption into networks of surveillance and control.

Taking into account *sekai-kei*'s properties of internal transmediation, however, one might argue that the limit point has already been crossed. The interactionist model of environmental media as a conduit to the world depends on a perceiving subject who can integrate fictional and nonfictional media images into its imagined world according to rational categories of real-world social relations: nation, class, ethnicity, religion, etc. The imaginative process of *sekai-kei* fictions reveals a very different relationship between mediated images and the world. To repeat Maejima's thesis, *sekai-kei* is a narrative of self enacted through the tropes of the otaku environment of imagination taken as a whole. *Sekai-kei* applies this same totalizing method of image-assembly to the global media environment. The effect collapses the hierarchies and intensities of *both* transmedia environments into a single horizon of perception. Steven Shaviro refers to this kind of imaginary as a "flat ontology," by which he simply means that "there is no hierarchy of representations" and "no image source or sound source is treated as more authentic than any other" (Shaviro, 2010, pp. 73–74). The "world" or totality of media environments is invoked as an undifferentiated genre-assemblage. Perhaps the purest instance of this endeavor, *Hoshi no Koe* "takes from otakus' common premises and types" a bare minimum of reference to recognize the space in which Noboru and Mikako's love-story unfolds (Maejima, 2010, p. 85). The tropes of robot anime and sci-fi films are woven into clichés from school dramas and coming-of-age stories.

Fantastic scenery is couched inside the cute language of a text message. Augmented reality and virtual displays are poised alongside normal cell phone screens. Critically, these are all interspersed with lingering stills of everyday objects like railroad crossings, telephone lines, and narrow streets (see Figure 12.7). Rather than a logically organized genre and world-setting which then "reflects" material conditions, fictional and nonfictional media images evoke shared categories of understanding and fuse them with sense-rich "real" images into a phenomenological collage comprising a "*sekai*/world." Mikako's opening soliloquy directly references this approach: "There's this word 'world.' Until middle school, I thought that 'world' meant the place where your cellphone reception could reach." The "world" is that field of engaged perception accessible through the representational and communicative tools at your disposal. In *sekai-kei* the fictional and non-fictional, the mediated and the direct, the large and the small, are all equal generators of experiences that can assemble into a subjective world.

Sekai-kei's prescient vision of the contemporary media environment, now sometimes referred to as the "post-truth" world, seems to sound a death knell for the interactionist model. A flat horizontal environment of undifferentiated media-images referring to each other in an endless disorienting web seems to foreclose the possibility of a situated social subject that can organize a representation of the world for itself or organize a representation of itself to others. A comic scene in *Iriya no Sora* seems to illustrate such futility. Naoyuki and Kana go on a movie date together, unknowingly observed both by Kana's military supervisors and by Naoyuki's jealous younger sister accompanied by his UFO-enthusiast classmate. The scene shifts between the two spy parties as they use surveillance technology to eavesdrop on each other and on Naoyuki and Kana, who are watching a movie composed of clichéd cinematic images. Both the supervisor Enomoto and Naoyuki's classmate continuously shift enthusiasm between the ostensible goals of their respective "missions" and Naoyuki's romantic success. In this space of mutual surveillance, the serious genres of spy drama and global conspiracy merge into locker room talk, sibling jealousy, and other trivial genres of social interaction, all bound together by the film screen which is itself a mix of genres. In this moment, *Iriya no Sora* creates a microcosm of its own futile desire to visualize totality and connection being constantly redirected through varying scales and emotions in the collapsed space of media images.

Nevertheless, *sekai-kei* fictions do visualize moments of coherence in the flat and fluid world without relying on rational subjectivity, through their very dependence on the collectivity inherent in fictionality itself. A subtle but telling moment in the *Saikano* manga reveals *sekai-kei*'s underlying premise that when the supposedly real bases of experience dislocate and dissolve, fiction as shared imaginary horizon has the power to temporarily hold a world together. After planning to run away together, Shūji waits for Chise in front of the train station, but she is prevented from meeting him by an order to sortie. Afterward, a two-page spread shows Shūji in the foreground

Figure 12.6 Shūj and Chise's missed encounter in *Saikano* (Takahashi 2000).
©高橋しん/小学館 © Shin Takahashi/Shogakukan Inc.

slumped in disappointment inside a phone booth, while behind him a massive bird-like aircraft moves across the sky (see Figure 12.6). This aircraft has not appeared before, nor will it appear in this form again. However, a certain curvature of the wings and arrangement of its metal tendrils allows a reader sharing *Saikano*'s environment of imagination to intuit that this is another form of Chise-as-weapon. The design elements of *mecha* anime-style machinery form a visual thread binding the concealed elements of the plot together; she is passing over in an attempt to inform him of what happened. Shūji's back is turned and the opportunity is missed. For the reader, however, the image is pregnant with the possibility not only of mutual recognition but of constructing a temporary schema of the structures and events which brought them to where they are. The collective exercise of the imagination that fiction entails creates threads of recognition that can bind experience together, and potentially connect people as well.

Counterpoised to the encompassing work of fiction are the everyday sensations which appear throughout *sekai-kei* texts as intensities within the horizontal flow of mediation. While they do not amount to Silverstone's sense of the everyday as an articulated social world, these moments seem to hold on to the promise of a basic reciprocity. *Hoshi no Koe*'s stills of mundane urban objects, a fixture of director Shinkai Makoto's style, serve

Figure 12.7 Everyday urban objects in *Hoshi no Koe*.

as anchors of experience and as confirmations of the shared space Noboru and Mikako inhabit before she leaves for space (Figure 12.7). Importantly, media technologies provide such reminders as well. Though Mikako can only use her cell phone to send text messages which will reach Noboru years later, throughout her galactic travels she is shown clutching it, retaining in the media object the promise of direct communication in its potential to transmit a "voice." Writing about *Saikano*, Stevie Suan characterizes Shūji and Chise's relationship in terms of Judith Butler's notion of "the mutual implication of the "you" in the "I."" As the two grow closer, Suan explains, "we can see an exposure of the fault lines of the bordered-whole individual," with the final image of their kiss "combining the two together" (Suan, 2018, p. 221). Beautifully actualized instances of this potential for mutual implication occur throughout the *Saikano* anime, where the most detailed animation is reserved not for battles or even the final apocalypse but for the couple's intimate moments. In one tragic scene, the two lie next to each other as Shūji reveals that he has cheated on her. As he confesses, she bites him on the arm, drawing blood (Figure 12.8). The close-up combines sensitive movement, hyperreal color, and frame-by-frame flow of the red blood seeping into Shūji's shirt to create a sense of presence rare in television anime. In *sekai-kei*'s fullness as visual transmedia, moments like these serve not to validate the transcendental identity of lone male subject, but to preserve the reality of the lovers' contact, even painful contact, to

Figure 12.8 Chise bites Shūji in the *Saikano* anime.

validate the intimacy and everydayness of human connection as it stands to be dissolved within a global flow of troubling images. The pair of eyes, the blood and organs supporting them, the push and pull of desires and anxieties, and the tenuous promise of recognition—for *sekai-kei*, these are potential beginnings of the social.

Sekai-kei and social imagination

Stimulated by an acute moment of social breakdown, *sekai-kei* fictions produce affectively charged experiences of the imaginative dislocation characteristic of neoliberal capitalism. Within the collapsed horizon of multiple media environments, they find potential for renewed social being in the collective imaginative process of fiction and in the simple sensations of everyday life. In this final section, I will consider how *sekai-kei's* imaginative dynamics have incorporated into the transmedia environment of otaku imagination via a look at *Suzumiya Haruhi no Yūutsu*, the franchise described by Saito as "a meta-commentary format for the participatory culture" which "self-reflectively mimics the way consumers explore multiple story worlds" (Saito, 2015, p. 157). Maejima recognizes *Haruhi* as a parodic descendent of *sekai-kei* which randomly assembles otaku world-settings and stock character types only to only to subsume them into an ironic narrative of youth subjectivity (Maejima, 2010, p. 117). The story follows the relationship between the imaginatively obsessive Haruhi and the cynically practical Kyon. Haruhi has decided that she has "no interest in regular humans" and continually attempts to enact plot elements from genre fiction in order to bring paranormal events into being. She is always frustrated in her quests, while Kyon's professed desire for everyday small-scale belonging is beset by the supernatural phenomena which Haruhi, the unwitting creator of the universe, generates without knowing. Each side character embodies a different genre paradigm—aliens, time-travelers, and superpower-users—whose overcomplicated details intertwine confusingly. The pleasure of *Haruhi*'s imagined world emanates from the unstable interactions between the genres that construct it, a complex sensorium of shifts between numerous fictional world-settings. In contrast to *sekai-kei*'s earnest use of fiction to hold a worldview together, *Haruhi* conspicuously enjoys playing with fiction's expansive ability to create alternatives to reality.

Haruhi contains none of the geopolitical panic or the melancholy fatalism which define the core *sekai-kei* fictions. However, it is even more saturated with mediated visuality. The original 2003 light novel established the influential character dynamic of "ironic boy meets obsessive girl," as well as the textual process of calling attention to its own haphazard use of the "quotes, archetypes, allusions, and references" it draws from otaku transmedia (Saito, 2015, p. 156). Put into the terms of this chapter's discussion, *Haruhi* turns *sekai-kei*'s scales of visuality and constructions of world-as-genre-assemblage into a mundane process. The lived experience it articulates becomes obvious in Kyoto Animation's 2006 anime series, which definitively actualizes *Haruhi*'s dynamics within an energized hyper-mediated environment. Scenes are fractured and reassembled through frenzied cuts, enhanced with extra-diegetic flourishes, blended with associative symbols, and shot through with endless moments of remediation—all unified through the subject-perception enacted by Kyon's persistent voice-over. In effect, the *Haruhi* anime simulates an experience of school life within a media-saturated world, reorienting *sekai-kei*'s social imaging techniques toward a manic celebration of the self-referencing media environment which it itself generates.

The intense connectivity of *Haruhi*'s world is characterized by an almost magical form of associative thinking on both the structural and the diegetic levels. Haruhi's plans involve assembling symbolic elements of a certain genre in a kind of ritual meant to summon the narrative events they represent. Her actions do affect the world but are endlessly warped, deflected, and recombined, as in the episode shown in Figure 12.9. Through a byzantine chain of sci-fi causality, Haruhi's handmade club logo allows an interdimensional cricket monster to awaken within computer networks. The sense of an intensified and disordered post-social space through which *sekai-kei* fictions grasped the social breakdown at the turn of the millennium persists inside *Haruhi*. The stable national imaginary of "normative notions and images" organizing social experience has long since gone, replaced by a phenomenology of perplexing fluctuations between media systems, fictional world-settings, aesthetic tropes, and narrative frames (Taylor, 2003, p. 32). If the original *sekai-kei* fictions were anxious apprehensions of the

Figure 12.9 Haruhi's mysterious logo unleashes havoc in the *Haruhi* anime.

collapse of the postwar social order and the initial phase of globalization, one might easily see in *Haruhi* a gleeful acquiescence in Japan's absorption into the fluid media environment of global communicative capitalism.

However, *Haruhi*'s narrative-based structure always grounds mediated experience in subjective perception. The logo incident ends with character shots of Kyon saying "I'm afraid" and pensively walking down a moonlit street. Here too, the ludic play of recombinatory images reflects and feeds a subjective social orientation—a pair of eyes looking at and trying to order their world. The physicality of the everyday also continues to reassert itself within the seemingly endless flow. The discomfort of the seasons—cold mornings in the winter and sweaty classrooms in the summer—are recurring themes, as is Kyon's grueling uphill walk to school. One full episode is given over to "long takes" of events moving in real time, showing the characters from a single angle as they silently relax in their club room, with only ambient school sounds in the background (Figure 12.10). The shock of this extended stillness after long periods of speed creates, at least for a moment, a hierarchy of perception with it at the center. It gives a sense of the delirious flow through spaces of possibility and fictional alterity created by media environments naturally and inevitably returning to the naked sensation of being physically situated in the world, experiencing it alongside other similar beings. In its own way, *Haruhi* also attempts to imagine the social through transmediation.

Through its adaptation and proliferation through franchises like *Haruhi*, *sekai-kei*'s problematics persist throughout otaku media culture: for example, in the recent popularity of *isekai* stories which dramatize the experience of casualized labor within a RPG-fantasy world, or in the "anime

Figure 12.10 An episode of stillness in the *Haruhi* anime.

pilgrimage" phenomenon of fans visiting real-world locations featured in anime, or in the online practice of creating anime personifications of political entities. All these cultural forms attempt to envisage the social through the lens of transmediation. All of them encounter the dual nature of media environments as both self-referencing consumption and communicators of experience, and all engage with this duality by shifting between the expansive and/or cohesive power of fiction and the stimulation of everyday affects. This tenuous movement constitutes what I see as the social imagination of otaku culture. Any new possibilities of social relation or potential politics its articulations of mediated sociality might produce are intriguing topics for further inquiry.

Notes

1 This chapter will follow Japanese naming conventions and apply macrons in transliteration, except in the case where an author's publication is originally in English. In this case, the name will appear as it does in the original publication. All English translations of Japanese text are my own.

2 "Otaku" is the longstanding term used to describe die-hard fans of Japanese anime and manga. However, the terms "otaku media" or "otaku culture" in this chapter refer, as they do in prominent Japanese discussions, to the transmedia flow of images and themes throughout this media ecology according to unifying forces of character-based affect (see Steinberg, 2012) and libidinal "affinity for the fictional context" (Saitō, 2000, p. 20). The essays in Debating Otaku can provide a more thorough elaboration of the term "otaku" for English readers (Galbraith et al., 2015). Azuma Hiroki's postmodern analysis of otaku, touched on in this chapter, also has an English translation (Azuma, 2009).

References

Akiyama, M. (2001). *Iriya no sora, UFO no natsu* [Iriya's sky, summer of the UFOs] (Vol. 1). Tokyo: Dengeki Bunko.

Azuma, H. (Ed.). (2004). *Bishōjo gēmu no rinkaiten* [The limit of bishojo games] (Vol. 1). Tokyo: Hajou Books.

Azuma, H. (2007). *Gēmuteki riarizumu no tanjō: Dōbutsuka suru posutomodān 2* [Japan's database animals 2: Game-like realism]. Tokyo: Kodansha Gendai Shinsho.

Azuma, H. (2009). *Otaku: Japan's database animals* (J. E. Abel and S. Kono, Trans.). Minneapolis: University of Minnesota Press.

Bauman, Z. (2000). *Liquid modernity.* Cambridge, UK: Polity Press.

Condry, I. (2013). *The soul of anime: Collaborative creativity and Japan's media success story.* Durham, NC: Duke University Press.

Deleuze, G. (1995). *Negotiations 1972–1990* (M. Joughin, Trans.). New York, NY: Columbia University Press.

Fujiki, H. (2019). *Eiga kankyaku to wa nanimono ka: Media to shakai shutai no kingendaishi* [Who is the cinema audience?: A modern-contemporary history of media and social subjects]. Nagoya: Nagoya University Press.

Fukuda, M. (2010). *Risuku komyunikēshon to media: Shakai chōsaronteki apurōchi* [Risk communication and media: A social survey approach]. Tokyo: Hokuju Shuppan.

Galbraith, P. W, Kam, T. H, & Kamm, B. (Eds.) (2015). *Debating Otaku in contemporary Japan: Historical perspective and new horizons.* London, UK: Bloomsbury.

Genda, Y. (2005). *A nagging sense of job insecurity: The new reality facing Japanese youth* (J. C. Hoff, Trans.). New York, NY: House Press.

Hagiwara, S. (Ed.). (2007). *Terebi nyūsu no sekaizō: Gaikoku kanren hōdō ga kōchiku suru riaritī* [Television's world-image: The reality created by foreign-news coverage]. Tokyo: Keisō Shobō.

Hamano, S. (2014). Jōhōka: Nihon shakai wa jōhōka no yume o miru ka [Does Japanese society dream of informationization?] In Eiji Oguma (Ed.), *Heisei-shi* [History of the Heisei era] (pp. 431–466). Tokyo: Kawade Shobō Shinsha.

Hook, G. D., & Takeda, H. (2007). Self-responsibility and the nature of the postwar Japanese state: Risk through the looking glass. *The Journal of Japanese Studies* Vol. 33, No. 1 (Winter 2007), pp. 93–123.

Ishihara, T. (Director). (2006). *Suzumiya Haruhi no yūutsu* [The melancholy of Haruhi Suzumiya] [Television series]. Uji: Kyoto Animation.

Itō, N. (Director). (2005). *Iriya no sora, UFO no natsu* [Iriya's sky, summer of the UFOS] [OVA]. Tokyo: Toei Animation.

Iwabuchi, K. (2007). *Bunka no taiwaryoku: Sofuto pawā to burando nashonarizumu wo koete* [Culture's power of dialogue: Beyond soft power and brand-nationalism]. Tokyo: Nihon Keizai Shinbunsha.

Jenkins, H. (2006). *Convergence culture: Where old and new media collide.* New York, NY: New York University Press.

Kasai, K. (2009). Sekai-kei to reigai jōtai [Sekai-kei and the state of exception]. In Genkai shōsetsu kenkyūkai [Limit-Novel Research Group] (Ed.), *Shakai wa sonzai shinai: Sekai-kei bunkaron* [Society does not exist: Sekai-kei cultural theory], pp. 21–61. Tokyo: Nan'un-do.

Kase, M. (Director). (2002). *Saishū Heiki Kanojo* [She, the ultimate weapon] [anime series]. Tokyo: Gonzo.

Kotani, S. (Ed.). (2017). *Nijūisseiki no wakamonoron: Aimai na fuan wo ikiru* [Twenty-first-century theories of the youth: Living with vague unease]. Tokyo: Sekai Shisōsha.

Maejima, S. (2010). *Sekai-kei to wa nani ka* [What is sekai-kei]. Tokyo: Seikaisha Bunko.

Orgad, S. (2012). *Media representations and the global imagination*. Cambridge, UK: Polity Press.

Saito, S. (2015). Beyond the horizon of the possible worlds: A historical overview of Japanese media Franchises. (F. Lunning, Ed.). *Mechademia: World Renewal* Vol. 10, pp. 143–161.

Saitō, T. (2000). *Sentō bishōjo seishin bunseki* [The psychoanalysis of beautiful fighting girls]. Tokyo: Ōta Shuppan.

Satō, S. (2004). Iriya no sora: Sukō wo megute [Iriya's sky: On the sublime]. *Majestic, 12*(01), n.p.

Shaviro, S. (2010). *Post-cinematic affect*. Winchester, UK: Zero Books.

Shinkai, M. (Director). (2002). *Hoshi no koe* [Voices of a distance star] [Cinematic anime]. Tokyo: CoMix Wave Inc.

Silverstone, R. (2007). *Media and morality: On the rise of the mediapolis* (Kindle ed.). Cambridge, UK: Polity Press.

Steinberg, M. (2012). *Anime's media mix: Franchising toys and characters in Japan*. Minneapolis: University of Minnesota Press.

Steinberg, M. (2014). Realism in the animation media environment: Animation theory from Japan. In K. Beckman (Ed.), *Animating film theory* (pp. 287–300). Durham, NC: Duke University Press.

Suan, S. (2018). Anime's identity: Performativity and media-form in our moment of globalization (Doctoral dissertation, Kyoto Seika University).

Takahashi, S. (2000–2001). *Saishū Heiki Kanojo* [She, the ultimate weapon] (Vol. 1–7) [Manga]. Tokyo: Shogakkan.

Tanigawa, N. (2003). *Suzumiya Haruhi no yūutsu* [The melancholy of Haruhi Suzumiya]. Tokyo: Kadokawa Sunīkā Bunko.

Taylor, C. (2003). *Modern social imaginaries*. Durham, NC: Duke University Press.

Tomlinson, J. (1999). *Globalization and culture*. Cambridge, UK: Polity Press.

Ueno, C. (2013). *Onnatachi no sabaibaru sakusen* [Women's survival strategies]. Tokyo: Bunshun.

Uno, T. (2008). *Zero-jidai no sōzōryoku* [The imagination of the 2000s]. Tokyo: Hayakawa Shobō.

Watanabe, O. (2007). Nihon no shinjiyūshugi: Hāvī no 'shinjiyūshugi' ni yosete [Japanese neoliberalism: Following Harvey's 'Neoliberalism']. In D. Harvey (Ed.), *Neoliberalism* (Japanese edition, pp. 289–329). Tokyo: Sakuhinsha.

Yoshimi, S. (2009). *Posuto sengo shakai* [Post-postwar society]. Tokyo: Iwanami Shinsho.

13 From media mix to platformization

The transmedia strategy of "IP" in *One Hundred Thousand Bad Jokes*

Jinying Li

In 2014, one of the most successful films in Chinese movie theaters was an animated feature film, *One Hundred Thousand Bad Jokes*. With a modest budget of merely 10 million RMB, the film earned 120 million RMB at the box office, becoming one of the highest earning Chinese animation films in the recent history. Like many successful animation films, *One Hundred Thousand Bad Jokes* was part of a tremendously popular transmedia franchise: it was initially a web comic series that began to be published on the online comic platform u17.com in 2010, which was then followed by an animated web video series that had gained increasing popularity on Chinese video-sharing platforms such as Youku, Tencent, and Bilibili since 2012. Before the feature animation film was released in movie theaters, the web comics and video series had already generated billions of viewership and a substantial fan base on China's rapidly expanding Internet platforms. To a large extent, the box-office triumph of the animation film *One Hundred Thousand Bad Jokes* was the result of an Internet cultural phenomenon rather than a cinematic one. Subsequently, the successful release of the feature film in 2014 was quickly followed by a popular mobile game, a live theatrical performance, and a feature animation film sequel, *One Hundred Thousand Bad Jokes 2*, which was released in 2017 with equal success as the previous one. Overall, the series' sizable online fan base was effectively transformed to powerful cultural synergy to propel a successful transmedia system.

The transmedia spread of *One Hundred Thousand Bad Jokes* also marks the profound impact of the localization of anime and its media mix culture in China. By "anime," I am not simply referring to a national form of Japanese animation as it is commonly known. Instead, the term describes a transnational cultural system of animation with a specific set of visual styles (e.g. flatness, stillness, and limited movement) that date back to the conventions of postwar manga and TV animation in Japan, as well as a transmedia franchising and merchandising system centering on anime and manga that is described as "media mix" (LaMarre, 2009; Steinberg, 2012). The transmedia franchise of *One Hundred Thousand Bad Jokes*, including the web comics, the animation video series, and the feature films, all demonstrate the characteristic features of anime and its media mix, though they were produced in China by Chinese authors and artists and targeting the Chinese audience. Not only are the visual styles of *One Hundred Thousand Bad Jokes* almost identical to those of Japanese manga and anime, but this Chinese web comic and animation series also frequently make references to famous manga and anime, such as *Neon Genesis Evangelion, Gundam, Detective Conan, Slam Dunk, Saint Seiya,* and *Attack on Titan,* all of which have widespread popularity in China. Its narrative form, which consists of a collection of comedic gags, memes, parodies, pastiches, sarcastic comments and humorous cultural references, is following the genre conventions of popular manga comedies such as *Gag Manga Biyori* and *Gin Tama.* So much so that *One Hundred Thousand Bad Jokes* is also described as the "Chinese version of *Gag Manga Biyori*" (Xu, 2014). Combining web comics, digital animation, and mobile gaming across multiple platforms to generate transmedia synergy and to expand the fan base, the franchising mechanism of *One Hundred Thousand Bad Jokes* appears to be similar to that of anime's media mix, which is also known in China as Japanese ACG (animation, comics, and games). The commercial success of *One Hundred Thousand Bad Jokes* thus demonstrates the extensive domestication of the transmedia strategies of anime and otaku culture in China.[1]

Unlike anime's media mix, however, the transmedia system of *One Hundred Thousand Bad Jokes* was not developed by the animation studio or the comic author who created the original content. Instead, it was developed, controlled and managed by u17.com (hereafter u17), one of China's earliest and largest online platforms for publishing original web comics.[2] Initially founded in 2006 as a comic-sharing website for fans, u17 quickly became a major digital content platform that is specially designed for original web comics. Since 2009, u17 has published some of the most popular web comics in China, and *One Hundred Thousand Bad Jokes* in particular was developed and celebrated by the platform as its most successful and valuable transmedia series that is often described as "IP." In fact, the box-office success of the animated film version of *Bad Jokes* in 2014 coincided with the rise of the co-called IP films in Chinese media industry. The concept of IP here refers to transmedia content as original intellectual property for cinematic adaptation, and the notion of IP films describes a trending strategy to attach film production to a larger transmedia ecosystem that proliferates various types of content, including cinema, comics, novels, games, music and television shows, through digital platforms (Li, forthcoming in 2020). With platforms as the new nexus in a transmedia ecosystem, IP and its development are thus controlled by China's largest platform providers such as Tencent, Alibaba, and Aiqiyi instead of content creators. Therefore, the notion of IP is not simply about intellectual property, but refers to a complex transmedia system that is based on the infrastructure and operation of platforms. And the rise of IP films, as I argued elsewhere, is the result of the platformization of Chinese cinema in the Internet era, which has profoundly transformed the production and consumption of film culture with new logics of content generation, management, and control that are dictated by the technology and political economy of digital platforms (ibid.).

The box-office triumph of *One Hundred Thousand Bad Jokes* is one of the prime examples of the commercial success of IP films. And its successful transmedia strategy for content creation, distribution, and consumption marks the transition of Chinese animation from anime's media mix system to platform-based IP system, a process that entails the ongoing platformization that has fundamentally reshaped the landscape of media cultures in China.

This chapter examines this process by comparing the emerging new strategy of IP in the transmedia system of *One Hundred Thousand Bad Jokes* with the existing model of media mix that has been established in anime culture. Whereas the media mix system relies on the world-character relation to regulate the transmedial process of production and consumption to maintain a certain degree of consistency in content control (Steinberg, 2012), the IP system rather operates through what I have called "affective modules" to establish, sustain, and manage affective parasocial contact with users, so that the massive data trafficking that is generated through such contact can be effectively captured, controlled, and monetized by the algorithmic infrastructure of platforms (Li, forthcoming in 2020). This platform-based enframing of affective contact is at the center of the transmedia strategy of IP system. Understanding how IP enframes affective parasocial activity, as well as how such affective enframing drives transmedia proliferation and consumption of content, is the key to understanding the operational logics of digital platforms and the ways in which they have transformed our social and cultural lives.

The affective modules of IP as a platform

Although the concept of IP refers to the intellectual property of a certain media content for transmedia franchising, its significance relies less on the adaptation of original texts than the transferability of users and fans to other media contexts (Yin & Liang, 2016, p. 6). With the notion of "IP transfer" at the center, this transmedia system blurs the distinction between content generation and information flow. The core value of an IP, therefore, is not simply the intellectual property of a media content, but is the monetizable data generated from the networked connectivity among the multitudes of users and contents. As such, the system of IP operates as less a process of textual adaptation than a networked assemblage of transmedia modules, which are often fragmented and highly affective. In other words, the key purpose of an IP is not simply to proliferate contents across different media, but also to assemble and operate these networked modules to generate, enhance, and manage user communication and informational contact for monetization. Thus, IP functions as the "connection point to realize the aggregation of audiences from diverse media arenas" (Wang & Wang, 2015, p. 164). Such is also the function of a platform, a communicative, informational aggregation system for putting users, contents, products, services, and money in contact (Gawer, 2011; Gillespie, 2010; Helmond, 2015; Li, 2017; Steinberg, 2017), which is the infrastructural foundation that the IP system is based upon. If the function of a platform is fundamentally to enable the digital lockdown of intra-user contact (with data, contents, products, and etc.) into a centralized information system for algorithmic control, management, and monetization, then the function of an IP, in a similar fashion, is to transfer, capture and contain fans' affective attachment into a transmedia ecosystem for generating valuable information flow.

For the aggregation system of a platform, a modular structure is crucial, because it allows standard interfaces for seamless exchange of data, contents, services, and commodities (Gawer, 2011). These digital modules, such as links, apps, or "like" buttons, are the operative sites where user interactivity and communication are enabled to generate big data and information flow (Langlois & Elmer, 2013). For the transmedia system of IP, the fragmented and affective textual modules, such as gags, songs, and dramatic scenes, are also the operative sites where fan attachment is created, captured and sustained to facilitate data transfer and management. From this perspective, *One Hundred Thousand Bad Jokes* is arguably one of the best examples of IP as a networked assemblage of affective modules, because this transmedia series, in either comics, games, or animation videos and films, is always structured as a highly fragmented complex composed with a collection of sketches and gags, rather than a coherent narrative with stories. By closely examining the ways in which the transmedia system is formed and operated in *One Hundred Thousand Bad Jokes*, I want to study how the affective modules of IP function as enframing devices to capture and contain affective communications, and how these devices transfer the textual meanings of media content to the monetizable values of informational contact. I will demonstrate that the affective modules function as contact points to evoke user interaction and communication, shifting the focus of a transmedia system from narrative content to informational contact. Such a shift entails a profound transformation of transmedia strategy, from the character-world relation in media mix to affective resonance in the platform-based IP system. The move from media mix to platformization suggests that parasociality has taken the priority over storytelling as the central mechanism of a transmedia system, leading to a change in the logic of media culture from narrative consumption to platformativity.

From content to contact

As the title suggests, *One Hundred Thousand Bad Jokes* is less about storytelling than about evoking audience reactions to humor. Fashioning itself as a seemingly random collection of "bad jokes," the series, either in web comics or animated web videos, is structured as a networked assemblage of short, disjunctive comical sketches. In the comics, each chapter is no more than ten pages, and one chapter is not necessarily connected to the next one in narrative or setting. And the numbering system of the chapters is non-sequential and appears to be random. For instance, chapter 99984 is part of a story called "The End of the World," which is followed by chapter 80012 that appears to be simply a parody of Chinese traditional poetry. The next is chapter 99035, which is a short comical sketch with a dystopian story about metamorphosis, followed by chapter 99984.5, which seems to come back to "The End of the World" story though with additional notes from the author about how to use the new commenting interface on the platform u17 where the web comic was published. The resulting structure is quite disjunctive, jumping from the fragment of one story to that of another, from a fictional universe to the author's comments, from the parody of one popular culture to the reference to another. The animated web video series is also structured in a similar fashion. The episodes are short—five to ten minutes each—and the order among them appears to be non-sequential. Episode 1 is titled "Nezha's Story 1," while episode 2 is "Pinocchio's Story," followed by episode 3 titled "Nezha's Story 2." Episodes 4 to 6 then tell a new story "Fulu" followed by episodes 7 and 8 "The End of World." And episode 9 comes back to "Nezha's Story 3." The structure is thus fragmented, disjunctive, and lack of closure. As such, the diegetic universe (or universes as there is not a singular, unifying story) is ruptured and flattened. There is no longer a linear progression with a cause-effect chain, but is a modular network consisted of disjunctive fragments that can be breaking apart and reassembled.

Although these short, disjunctive fragments in the comic and animation series are not connected by any narrative logic, they are united by an affective one, that is, to *make you laugh*. As gags, jokes, or memes, the disjunctive fragments in *One Hundred Thousand Bad Jokes* are highly affective. The graphic style of the comic and animation is often crude but explicit, and the humor is often quite visceral and even infectious. It is evidently clear that the intension of this transmedia series is not storytelling, but is to evoke affective response and connection with the viewers. In fact, generating active user interaction and participation is the key to the development of the transmedia system of *One Hundred Thousand Bad Jokes* as a successful IP. The structure of the comic and animation is purposely designed to be fragmented and disjunctive so that it can effectively stimulate user participation—the viewers have to constantly rearrange the fragments and to actively establish the missing links to make sense of the narrative themselves. The nonlinear assemblage of affective fragments is uniquely powerful to enable user attachment. And almost every element of *One Hundred Thousand Bad Jokes* is intended to sustain an open, interactive, and participatory media environment. For instance, the characters in the stories constantly break the fourth wall to give self-reflective comments. And the comic author, who uses the name "Han Wu" and is drawn as a young man with a knife stuck in his forehead, frequently appears in the comic and animation videos to directly address the readers and audiences.

In sum, the transmedia system of *Hundred Thousand Bad Jokes* is driven less by the narrative content for storytelling than by the affective contact for fan attachment. And the contact is not only affective but also intertextual. The comical gags in the series are often parodic references to or satirical comments of certain popular cultural elements such as Japanese anime, Disney cartoons, and Hollywood superhero movies that are especially recognizable among China's otaku generation who grew up with the expanding global networks of geeky subcultures. In fact, most of the stories in the series are not original narratives, but are parodic sketches or satirical pastiches that make fun of well-known cultural objects. "Nezha's Story," for instance, is a spoof of a mythical character in Chinese traditional folktale, and "Pinocchio's Story" and "Snow White's Story" are evidently lampoons of Disney fairytales. And "The Hero's Story" is a satirical take on glitches and clichés in video games. Identifying these intertextual references and parodies, which is like interactive gameplay between viewers and contents, is the main part of the pleasure to enjoy these "bad jokes."

Evoking affective and intertextual connections, *One Hundred Thousand Bad Jokes* presents its transmedia content as contact. These affective modules—jokes, gags, and spoofs—are the contact points where the texts, viewers, meanings, and affects meet. In other words, the function of the transmedia content in *One Hundred Thousand Bad Jokes* is not telling stories, but is generating affective contact. The shift from content to contact marks the key characteristic of IP as a platform-based transmedia system, because the central logic of a platform, as I have argued earlier, is to pave a space to establish effective contact of a certain kind (Li, 2017). The focus on contact also distinguishes IP from conventional strategies of transmedia content generation whereby consistency in narrative tropes and character designs is still very much at the center for expansive world building. The IP system, in contrast, is not so much concerned with controlling and proliferating contents as with generating, sustaining, and managing as many contact points as possible. Like a platform that relies on various digital apps or functions (e.g. "like" buttons, face lenses, emoji stickers) to maintain user stickiness, IP uses affective modules as contact points to capture, contain, and control users' attachment within its transmedia ecosystem. As contact points, the affective modules demand constant interactions with users, locking them down into the platformed system of IP by sustaining and managing affective contacts that are algorithmically encoded, enhanced, and enclosed as data traffics.

In the platformed transmedia system of *One Hundred Thousand Bad Jokes*, those affective modules ("bad jokes") as contact points also visually manifest themselves through a unique interface effect called *danmaku* (or, "danmu" as it is pronounced in Chinese), which renders user comments overlapping the visual content on screen. Originally designed by Japanese video-sharing platform Niconico, the *danmaku* interface was quickly popularized in China and was widely spread from video-streaming platforms to television to cinema to social media, becoming almost a signature interface in Chinese digital culture (Li, 2017). U17.com, where *One Hundred Thousand Bad Jokes* was originally published, was the first comic content platform in China to have incorporated the *danmaku* interface, which quickly became its most popular feature. On u17 or elsewhere, the key function of the *danmaku* interface on media platforms is not so much to generate user comments or derivative content as to stimulate and sustain active, communicative contacts—between content and users as well as among users themselves—by rendering these dynamic contacts highly visible on screen. As Marc Steinberg (2017) notes, the purpose of *danmaku* on Niconico is to sustain active communications, because "communication is more important than content" for the ecosystem of a transmedia platform.

As a comic content platform that is famous for its *danmaku* interface, u17 foregrounds its central objective of sustaining communicative contact. It describes the function of user comment on *danmaku* as "*tucao*," a popular term in Chinese otaku culture that was borrowed from the Japanese word *tsukkomi*, which means to point out or comment on something that is ridiculous, silly or nonsensical in comedy. In its original Japanese cultural context, *tsukkomi* often acts in pair with *boke* in a stand-up comedy duo, and thus it is a communicative action in a conversational setting. Emphasizing the sense of interactivity and communicativeness in the original Japanese term, *tucao* in its Chinese context is recognized as a central element in participatory fan cultures, for writing funny or satirical comments is one of the most common activities for fans to participate in content generation. On the platform u17, all user comments on *danmaku* are called *tucao*, regardless of whether they are comical or not, because they are all communicative and participatory in nature. By equating *danmaku* comments with *tucao*, the platform emphasizes the interactive and communicative dimension in *danmaku* interface. Thus, *tucao* is the act of contact among users, content and platform, and *danmaku* is a dynamic contact zone where such contact takes place in a highly visible and affective manner.

Developed by the platform u17, the transmedia system of *One Hundred Thousand Bad Jokes* highlights the platform's unique interface effect of *danmaku*, by incorporating comical *tucao* in its texts and paratexts. Since most of the "bad jokes" are satirical comments that make fun of the silly clichés in popular culture, the series almost appears as an assemblage of various kinds of *tucao*, and its object of *tucao* comments is often itself. Like a typical *tsukkomi* in Japanese stand-up comedy, characters in *Bad Jokes* often self-reflectively point out the ridiculousness in the story, the setting or other chatterers. The fictional characters also frequently comment on or make fun of the comic author himself, telling the viewers that the incoherence of the story or the poor character design are the result of the author's laziness. Overall, *tucao*, or self-*tucao*, is the central theme that unites the seemingly chaotic structure of the series. Such a gesture of self-mockery is also a gesture of invitation, inviting the readers and audiences to participate in the collective activity of *tucao*. In fact, the author even appears in one chapter of the comic to directly address the readers, discussing with them about how to effectively use the *tucao* function on *danmaku* interface. And the viewers respond to this invitation enthusiastically by entering overwhelming comments on *danmaku*: the first page of this web comic received more than 7,000 entries of *tucao* comments on the *danmaku* interface of u17. The fan participation through *danmaku* comments made *One Hundred Thousand Bad Jokes* one of the most popular web comics in China. Since the platform u17 is the owner and developer of the IP, its interface effect of *tucao* on *danmaku* is not only highlighted in the web comic series, but is embraced as a central nexus that organizes the whole transmedia system of the IP. For the animated web video series, u17 collaborated with Bilibili, a leading video-sharing platform that features *danamku*, as a co-producer and distributor, because the video platform's *danmaku* interface is a perfect match for the series' emphasis on *tucao* commenting. The mobile game version also features *tucao* function on *danmaku* interface, and the player' commenting activity is one of the key elements in the game play that emphasizes social interactivity as much as competitive combat.

More importantly, the series not only takes advantage of the commenting function on *danmaku* as a core mechanism to organize its transmedia ecosystem, but it also features *tucao* commenting as a central motif in its narrative and visual design, converging content with the logic of platform and its interface effect. As an assemblage of "bad jokes" (instead of stories), the series is not driven by narrative, but is almost entirely driven by the sensibility of *tucao*. As many commentators have observed, *One Hundred Thousand Bad Jokes* is not so much a transmedia system of storytelling as that of *tucao* commenting (Han, 2015; Xu, 2014). If *tucao* marks the interface effect of *danmauku* on the platform u17, it is also the central force that unifies the transmedia series of *Bad Jokes* and attracts its fan base. The quality of the platform is thus transferred to and converged with that of content. Since *tucao* is more aligned with communicative contact than with narrative content, it also shifts the focus of the transmedia system toward platformed connectivity.

The series *One Hundred Thousand Bad Jokes* demonstrates the centrality of *tucao* commenting most explicitly and dramatically in the story called "The End of the World." Its hero is an anonymous male character whose super power is nothing but *tucao*, which is channeled and enhanced through advanced alien technologies to become tremendous energy and combat power. The hero unleashes his *tucao* power to defeat the alien enemy and saves the whole world from apocalypse. The story was so central to the whole transmedia series that it became the narrative base for the feature animation film that has the same character with a similar narrative trope. As ridiculous as it may appear to be, the story is actually quite a playful self-reflection of the cultural power of participatory viewership that is enabled by platform-based transmedia systems. The male hero, who remains anonymous throughout the whole series, is the alter ego of the viewers themselves, whose continuous communicative activity—in the form of *tucao* commenting on *danmaku*— is the ultimate driving force that propels the engine of a transmedia system. Indeed, the real production force that generates and sustains the transmedia system of IP is neither the author nor the platform, but is the collective, free labor of participatory fans, whose communicative energy—like the *tucao* energy of the fictional hero—is technologically encoded and enhanced by digital interfaces such as *danmaku* to drive the proliferation of transmedia content on platforms. In the climax of the animated feature film, the hero's superpower of *tucao* is literally visualized in the form of *danmaku* with lines of *tucao* comments flying over screen in seemingly real time. Enhanced by the *danmaku* effect, the tremendous *tucao* energy that the hero unleashes through this overwhelming amount of onscreen comments eventually defeats the enemy and ultimately saves the world. The story makes it blatantly clear that the real power is not from creating a story or a character, but from *tucao*, that is, user communication and participation. In other words, what drives the transmedia IP of *One Hundred Thousand Bad Jokes* is not its content but the contact—the interactive and affective act of *tucao* commenting that collectively creates a transmedia environment where people are communicating with each other by laughing, joking, and spoofing together with silly comments. Such a function of participatory sociality is the key element of not only transmedia IP but almost any digital platforms.

From "worldview" to "affective resonance"

The shift from content to contact, from storytelling to social networking, also entails a radical departure from the well-established model of transmedia strategy that is commonly known as media mix in Japan or convergence in Hollywood. The central elements for developing a successful transmedia franchise are expansive world building and consistent character design. Transmedia franchising, as Henry Jenkins (2006, p. 21) points out, "is the art of world making. To fully experience any fictional world, consumers must assume the role of hunters and gatherers, chasing down bits of the story across media channels." The character-world relation, in particular, is the guiding principle in the operation system of media mix. Since a transmedia system is always an expansive network of fragments with increasing number of variable and derivative contents, the character-world relation provides an effective model for the producers to maintain a certain degree of control, by proposing "to develop multiple narrative fragments on the basis of a single worldview" (Steinberg, 2012, p. 17). The "worldview" (*sekaikan*) is the grand narrative that unites all the small narratives in the media mix system. Fans consume a great amount of small narrative frag-ments across many different media—comics, animations, games, or toys—in order to gain access to the grand narrative, the worldview. Amidst the expansive system with proliferating variations and fragments, the character design is centrally controlled by the producer and studio, providing a reg-ulatory mechanism to maintain a certain degree of consistency (Steinberg, 2012, pp. 176–183). This model of media mix is first theorized by Otsuka Eiji as "narrative consumption" (Otsuka, 1989).

Compared with this media mix strategy that centers on the character-world relation, the transmedia system of *One Hundred Thousand Bad Jokes*, in a sharp contrast, is completely lack of a unifying worldview. As an assemblage of comical sketches, the series tells many small fragmented stories that are never intended to be united by a central grand narrative, though there may be some subtle clues or connections among them in terms of genre, style, or subject. Instead of a singular worldview, the transmedia series of *Bad Jokes* rather features a network of multiple diverse worlds that appear to be unrelated to each other without a sense of unification. The universe of Superman that is saturated with loads of clichés from Hol-lywood and DC comic merges with the world of Ultraman, the superhero from a Japanese TV series that was incredibly popular in China in the 1980s; the world of Nezha in ancient Chinese myth is juxtaposed with the worlds of western fairytales of Snow White and Pinocchio; the science fiction universe of an anonymous hero saving humanity from Godzilla-like alien monsters suddenly jumps into the world of martial arts with two fa-mous kung-fu masters caught in a perpetual duel on a rooftop; the world of teenage romance with a magical girlfriend that follows the conventions of Japanese manga is intermingled with the legend of Monkey King and his fantastic adventure in the mythical landscape of ancient China where the "original" Monkey King meets Goku from *Dragon Ball*.

Without the central unification of a grand worldview, however, these diverse, fragmented "small" worlds are rather connected by the shared af-fective responses that are evoked: they make you laugh while at the same time generate nostalgic feelings toward these canonic stories and characters in children's entertainment—Monkey King, Snow White, Pinocchio, Su-perman, and Ultrman—that are fondly remembered and enjoyed by global youth. Consuming these small worlds through the transmedia IP is akin to sharing our collective childhood memory on social media platforms, though with a little kinky tone and a comedic touch that betrays the loss of innocence in adulthood. This collective experience of memory-sharing evokes nostalgic and sentimental feelings that are deeply affective. Viewers' comments often openly admit that they enjoy the series with both laughter and tears. These shared affective feelings unite this otherwise chaotic and fragmented assemblage of diverse universes, giving it a certain degree of emotional—rather than narrative—consistency across different worlds and variations, and ultimately gather viewers together in this transmedia system of the IP. What drives viewers to consume these diverse small stories across different media is not the desire to access to a grand worldview, but is the evocation of shared affective feelings that connect the fans with the IP as well as with other fans through a strong, affective parasocial bond. Indeed, on forums, discussion boards, and social media platforms, what have been mostly commented on and discussed about among *Bad Jokes'* millions of fans are neither particular characters nor the worldview (or the lack thereof), but their shared affective feelings: the naughty laughter on Nezha's birth and the teary sorrow upon his death; the surprising amusement and kinky delight of seeing Snow White falling in love with Pinocchio; the nostalgia and excitement when witnessing Ultraman and Superman, two of our favorite childhood superheroes, meet together to crack a stupid joke. Rather than "chasing down bits of the story" to gain access to the worldview, the fans of *Bad Jokes* pursuit those diverse and disjunctive fragments across different media in order be connected with shared affective feelings. In fact, it is such affective contact, rather than the character-world relation, that organizes the transmedia ecosystem of *One Hundred Thousand Bad Jokes* as an effective and valuable IP. As such, IP is a generative platform that enables, sustains, and controls these affective connections.

The crucial role of affective contact in establishing a transmedia system of IP is well known in Chinese media industry, especially among platform operators such as Tencent and Alibaba who first introduced the concept and business model of IP. They call it "affective resonance" (*qinggan gongming*), which is the core element in the transmedia strategy of IP. Describing IP as the "container of user's affect" Tencent's senior executive Cheng Wu highlights the significance of affective resonance to generate and sustain continuous user contact, that is, to maintain user stickiness and enclosure within a transmedia system of IP. It is through affective resonance that a user communicates with and participates in the IP system, a process of constant informational contact that produces valuable data traffics for platform operators (Cheng & Li, 2015). In other words, to establish a transmedia system of IP, affective resonance is the core engine, and data mining is the operative mechanism.

Affective resonance is indeed the key engine that drives the transmedia system of *One Hundred Thousand Bad Jokes*, especially for the box-office success of its feature film, as some reviewers have observed (Liu, 2014). Not only do the sentimental, nostalgic feelings that the series evokes generate affective resonance between viewers and the contents (as well as among viewers themselves), but the series' emphasis on *tucao* comments also resonates well with users' daily experience on popular media platforms that rely on their participatory commenting as the driving force. The characters in the series are constantly commenting or self-commenting on the ridiculous elements in their fictional worlds, which mirrors the common activities of the viewers, who are probably entering their *tucao* comments on *danmaku* right at the moment when they are reading the comics on u17 or watching the animation videos on Bilibili. The anonymous hero in the feature film, as I have argued earlier, is particularly designed as the alter ego of the audience. Like the hero on the screen, the viewers in front must also have realized that their interactive and communicative activity of *tucao* is the source of real superpower, the ultimate production force that propels the increasingly platformed media industry. Such recognition is where resonance takes place. Experiencing this resonance by recognizing oneself on screen also generates affective feelings of intimacy, familiarity, and proximity. It creates a sense of mutual connection and communication, a sense of belonging to a community, which points the function of IP toward the dimension of the social and the parasocial.

From narrative consumption to platformativity

The paradigm of storytelling is often considered the center of trasnmedia strategies, for the production and consumption of narratives are believed to be the forces that drive transmedia synergy. For example, the character-world relation, which serves as the guiding principle of media mix, is theorized by Otsuka Eiji (1989) as the mechanism of narrative consumption. In this mechanism, every unit or fragment in a transmedia system—a comic, animation, toy, or sticker—is consumed by fans as a small narrative. But the fundamental driving force that motivates this excessive, transmedia consumption is not the variation of small narratives themselves, but is the grand narrative (the worldview) that unites them all. The bigger amount of small fragments that consumers consume, the closer they get to the totality of the grand narrative. But what makes the grand narrative desirable is the fact that it is never fully presented but only hinted: its superseding power that unites all small narrative resides in its perpetually negative status of being absent. Consumers desire the grand narrative precisely because it is never there.

It is difficult not to interpret Otsuka's emphasis on the totality and elusiveness of the worldview along the lines of postmodern theories that center on the collapse of grand narratives and textual closure (Derrida, 1978; Lyotard & Jameson, 1984). In fact, Azuma Hiroki, a Japanese media theorist who further developed Otsuka's theory, characterizes narrative consumption precisely as a symptom of the early-stage postmodernity, whereby the worldview in a media mix system is simply a popular culture's substitute for the loss of the actual grand narrative and its implication in modern subjectivity (Azuma & Abel, 2009). This postmodern paradigm that challenges narrative closure, as Thomas Lamarre suggests, also points to the liberation of story from narrative discursiveness and its media formats (Lamarre, 2018, p. 179). This liberation of story, more importantly, coincided with a tendency to liberate content from materialized media conditions, facilitated by the legal and economic structure of intellectual property and licensing, as well as the rise of digitalization in cultural industries, which, by then, had also been widely known as "content industries." "Content is the king" became a new motto. In fact, the concept of media mix in Japan, as well as the concept of convergence in North America, came to the public attention at the precise moment when contents are believed to have taken the priority over material goods as major commodities. Both the concepts of convergence and media mix assume a certain degree of autonomy of content that can be freely transferred to any media contexts, a condition and implication of convergence that is often described as "spreadable" (Jenkins, Ford, & Green, 2013) Otsuka's theory of narrative consumption, to a certain degree, is also part of this content-centric paradigm in postmodern society that is dictated by the overwhelming diffusion of communicative signs in commodity environments for excessive consumption, or, in Otsuka's own words, "the endless play of *things* as signs" (Ōtsuka, 2010, p. 113, quoted from Steinberg, 2012, p. 180).

With the rise of digital platforms in the recent decade, however, the focus began to shift from content to platform. As Marc Steinberg (2017) observes, the rise of mediating platforms such as Niconico, whose *danmaku* commenting interface emphasizes as much social networking as content delivery, effectively merges contents with platforms, which puts forward transmedia convergence of another kind. For Chinese media industry, the rise of IP system marks a transitioning and converging point between content and platform. Although the terminological root of IP in intellectual property links it to the centrality of content, the fact that it is platform providers, instead of content industries, who raised the concept and proposed the model of IP complicates the situation by aligning the genealogical and operational origin of IP with the techno-economic logics of platforms. Indeed, as my case study of *One Hundred Thousand Bad Jokes* suggests, the transmedia system of IP operates more like a platform than content. It prioritizes social connectivity over storytelling, contact over content. Like a typical platform, IP relies on capturing and containing user attachment within an enclosed ecosystem through affective connections. And the key power of IP, as Tencent's senior VP Cheng Wu suggests, is its effectiveness in aggregation of core users who can be algorithmically matched with their desired products (Cheng & Li, 2015, p. 18). Such digital mapping between people and things is the typical function of a social graph for any popular media platform, be it Facebook or YouTube.

IP, in essence, is the result of the platformization of content. *One Hundred Thousand Bad Jokes* clearly demonstrates the effect of platformization: its lack of narrative consistency and unity (or, more precisely, the lack of narrative as such) and its devoid of a singular worldview. What drives consumers into the transmedia system of IP is no longer the desire of narrative consumption but is that of affective resonance. The platformization effect is most explicitly displayed in the series' first feature film, when *danmaku* comments are unleashed on screen as the hero's ultimate superpower, which playfully converges the platform logic and its interface effect with the dramatic elements of the narrative. If narrative consumption is the signature of a society with "the endless play of *things as signs*," the desire of connectivity in *One Hundred Thousand Bad Jokes* seems to suggest that we are now living in a society that has displaced signs with signals, which are more concerned with information relay than exchange of meanings.

The shift from narrative consumption in media mix to affective connectivity in IP also suggests a move away from the paradigm of storytelling in transmedia strategies, because storytelling cannot address the significance of contact that has become the central effect of platformization. Unlike content that focuses on individual units (a story, a film, or a novel), the notion of contact rather situates in the space and relation in between. The shift toward contact in IP as platform foregrounds the questions of what Thomas Lamarre (2018) describes as "intra-action and infra-individual resonance" (p. 114). To address these questions, Lamarre agues for a paradigm shift from transmedia storytelling to transmedia ecology, because "the ecological approach explores the infra-individual intra-actions that are brought into relations" (p. 115). Platforms are the infrastructures that mediate and contain these relations and contacts. Like platforms, IP also functions as a transmedia ecological system that brings users, contents, and platforms (the actual digital platforms such as u17 and Bilibili) into contacts through infra-individual intra-actions, that is, the affective resonance that IP generates and enframes.

If we consider IP as a generative platform, we have to understand it less as a system of transmedia storytelling than that of transmedia ecology, a system where the infra-individual intra-actions of affective resonance blurs the boundaries between content and platform, between signs and signals, between the individual and the infrastructural, between living organism and non-living things. This is a system of what Lamarre calls "platformativity," a concept that "is intended to address the infra-individual intra-actions between platform and human, and individual and collective – a kind of performativity via platforms" (Lamarre, 2017, p. 301). Overlapping the performative dimension of human culture with that of technological platforms, the concept invites us to think beyond an individual content or story, but to focus on the intermingled, "platformative" relations among humans, cultures, societies, and technologies.

In the system of platformativity, the affective quality of infra-individual intra-actions is more important than the representation of or interaction among individuals (Lamarre 2017, p. 302). It is precisely the case in the transmedia system of IP, whereby the infra-individual, affective resonance proves to be crucial. In the transmedia system of *One Hundred Thousand Bad Jokes*, the infra-individual, intra-action of participatory *tucao* commenting, as well as the affective feeling of collective nostalgia, is far more important than storytelling (if we can even consider its fragmented narrative a kind of storytelling). Almost all elements of the series, including its narrative, visual style and character design, are intended to enhance the affective resonance of the infra-individual, intra-action: the characters are familiar ones from collective childhood memories, who are doing a familiar thing (*tucao* commenting) on a familiar interface (*danmaku*). The infra-individual semblance, or, the platformative relation, among the characters, users, and the interface effect of platforms generates affective resonance that drives the IP system of *One Hundred Thousand Bad Jokes*. Without the totality of a singular worldview, the system is united by this affective resonance among the individual, the collective, and the infrastructural, as well as among users, content, and platform. In other words, it is the infra-individual, intra-action of platformativity that organizes the IP system of *One Hundred Thousand Bad Jokes*.

The infra-individual connections in the platformativity of IP are often intimate and ephemeral. The affective resonance between users and IP forms a kind of parasociality that captures the users in a social limbo that feels both familiar and distanced. However, for an Internet generation that is claimed to have increasingly been alienated, parasociality can sometime become the genuine, or even the only, sociality that one engages with. This brings a quasi-therapeutic function to the platformative, infra-individual connections in IP, for the affective resonance can breed a sense of belonging and intimacy. In fact, the parasocial aspect of platformativity is quite crucial for IP, whose transmedia system relies on the collective and participatory fan activities, which are almost always parasocial in nature, as the primary production force. This parasocial dimension in IP strategy is described as "crowdsourcing of feelings" (*qinggan zhongchong*), because participatory fans and users "invest their affective feelings into the creation and circulation of IP" (Yin & Liang, 2016, p. 6). It is probably also worth mentioning that the feature animation installment of *One Hundred Thousand Bad Jokes* is one of the first Chinese films to have used crowdfunding in its fundraising process. Although the fund that was raised through crowdsourcing was only a small part of the film's overall budget, the strategy generated active parasocial participation among fans, inviting them to further invest their affective feelings if not their money. No matter money or feelings, the reliance on crowdsourcing in the development of IP points to the central significance of parasociality in generating and sustaining a transmedia system in the era of platformativity.

Notes

1 The term "otaku" usually refers to the devoted fans of anime and manga in Japan and elsewhere. Translated as *"zhai wenhua"* in Chinese, the notion of otaku culture in China characterizes not only the transnational fan culture of anime's media mix but also the broader cultural spectrum of Internet-based media consumption that is often excessive, participatory, and technologically enhanced.

2 The Chinese name for the platform is *"youyaoqi,"* which means having demon spirit, a homophonic pun of the pronunciation of "u17" in Chinese.

Bibliography

Azuma, H., & Abel, J. E. (2009). *Otaku: Japan's database animals.* Minneapolis: University of Minnesota Press.

Cheng, W., & Li, Q. (2015). IP热潮的背后与泛娱乐思维下的未来电影 [The future cinema behind IP fever and pan entertainment thinking]. 当代电影 *Contemporary Cinema*, 9, 17–22.

Derrida, J. (1978). *Writing and difference.* Chicago, IL: University of Chicago Press.

Gawer, A. (2011). *Platforms, markets and innovation.* Cheltenham, UK: Edward Elgar Publishing Inc.

Gillespie, T. (2010). The politics of 'platforms.' *New Media & Society, 12*(3), 347–364.

Han, W. (2015). 电影《十万个冷笑话》成功背后的互联网思维 [The internet logic behind the success of the feature film One Hundred Thousand Bad Jokes]. 新闻知识 *News Research*, 6, 51–52.

Helmond, A. (2015). The platformization of the web: Making web data platform ready. *Social Media + Society, 1*(2), 1–11. doi:10.1177/2056305115603080

Jenkins, H. (2006). *Convergence culture: Where old and new media collide* (illustrated edition). New York, NY: NYU Press.

Jenkins, H., Ford, S., & Green, J. (2013). *Spreadable media: Creating value and meaning in a networked culture.* New York, NY: NYU Press.

Lamarre, T. (2009). *The anime machine: A media theory of animation.* Minneapolis: University of Minnesota Press.

Lamarre, T. (2017). Platformativity: Media studies, area studies. *Asiascape: Digital Asia, 4*(3), 285–305. doi:10.1163/22142312-12340081

Lamarre, T. (2018). *The anime ecology: A genealogy of television, animation, and game media.* Minneapolis: University of Minnesota Press.

Langlois, G., & Elmer, G. (2013). The research politics of social media platforms. *Culture Machine, 14*, 1–17.

Li, J. (2017). The interface affect of a contact zone: Danmaku on video-streaming platforms. *Asiascape: Digital Asia, 4*(3), 233–256. doi:10.1163/22142312-12340079

Li, J. (2020). The platformization of Chinese cinema: The rise of IP films in the age of internet+. *Asian Cinema.* Forthcoming.

Liu, C. (2014, November 7). 首部众筹电影《十万个冷笑话》将上映，众人拾柴真能推动影视市场? [The first crowdfunded film, One Hundred Thousand Bad Jokes, will be released in theaters]. 南方日报 *The Southern Daily.*

Lyotard, J. F., & Jameson, F. (1984). *The postmodern condition: A report on knowledge* (1st edition; G. Bennington & B. Massumi, Trans.). Minneapolis: University of Minnesota Press.

Otsuka, E. (1989). *Monogatari Shohiron (Theory of narrative consumption).* Tokyo, Japan: Shin'yosha.

Ōtsuka, E. (2010). World and variation: The reproduction and consumption of narrative (M. Steinberg, Trans.). *Mechademia, 5*(1), 99–116.

Steinberg, M. (2012). *Anime's media mix: Franchising toys and characters in Japan.* Minneapolis: University of Minnesota Press.

Steinberg, M. (2017). Converging contents and platforms: Niconico video and Japan's media mix ecology. In J. Neves & B. Sarkar (Eds.), *Asian video cultures: In the penumbra of the global* (pp. 91–113). Durham, NC: Duke University Press.

Wang, W., & Wang, Y. (2015). 腾讯电影的受众整合路径分析 [Audience integration path analysis of the Tencent film]. *当代电影 Contemporary Cinema*, 1, 161–164.

Xu, X. (2014). 中国动画电影进入媒体融合时代了吗?——结合《十万个冷笑话》个案 [Has Chinese animation cinema enter the age of media convergence? — The case study of One Hundred Thousand Bad Jokes]. *电影艺术 Film Art*, 6, 33–38.

Yin, H., & Liang, J. (2016). 通向小康社会的多元电影文化 ——2015年中国电影创作 [Diverse film culture leading to a well-off society: The Chinese film production in 2015]. *当代电影 Contemporary Cinema*, 3, 4–12.

Index